To the memory of my beloved son

Contents

List of Abbreviations

CS = Cortland Standard
DN = Daily News
NYRB = New York Review of Books
OT = Our Town
P = New York Post
T = New York Times
TSB = New York Times Book Review (Sunday)
TSM = New York Times Magazine (Sunday)
USA = USA Today

1

Introduction

And on that day, says the Lord God,
I will make the sun go down at noon,
*   and darken the earth in broad daylight*
I will turn your feasts into mourning,
*   and all your songs into lamentation;*
I will bring sackcloth upon all loins,
*   and baldness on every head;*
I will make it like the mourning for an only son,
*   and the end of it like a bitter day.*
                                                Amos 8.9-10

Grief fills the room up of my absent child,
Lies in his bed, walks up and down with me,
Puts on his pretty looks, repeats his words,
Remembers me of all his gracious parts,
Stuffs out his vacant garments with his form;
Then, have I reason to be fond of grief?
                        William Shakespeare, *King John*

Norman Mailer was awarded the Pulitzer Prize for writing a 1,050-page "true to life" novel about a murderer, Gary Gilmore. He called it *The Executioner's Song,* and like other writers who have become rich and who will become rich by concentrating on those who kill, Mailer paid little attention to the victims of Gilmore's crimes. I dedicate this book to all the suffering human beings whose lives have been destroyed by animals like Gary Gilmore. This is *The Victim's Song.*

And it is a song that is sung in hatred, not in love or forgiveness. In 1964 Max Wylie wrote a book about his murdered daughter called *The Gift of Janice.* He concluded his poignant memoir of his murdered daughter with the words: "I come not to participate in hatred but to share in love" (42). He described how he had scattered the ashes of his beloved daughter over the Adirondacks that she loved. What enabled Wylie to live with the horror of his daughter's brutal murder was the knowledge that he had the gift of his daughter's love for twenty-one years. That fact alone made him lucky and rich, and made her "live" for as long as he lived.

I am not Max Wylie. I cannot and never will accept the loss of my only child, Eric, or find the platitudes to wash away my anger, and my despair. Jesus in the Sermon on the Mount said: "Blessed are those who mourn, for they shall be comforted" (Matthew 5.4). Perhaps those who forgive can be comforted. Patrick Kehn, a thirty-eight-year-old lawyer, was robbed and stabbed to death in Manhattan by one of the countless juvenile vermin that roam the streets of New York. His mother chose the following selection to be read at his funeral: "If a man finds it's hard to forgive injuries, let him look at a crucifix and see that Christ shed all his blood for him and not only forgave his enemies, but even prayed to his heavenly father to forgive them also." The Pope pardoned Agca, the man who attempted to murder him. But I do not believe in the Christian doctrine of forgiveness. I despise a world in which young innocents are murdered, while the evil and the depraved rob and kill and live to be old. When I think of the years that my dead twenty-two-year-old son will never live to enjoy, the pleasures he will never experience, the wife he will never have, the children he will never know, the money that I have saved for him that he will never spend, the music he will never hear and play, I cannot help but hate those who destroyed his future. I cannot help but hate the conditions in New York City that make it possible for murder to thrive like garbage in a sewer.

Like Max Wylie I give thanks for the life of my child, but I also curse the evil that murdered him. Unlike the many hopeless and silent crippled souls whose lives have been ruined by violent crime, I refuse to be one of the silent, secret mourners. I write to accuse those in New York who have permitted crime to flourish: the politicians with their empty rhetoric, the judges and lawyers who are more concerned with the technicalities of the law than with justice, and the citizens whose apathy is an invitation to disaster.

Back in 1964 Max Wylie insisted that no one was safe in America. "Don't think," he warned, "you're safe just because you're home. It is possible you are being spied upon at this moment. . . . All of American cities are aswarm with roving psychotics" (36-37). But he did not know how unsafe those cities would become, how the "sanguinary savage slaughter" of his daughter would represent the stereotype of violence in America. Because his daughter was murdered in mid-morning in her apartment in Manhattan, Wylie warned his readers to protect themselves with new locks. How naive his advice seems to us today, for we know that violence erupts anywhere, anytime, in the streets, in the subways, in mansions, in slums, among the rich and the poor. It is no respecter of persons, and it is more often than not committed gratuitously by those who are very young.

For years I read about the violent crimes in New York City. The day after Helen Mintiks was murdered in the Metropolitan Opera House, I spoke to my son and warned him to be careful because the murdering savages were everywhere in the city. But as La Rochefoucauld said, "It is impossible to stare continuously at the sun or at death." Besides, murder was something that happened to people in books that I taught and read or in movies that I watched. It could not happen to me. And then it did happen. And it could happen to you; your loved ones might be murdered, and you might join the many who, like me, wail the victim's song.

The Pope is supposed to have said, after Agca attempted to kill him, "How could they have done this?" Presumably he meant how could they have done this to a pope. But I prefer to think the Pope believes that in God's eyes all men are equal, and that he was asking the question that all men of good will and peace ask, "How could they have done this to any human being?" Isaac Bashevis Singer said it best: "Every kind of killing or shooting, when I hear about it, it really shocks me. There are important people and less important, but when it comes to life and death every human being is dear to me. I tell you the truth, I feel that we are living in Sodom and Gomorrah. What has happened to humanity?" (T, May 14, 1981, A5).

What has happened to humanity? John Donne's famous line, "Any man's death diminishes me, because I am involved in mankind," has very little meaning for us in the modern world. We have come to accept assassinations. When a young man attempts to commit suicide, onlookers in the city of New York scream at him as he stands on the ledge, "Jump, Jump!" They run after a terrified man, chasing him to his death on the subway tracks. The most vicious crimes are committed by children. Perhaps we have been anesthetized by violence, and no longer have the capacity to be shocked by it.

When a mother writes about her murdered son, readers want her book to be hopeful and uplifting. If I had said to my son's murderers what Pope John Paul II said to Agca, "I speak to my brother whom I have pardoned," then this book could be placed on the shelf with all the "self-help" works that offer instant solutions to all problems. Some critics are dismayed when the treatment of murder is not "cool." For example, one *New York Times* reviewer criticized Willard Gaylin for not being objective enough in writing his excellent study of Bonnie Garland's murder; Gaylin was too passionately involved in the subject of injustice (May 18, 1982, C12). Similarly, another *Times* reviewer complained about the excessive feeling in Nicholas Gage's moving story of his search for his mother's murderer in *Eleni:* "When sorrow is distilled by art, we can share it better than when we are inundated with it" (Apr. 15, 1983, C31).

To distil the obscenity of murder through art is a very decorous, pleasant way of dealing with evil. I have written *The Victim's Song* precisely because I want to inundate the reader with anger, which is, as Carol Tavris states, a "moral emotion." She tells us that she watches "with admiration those who use anger to probe for truth, who challenge and change the complacent injustices of life, who take an unpopular position center stage while others say 'shhhh' from the wings" (23).

In December, 1984, Caroline Isenberg, a twenty-three-year-old Harvard graduate and aspiring actress, was murdered on the roof of a New York City apartment building. Her father,

Dr. Philip Isenberg, a psychiatrist, said that he felt no anger towards the man who had robbed and attempted to rape his daughter, and stabbed her many times until she died. Dorothy Rabinowitz, an astute critic of the media, was appalled by Dr. Isenberg's response to the murder of his daughter. She noted that Dr. Isenberg had told reporters that (1) the socializing systems of our society had not worked for this killer who lacked control; (2) he was sorry the killer ran into his daughter; (3) it was "bothersome" that the killer was still out there; (4) but, of course, the killer had a right to exist. Dorothy Rabinowitz asked: "What could psychiatrists make of this psychiatrist father of a murdered young woman who cannot find it in himself to express anger or blame?" To her he seems to be "the quintessential product of an age" using the language of the liberal sociologists, which has helped to "create the climate for a criminality more murderous than anything known in our history. Here, once again, even in the midst of bereavement, we have heard rationalizations for criminality" (P, Dec. 7, 1984, 49). In Rabinowitz's view, our progressive sociology, which was supposed to enlarge our humanity, has resulted in an extraordinary dehumanization and involved us in "lies about what constitutes a civilized attitude towards the murder of one's child." I do not intend to lie.

I hate the murderers of my son. I write to express my repugnance for the basest evil a man can commit: murder. I write because I do not want my son to be a forgotten victim like the 1,814 people who were killed in the city of New York in 1980, the year my son was killed. In that year more people were murdered in New York than in any other city in the country. Who cares about them? Who thinks about them? Who remembers them? On July 31, 1977, the Son of Sam killed twenty-year-old Stacy Moskowitz. Her boyfriend, Robert Violante, who was also shot by the Son of Sam, survives. On July 3, 1983, he said that he wanted to write a book called *The Forgotten Victim* because people forget too easily the victims of crime.

Diana Montenegro's sixteen-year-old daughter was stabbed to death in Brooklyn by a member of a teen-age gang. Mrs. Montenegro said: "I buried my daughter, but I cannot bury my anger and my pain. Time and again we see short-term sentences given to the criminals, while we, the victims, serve lifetime sentences of fear, grief, and violation" (T, Apr. 21, 1981, B1).

Like Mrs. Montenegro, I face a lifetime sentence of grief and pain. Like her I will not bury my anger. I have put it to use, not only to write this book as a memorial to my son, but also to offer what may well be the first documented study of what it means to be the mother of a child who was murdered in New York City. Let this city stand as paradigm for all the cities in which violence is a pervasive and accepted phenomenon.

2

The Ultimate Horror

*A writer's real material comes from his suffering. The truest
memory is the kind that leaves scars on the heart.*
Anatoly Rybakov, spoken at Yuri Trifonov's
funeral in Moscow, April, 1981

My son, Eric Kaminsky, twenty-two years old, walked into the
Eighth Avenue Subway at 181st Street on a beautiful Saturday
evening, between 9:30 and 9:45 on September 13, 1980. He had,
as always, spent the entire day practicing. He wanted to be a
concert pianist. Sometime before 10:00 P.M., at the very moment
that I was telling a friend of his hopes and plans, and of how
proud I was of his musical attainments, he was attacked in
that dangerous cavern known as a subway station. Two young
Dominicans robbed him, stole his wallet, and one of them
stabbed him. Eric fell to the ground. The stabbing was done so
efficiently that it cut the aorta, and, according to the coroner's
report, my son immediately bled to death. To make certain
that he could not retaliate, they threw his body on the tracks,
presumably hoping that an oncoming train would smash him
to a pulp and obliterate all traces of his identity. Several
witnesses rushed to his aid and pulled him up from the tracks.
But when the ambulance arrived from Harlem Hospital, Eric
was dead.

Then this son of mine, upon whom I had lavished such
loving care, whose every move I had scrupulously watched,

whose every pain I had tried to alleviate with love and attention, this son of mine lay all night unidentified in the Harlem Hospital. On Sunday the police of the Thirty-fourth Precinct walked the streets of Washington Heights with a picture of his dead face until someone recognized him as the boy who lived on 183rd Street. My husband's sister Ann had listened to the story of Eric's murder on television, but she did not know that Eric was the unidentified boy on the subway.

On September 14 at 3:00 P.M., Detective Gonzalez called us in Cortland. When I picked up the phone, I thought he was the detective who had talked to us in the morning about a robbery in our house. When he asked to speak to my husband I was not concerned since I assumed he wanted to discuss the robbery. After all, only material things had been stolen: silver, a fur coat; no one was home, no one had been hurt when these things were stolen on the evening of September 13. But as I looked at my husband as he listened to the voice on the phone, I knew at that moment that our lives had changed irrevocably. On that same night that we had been robbed of things, we had also lost what we loved most in the world, our beloved son, and we would never be the same again.

How many times have you read the story of a murder victim in a newspaper or heard it on television? Momentarily horrified by the details, you then returned to drinking your cup of coffee, or washing your floor. The real horror of murder is never described by the media or in fictional accounts of murder. For years I had read mystery fiction for *relaxation,* for *enjoyment.* I had, like millions of others, like some presidents of the United States, read in bed a mystery murder story to relax my mind. I also taught a course in mystery fiction at the State University College at Cortland where I am a professor of English. How ironic that the foul act of murder should have been for me nothing more than a form of entertainment.

Who cares to describe what a mother and father do after they are told their son is murdered? It is never a simple matter of fainting or crying or being sedated. When I learned of my son's death, I wished at that moment that I would faint, that I could blot out the reality. But I did not faint nor could I blot out the truth. That same day my husband and I drove from Cortland to New York City, to the city where we always visited

Eric, to the city where we expected Eric to perform in a concert. Instead we slept, drugged, in my sister-in-law's house, and the next morning set out on our journey of horror. How we both lived through that morning I shall never know. I wanted to die. But my body kept moving, and I did what I was supposed to do. The police officers had told us what our chores were to be that morning.

First we had to go to the morgue. I had read about morgues. I had seen them on television and in the movies. But a morgue is only a place where they keep dead bodies—until the day that one of those dead bodies is someone you love. Then a morgue is worse than a grave.

For one hour we waited in the nondescript lobby of the Medical Examiner's building on Twenty-eighth Street. When I first learned of my son's death, I said, "Oh no, there must be some mistake." Then our neighbor called his apartment in New York, and assured us no one was home. Now once again we sat, hoping that the police had made a mistake. Sometimes identifications were wrong. I sat there thinking that perhaps he was really at the Manhattan School of Music, playing the Liszt Sonata he was preparing for an audition. When the clerk finally arrived, we were sent to his desk and asked questions by a black man whose sad face revealed the wearing effect of constantly listening to bereaved people. He asked me whether I wanted to view the body, and I said that under no circumstances would I permit my husband to go alone.

We were led to a room where a body was wheeled out, and we looked down into the strange face of a stranger. The finely chiseled features of my son's face were swollen beyond recognition. My husband doubled over in pain and almost fell, but I held on to him. Then I leaned over and kissed Eric on his forehead. It was cold, ice cold. I felt as if I were kissing a stone.

Then we were driven to the Thirty-fourth Precinct in the Bronx, and three somber, well-dressed detectives talked to us in a small room. We were given the keys to our son's apartment, and one of the men said sadly as he looked at the hopeless grief in our eyes: "There's a hard core of horror in the city. No one is safe."

Then we drove to the Riverside Chapel in the Bronx, the same funeral home we had visited the previous Thanksgiving

Day to make arrangements for the funeral of my brother-in-law Paul, who had died of a heart attack. We had gone alone to pick the coffin, for his wife, Rose, was too distraught to accompany us. But she was with us now as we ordered the same kind of coffin for our son, and a grave plot next to Paul's grave.

We left the Riverside Chapel and returned to Rose's house. I do not remember what happened that night except that we all wept.

On Tuesday, September 16, 1980, we returned to the Riverside Chapel, where friends and relatives joined us for the funeral. I remember thinking as I walked into the chapel, this is not happening; it is part of some dream. When Christi Witker of the Independent Network News program walked over to me with her microphone and asked us some questions, I felt for a moment as if we were in the midst of a television drama that we had watched over and over again—a child killed, and the parents in the midst of their agony asked by a totally unconcerned and uninvolved newshound, "How do you feel about the murder of your child?" I do not remember what she asked me. I do not remember what I replied or what my husband said. We sat through the memorial service, which we had asked the Reform rabbi to make as brief as possible so that we could maintain our control. Numbed we listened to his eulogy. Numbed we walked out into the limousine which drove us to the cemetery. There we looked at his coffin as the rabbi uttered the required words. But I do not think that even then I believed Eric was dead.

It was two days later, when we visited his apartment, his empty apartment, and looked at the concert grand Baldwin that he would never play again that I fully grasped the horror. My husband cried, "It's not fair!" We donated his piano to the Manhattan School of Music. I could not bear the thought that he would never play that piano again, or listen to his records; he would never call me again from his flat; he would never call me again and I would never see him again. I have taught *King Lear* in my Shakespeare class for many years, but I never really *felt* the lines Lear speaks so eloquently when his daughter Cordelia dies, "Never, never, never, never." Now I know what they mean.

The wife of a murdered policeman told a *New York Times* reporter that grief is a private affair. She refused to have her husband's brother live with her for that reason. Grief is private and no one can really share it with you. But I have made a vow to my son. His death shall not be a forgotten statistic in the sordid history of crime in New York City.

How easy it is to be a forgotten statistic. For so many terrible, violent events occur every day that the death of one person, no matter how much it affects people when it first happens, soon recedes in the memory of those who are inundated with the stories of assassinations, catastrophes, and terrorist activities. Since my son was murdered, we have had the murder of Dr. Michael Halberstam, the noted cardiologist, the murder of John Lennon, the murders of twenty-eight black Atlanta children, the deaths of three thousand victims in the earthquake in Italy, the burned bodies of more than a hundred victims in the Las Vegas and Stouffer Inn fires, the attempted assassinations of Ronald Reagan and the Pope, the assassination of Sadat, and the slaughter of the Marines in Beirut. The Pope was shot on May 13, 1981, and for a few days everybody wrote about the terrible act performed against the Holy Man of Peace. But the interest in the Pope also will abate, and his story will gradually be relegated to the back pages of the newspaper until someone writes a book about the man who tried to kill the Pope. Indeed, on the day he was shot, irate soap opera addicts besieged many stations insisting that the news coverage of the shooting of the Pope be stopped immediately so that they could watch their soap operas. What do all the bereaved families do when they suffer the loss of a loved one through violence? Some of them may make a few bitter comments which are quoted in the press, but almost all of them remain silent. I believe that an entire city could lose all of its children, and the unaffected population would quickly resume the normal activities of everyday life. For as La Rochefoucauld said, we can bear the sufferings of others with equanimity.

As each day goes by, I miss my son more and more. I think each day as I wake up, remembering once again that he is dead, that I will not be able to cry. But sometime during the day, a memory, the sight of his room, the place where he played, the door opening and a "Hi Mom" that I hear in my mind, all of these bring back the tears.

My loss has taught me a great deal about human nature. People react to the tragedy of death in different ways. Some are so terrified by the graphic evidence of their own mortality that, unable to face it, they ignore it. Others are professional mourners, so fascinated by death that they do not miss any opportunity to visit those who have suffered bereavement— even those whom they know only slightly. But the feeling, compassionate friends visit and try to comfort you and try to help you through the terrible days when the pain is unbearable. These are the ones you can never forget.

Our relatives live in New York City and we live in Cortland. The close ones tried to help by using the telephone. But they were not with us during our darkest hours. Nor were the relatives whom we had met at parties, at weddings, at happy affairs. In fact, most of them did not bother to call because they did not know what to say to us, how to speak to us. Hundreds of letters of sympathy poured in from strangers. Brief notes came from friends whom we expected to write long letters. Long letters came from those whom we did not know well. Obtuse friends wrote to tell us that they knew how we must have felt because they had children of their own or they had an only child, or they had gifted children who played the piano. Somehow whatever was said to us was wrong. Nothing could comfort us. But I shall never forget what so many good people tried to do, and I shall never forget what was not done.

Several months before my son was murdered, he visited us in Cortland to attend the wedding of his high school friend Peter. He had called Eric and asked him to be an usher at his wedding. Eric bought a gift for the bride and groom, and rented a tuxedo. We all attended the wedding.

Five years have passed and Peter, who lives just a few blocks away from us, has not visited us; he has not telephoned, or talked to us. He has everything now that my son will never have: a wife, a job, perhaps a child. But I do not understand why a young, decent person who used to spend time in our home, who even after he graduated from high school visited us to talk about his future plans, could not pick up a phone and speak a few brief words of consolation. He alone knows what has kept him from expressing the sympathy that one expects from a friend of the deceased. He alone will have to live with that knowledge.

But then there were the classmates at SUNY-Binghamton who dedicated a concert to Eric. The Juilliard String Quartet dedicated their concert at SUNY-Binghamton to Eric, and some of his friends showed that they would not forget him. Besides the close members of our family who cared about us during the darkest hours, we can never forget the friends in Cortland who tried to help us in ways that we shall always value. We shall always remember the so-called friends who were so desperately afraid of their own mortality that they did not even try to talk to us; instead they donated money to the Manhattan School of Music or the Cortland Library in Eric's memory, as if to assuage their conscience.

Does losing your child through an accident or through illness make you feel different about loss? I do not know whether a mother whose child has died from leukemia or an accident feels the same kind of despair that a mother feels whose child has been murdered. But I know that my bitterness was not directed against an unknown or intangible force but against two living human beings who had done their terrible deed in a society that permitted them to function as murderers.

What have those who tried to comfort us said? A few, a very few, spoke of God and of their belief that there is a purpose to life. These were, I remember, the consoling words of the husband of a friend after the funeral. Recently his wife died suddenly, and I noted that he never once repeated the words about God that he had used to console me. Several kind souls who had suffered the loss of a child wrote to assure me that eventually I would survive the tragedy and come to accept it. Jim Jensen, the TV anchor man on Channel 2, sent me a compassionate letter.

Dr. James Ferrante wrote a very moving guest editorial in *Modern Medicine* in which he described his reactions after he learned that his thirteen-year-old son had been struck down and killed by a car in a parking lot. Nothing in his fifteen years of medical practice and ten years of teaching prepared him for the mental anguish and physical illness he suffered.

He described what I felt: "I wanted to die, kill, maim, and retaliate. To do all the things I was never permitted. I was a doctor. I was used to tragedy and the senselessness of death." He remembered how many times he had left grieving parents to fend for themselves. But when he had his own tragedy, he could not cope. He had become a doctor because of his "fear of and hatred of death. And the sanctity, joy and pricelessness of life." And he asked himself, "Ferrante, how can you possibly survive the greatest of all human tragedies?" The main thrust of his moving article was that physicians should be trained to cope with bereavement. In my despair I wrote to Dr. Ferrante to tell him how much I empathized with all that he had written and to ask whether he could offer me any advice in the light of his experience with such tragedy. His answer revealed that he did not understand any more than I did the reasons for the ineffable horror of loss.

I would ask myself, "How can I survive the greatest of all human tragedies?" I would teach my classes, mark my papers, but always the recurring nightmare images of how Eric died would incapacitate me. The mornings were the worst time when I would awake from a deep sleep and remember what had happened. I have the love of a remarkable husband (*kayn aynhoreh*), and we tried to comfort each other. But I could not overcome the despair and hopelessness. Finally I began to feel physically ill; I lost weight and felt nauseated and depressed most of the time.

Every day I would think about how my son died. My hatred for those who had caused his death was so overwhelming that only the thought of inflicting suffering upon them could moderate my agony. I imagined that in jail they had been stabbed a thousand times in every part of their bodies and were so brutally sodomized that they had to be castrated because of diseased organs. I could see them lying in a pool of blood, their eyes gouged out while they were slowly and painstakingly disemboweled. I would talk to that power called God: "I will believe in you," I said, "if the phone rings at this moment, and I learn that the two criminals are screaming like the creatures in Dante's *Inferno,* unable to die, but doomed to an eternity of unbearable suffering." But I never received any such telephone call. These dark thoughts overwhelmed me, and I realized that I needed help; my despair was destroying me.

I had never been to a psychiatrist. During the years I had read the classic works in psychology and listened to the stories relatives told me about their disturbed children's experiences with therapists. Some of my best friends were psychologists and psychiatrists. But I did not seek psychiatric counseling, not when my first husband died, not when my parents died, not when my friends died. In the past I had learned to accept the deaths of those I loved. But I could not accept the murder of my son, and during a two-year period after his death I sought help from seven psychiatrists.

The first psychiatrist listened to me for one hour and a half, and assured me I was suffering from a typical reactive depression which would ultimately disappear. He gave me some drugs and told me there was no need to see him again. Then I went to see a woman psychiatrist. She listened to my tale of sorrow, wrote in a notebook, and occasionally interjected a note of sympathy. She informed me at the conclusion of the interview that it would take five years for me to recover from the trauma of the loss. I went back once more to talk to her and found it to be an exercise in futility. Once again she expected me to talk, and she listened with her eyes closed, nodding her head and offering the choice bit of wisdom: "You really should get out and do some yoga exercises." Then in desperation I tried one more psychiatrist. Although she was pleasant and empathetic, she followed the same procedure of mainly listening to me for two sessions. The only difference was that she honestly admitted at the outset that she didn't know whether she could help me.

All kinds of contradictory advice have been offered to the grief-stricken, including the following. By all means get regular therapy; do not expect help from the shrinks. Cry and rage, and time will heal your wounds. Control your grief and take medication; don't take medication; drugs inhibit the normal mourning process and have unpleasant side effects. Visit your family to be comforted; do not visit your relatives for they will merely rub salt on the wound; try to forget the past; let everything that happened flow through your mind without restraint. While a great deal has been written about loss and grief, nobody really knows how to comfort the bereaved.

None of the books on bereavement helped; not the scientific ones by authors like John Bowlby, the compassionate ones written by Harriet Schiff and Judy Tatelbaum, the many studies of depression and suicide, nor the literature provided by such organizations as Compassionate Friends and the Parents of Murdered Children (POMC). Charlotte Hullinger and her husband formed POMC after their daughter was beaten to death by a rejected boyfriend in Germany. When Mrs. Hullinger kindly called me from Ohio to comfort me, she told me that her daughter's murderer had been freed after he spent several years in a mental institution in Germany and he had graduated from a college in America. Her husband is a minister; does this mean he is required to forgive?

Forgive the murderer! Trust in God. Time will heal. Life must go on. None of the platitudes is of any value. Only the pain persists.

On the day before Christmas, four months after my son died, I suddenly came face to face with Tom, one of Eric's high school friends. "Sorry I couldn't come to see you," he mumbled sadly. "I just couldn't do it." As I looked at him, a pleasant boy who used to ride the streets on Eric's bicycle and run with Eric on the track team, I felt that it was unjust that he should be alive while Eric was dead. Tom did not attend college and worked at menial jobs. Why was my talented, vital, motivated son dead when every one of his friends in Cortland was alive?

I felt the same kind of bitterness when I began to read the obituaries. I had never paid any attention to them, but after Eric died I began to notice the age of every person who died. It amazed me how long-lived famous people can be. Invariably they lived to be eighty-five, ninety, or even one-hundred. I hated them for living so long while my son was dead at twenty-two. Sorrow and hatred are the terrible twin sisters of psychological anguish. I found myself so depressed that for the first time in my life I had suicidal thoughts. Walking through my house, each step reminding me of my son as he grew up in the house for seventeen years, I felt I could not go on, I could no longer teach, I could no longer function in a normal fashion, I could no longer enjoy any of the activities that had made me a happy and fulfilled wife, mother, and teacher-scholar.

The psychiatrists had not helped me. I began to write this book to exorcise my pain and to fulfill the vow that I had made to my son that he would not be forgotten.

As I sit and write this particular passage it is April 3, 1981, Eric's birthday. He would be twenty-three years old today. Instead of celebrating his birthday, I think of him lying in his grave and I think of suicide. Since I am a teacher I see young people all day; some in my classes look like him as they walk by in their tight blue jeans and polo shirts. I almost call out to one of them, "Eric," because he looks so much like Eric. In the beginning I hated them for being alive while my son was dead. Now I look at them and my heart aches, but I no longer resent them. I pity them for starting life in a world that will ultimately destroy them, no matter what they do, no matter what path they take.

There is a famous passage at the end of Camus's *The Stranger*. Meursault, who is about to die, says, "I'd passed my life in a certain way, and I might have passed it in a different way, if I'd felt like it. I'd acted thus, and I hadn't acted otherwise; I hadn't done *x*, whereas I had done *y* or *z*. And what did that mean?" To Meursault it meant nothing, for in the end "there was only one class of men, the privileged class. All alike would be condemned to die one day . . ." (151-152). But is Camus right? Does not what we choose, *x* or *y* or *z*, determine the quality and length of our lives? Does not one path give us a healthy, satisfying life so that when we die at ninety-five we can not really complain, while another path leads us to early sorrow and death?

If Camus is right, and we all face the ultimate absurdity of death, then what we do does not matter. It will all come to the same thing in the end. And it is futile to wonder about what might have been. But while it is possible to accept philosophically the fact that all men come to the same end in a world in which even one-hundred years is an infinitesimal amount of time, emotionally it is not possible to accept the death of a loved one. And I keep thinking of what we might have done to prevent his death.

My husband and I ridicule superstitions in our book on logic. But Eric was killed on September 13. That night, speaking proudly about him to friends, I neglected to do what my mother always did when she wanted to keep the devil, or evil eye, from hurting those she loved. My remark about Eric's achievements should have been preceded by the words "*kayn aynhoreh*," which is a mixture of Yiddish and Hebrew, meaning, "no evil eye," a form of protection against tempting the evil spirits to action. By not using the expression, I failed to protect my son against the evil spirit that murdered him. For as a Jewish mother I should have used "*kayn aynhoreh*" every time I referred to the good or beautiful qualities of anyone I loved. Instead in the evening of September 13, at the very moment Eric was being stabbed to death, I spoke to my husband as we were driving back from Ithaca on Route 13 about how happy I was and how I wished time would stand still.

We had accomplished what we wanted to in our lives; we loved each other and our son. He was supposed to graduate in June, and we were very content. But according to superstitious belief, I should not have said that I was content, at least not without throwing salt over my shoulder, or placating Satan in some way.

Oddly enough, at that time I was writing a short story about a woman who appeared in one of my dreams. She waits for the return of her young son from school. The son never returns because he has been dead for a year, but she refuses to accept this fact and calls the police every day to report his disappearance. When Eric first went to school, like the woman in my story, I used to stand near the door, looking out for him, unable to do anything until he arrived home.

Some other strange coincidences came back to me. Picasso's *The Tragedy* hung on the wall in Eric's bedroom. Reluctantly I had given to the Salvation Army an old, favorite coat that I had kept for eighteen years. A black cat continually appeared before our house in the two weeks before Eric died. That cat has not appeared on our street since he was murdered.

Since he was murdered. Since he was murdered. I write these words as if I were writing some strange fact about some strange person. Like the woman in my story, I keep waiting for my son to return. In my more rational moments I keep thinking of the paths Eric might have taken, paths that might have led him to a long and happy life. If-then. That is what the philosophers call a counterfactual. The counterfactual will plague me for the rest of my life. If Eric had done x, then he might have had y.

3

Beginnings

Things are always at their best in their beginnings.
Blaise Pascal, *Lettres Provinciales*

I was born in Manhattan to Jewish parents who had come
from Kiev, Russia. They had immigrated to America to escape
a demoralizing existence in an anti-Semitic country. They
bought a farm in New Jersey and had the hard but free life of
poor farmers. Unfortunately, my father was not able to raise
enough to feed his five children (one of them died at an early
age of pneumonia), and after some years of desperate effort he
lost the farm. I grew up in Manhattan and never knew about
my father's country life; no one talked about it. We lived in
what would be described today as the Jewish ghetto, in a large
railroad flat on Henry Street. My father had a small hand
laundry, and we were poor but not impoverished. I did not
know I was in a Jewish ghetto. I had the kind of youth that
only rich children are supposed to enjoy, for we lived one block
from a most remarkable organization, the Educational Alli-
ance, the greatest source of pleasure in my youth.

The Educational Alliance was founded by a Jewish
philanthropic agency. In its huge brick building activities of
every kind were offered to the children of the neighborhood.
They could learn Hebrew, learn how to act, dance, sing, sew,
paint. Many of the teachers were famous artists who donated
their time. A member of Martha Graham's dance group taught

31

me modern dance. There was not enough time in the day to take advantage of all the free cultural activities. We produced ballets and plays, and were incredibly creative and cooperative. No "Y" in the country today provides what the Educational Alliance gave to the youth of the ghetto.

But those happy carefree days came to an end when my brother obtained a job in the Post Office. He was evidently one of the very few people in the depression era who managed to obtain what was then considered to be a very good civil service position. As a result he moved us out of the ghetto to Riverside Drive and convinced my father that he should retire. I had been happy in the slums of Henry Street, but I was miserable in the grandeur of Riverside Drive because I had no friends. After two years we moved to Bensonhurst in Brooklyn to be near my sister, who was married and had a young boy. The neighborhood was pleasant; we lived in a small private house on a street lined with trees.

On this street I met my first love, Frank Nutis. We knew each other for several years before he was drafted and sent to the Boca Raton Army Air Field in Florida. We were married and lived in a small house near the army base. On the very day of our anniversary, a year later, he died.

He had been admitted to the army hospital a few days earlier for what seemed to be an ordinary stomach disorder. The orderly on duty, who observed how nervous and concerned I was, said, "Don't worry, he isn't going to die." But Frank lay in the army hospital for two days, vomiting and ignored until he went into a diabetic coma. They could not save him. His young doctor wept. "We didn't know," he repeated over and over again. The army killed Frank through neglect just as surely as if he had been killed by a German soldier in Europe. Too many ill men lay on those mattresses on the floor in the army hospital at Boca Raton, and the doctors had not tested him. They had merely assumed he was suffering from indigestion or the flu.

I rode alone with Frank's dead body in the train that took me back to New York. My father, my gentle, kind, religious father, stood waiting for me at the station. He had spent his entire life loving God, and living the life of a Talmudic scholar. Yet he could only weep when he saw me, just as he would weep a year later when he was himself near death, and his God did not seem to be there in the end to comfort him. It seemed to me that he felt only the pain of his suffering. The beatific vision eluded him, for when we tried to please him by praying in his room, he turned his face to the wall and said, "Enough. It is all nothing."

A few weeks after Frank died the war ended; joyful celebrations erupted everywhere in the country. But I felt like the thousands who had lost their husbands or sons in actual battle. The death of Frank, a good, kind, intelligent person, made me acknowledge, for the first time in my life, the existence of evil, made me feel the bitterness of lost innocence. I loved Frank's parents and lived with them for a while, hoping to comfort them and to hold on to the past. But when my brother was released from the army, he convinced me that I should live with my parents.

When at the age of twenty-one you lose your husband after a happy year of marriage, you feel that your life is finished. No one I knew or loved had died before Frank died. Like a nun I renounced life and retired into what was to be the nunnery of education. I went back to college and finished my senior year at New York University. This university awarded me a tuition scholarship for the master's degree.

The great medievalist Margaret Schlauch had a profound effect on my life at this time. I took every course she gave, inspired by her knowledge and devotion to scholarship. She was the model of what I wanted to be. I would never love again. I would become a great scholar and teacher. I deliberately wore my wedding ring so that everyone would think I was married.

In the summer of 1946 I planned to go to Vermont with a friend, but when she could not join me, I decided instead to take Schlauch's linguistics course, my first graduate course. Behind me sat two young men who were always whispering and smiling in a friendly fashion when I turned frowning and asked them to be quiet. For whatever Margaret Schlauch had to say about Icelandic sagas could not be found in any texts, at least not until she did the translating. One day after class, one of these two students walked out of the building with me and asked if I wanted a lift to the subway. He was a slender, dark, good-looking young man. His car was an old, incredibly old jalopy that looked as if it would fall apart with more than one passenger. Perhaps another time, I said. And that was how I met my husband Jack. For some strange reason he did not notice my wedding ring. The next day he again asked me if I would drive in his car. This time I agreed on condition that my two friends would join us. But as we sat in his car, the back end seemed to droop, and the car would not start. Embarrassed, he told us that it didn't do very well with more than three people sitting in it. We left the car, laughing, waving goodbye as his motor sputtered and he barely managed to move the broken-down piece of junk. As it turned out, this was the car I was to ride in for a year. One door was held together with wire, and we stopped every few miles to fill the oil tank with oil we carried in a large can.

Jack had lived through the Battle of the Bulge, had won his Bronze Star, and never forgot that he had survived the war while many of his friends had died under horrible circumstances. All he wanted to do was study philosophy, and this is what he did for the next four years until he received his doctorate. We had a glorious time studying together at the Graduate School of Arts and Science at New York University. Those were our halcyon days in New York. We would spend a great deal of time at the New York Public Library, one of the most wonderful libraries in the world, poring through hundreds of books to prepare the many term papers we had to write. Very often we worked till the library closed at 10:00 P.M. and then we strolled along Forty-second Street until midnight. Yes, we would stroll. In those days it was safe to walk the streets of New York. There were no drug addicts, no muggers with knives, no frightening subculture groups to intimidate us. Many young people on dates walked without fear, enjoying the sights and sounds of the city. They could go to the movies in that area without worrying about crime and murder. At midnight Jack would take the subway to the Bronx, and I would take the subway to Brooklyn. On the subways were decent, law-abiding people, many of them returning from work or the theater.

Very often after attending classes, Jack and I would sit in Washington Square Park late in the evening. It is now considered the most dangerous park in the city. With our friends we would enjoy walking through Greenwich Village and eating good food at cheap restaurants. A former teacher I know lives in that area now and never ventures out after dark. She is a virtual prisoner in her apartment.

Those were the days. If Frank was my childhood sweetheart, Jack has been the lover of my life. Together we have enjoyed intellectual and emotional fulfillment and professional success (*kayn aynhoreh*).

Jack received his doctorate in philosophy and his first full-time teaching appointment at Akron, Ohio, a one-year temporary position at the generous salary of $2,500 a year. Since we had been living on my $1,200 a year assistantship in English from New York University, we felt that we had greatly improved our economic status when we went to Akron.

We returned to New York after spending a pleasant year in the rubber capital of the world. But we vowed that we would never leave New York again. Even then it was difficult to obtain decent living quarters in a good neighborhood. A lawyer, acting as a rental agent, made us pay him money "under the table" to obtain a desirable apartment in a brownstone on East Ninety-first Street between Lexington and Park Avenues, an apartment that was just a few blocks from the "Y" that my son was to live in thirty years later. I completed my doctorate and obtained a teaching position at Hunter College. I say "teaching position," but an instructorship that involved teaching four freshman composition courses and marking 120 papers a week hardly constituted anything more than a form of drudgery. During that year I often thought about leaving the teaching field, for I could not understand why one needed a doctorate to do such menial work.

From nine to five, Jack was a communications engineer at Western Electric, and in the evening he taught philosophy at City College. He worked very, very hard. Thus, despite our love of New York, when an assistant professorship in philosophy was offered to him at Harpur College in Binghamton, he accepted the position. With great regret we left New York City. In the first few years we missed this "lovely" city and spent many weekends there. But gradually we began to enjoy living in Binghamton and visited New York infrequently.

Ambitious and naive, I was elated when I obtained a lectureship in the English Department at Cornell University. Giving me the title of lecturer enabled Cornell to pay me half the salary of every instructor, $1,500, for a full load of teaching. I was so euphoric about the honor bestowed on me by Cornell that nothing fazed me, not even the tedious journey I made three times a week from Binghamton to Ithaca—in the Greyhound Bus Station at 5:30 A.M. to take a bus to Ithaca, to arrive at 7:15 A.M. and then to take a bus up the steep hill to Cornell. The Greyhound bus drove to Ithaca through the fiercest snowstorms, and I would arrive to teach my classes when faculty living in Ithaca could not move their cars in the snow.

Cornell is a magnificent university. It has one of the most beautiful campuses in the country. It has brilliant scholars and teachers. But after teaching there for three and a half years I lost my illusions about life in academe. In those years my freshman class consisted of mediocre students drawn from the hotel school. The best students were assigned to the full professors. A "star" in the English department taught a very popular course, and I was elated when I learned that I would assist him and have the opportunity to lecture to his four hundred students several times during the term. What he also required was that I mark all of the exams and papers in the course. When the chairman discovered that I had marked these hundreds of themes *and* taught my regular classes, he expressed surprise, and that was all he did. In the Halls of Ivy, and especially in the big universities, women instructors in those days were academic slaves.

Jack received his tenure at SUNY-Binghamton, he became a full professor, and as chairman of the department he watched it grow over the next ten years into a body of nineteen members.

He wanted a child. I had resisted the idea for years because after Frank died, I had developed a fear of loss and a fear of hospitals and doctors. But I loved Jack and decided to have a child. Eric was born at Lourdes Hospital in Binghamton on April 3, 1958. During the year I carried him, I also gave birth to a book on criticism which was published when he was born.

To be near Eric, I taught at a community college. This proved to be a disastrous experience. English teachers had to sign their names in a black book when they left their offices, even when they went to the bathroom! During the year I spent at this "college," I taught logic, history, and philosophy, as well as English. Since it was less stressful to teach at Cornell, I returned to the university. No longer a lecturer, I was promoted to the rank of instructor! But after four more years of teaching I wanted to stop traveling and build a home in Binghamton. I therefore applied for a part-time teaching position at Harpur College (the original name of SUNY-Binghamton). It was then that I encountered the betrayal of friendship.

Professor Nevid was a powerful force at SUNY-Binghamton when he hired my husband to teach philosophy. When Nevid got into difficulty with the administration, Jack, without tenure, loyally wrote a letter to the president in defense of Nevid's activities as the head of an innovative program. But when I applied for a position at Binghamton, it was Nevid who adamantly refused to allow me to teach even one freshman course; he did not want faculty wives teaching in the college. He was a good friend who had spent many hours in our home. So Nevid involved me in still another counterfactual.

Would my son be alive today if Nevid had permitted me to teach at Binghamton? Surely we would not have moved to Cortland.

For it was at the State University College at Cortland that I received an assistant professorship, and we moved to Cortland when Eric was five years old. The president of SUNY-Binghamton did not want Jack to move to Cortland. He told me in a private interview that I should devote my time to helping my husband with his research and give up my ambition to be a teacher. I left his office wondering why I had ever bothered to obtain a Ph.D. An administrator of a college would not talk to a woman in that way today. He might think the same thoughts, but he would not utter them. And yet the president of Binghamton was a kind, fatherly figure who thought that all wives should play the same role that his own wife performed so well. If I had listened to the president and remained in Binghamton, I might have lost a professorship, but gained years of life for my son. For then Eric, living in Binghamton, might not have taken the road which led him to New York

City. Like Faust I would willingly have made a pact with the devil to save my son's life. But when we moved to Cortland, I had no premonition of disaster. I lived there happily for seventeen years, teaching at Cortland while Jack commuted to Binghamton forty miles away.

Cortland was good to us. Eric thrived there, growing up in a safe country environment. I became a full professor of English, wrote books, and enjoyed the kind of professional and personal fulfillment that makes for happiness.

Eric attended the campus elementary school run by the college. He was a bright, lively, handsome boy with an ingratiating smile. When Lou Bradley, his first grade teacher, learned of his death, she wrote me a long letter revealing that after eighteen years she still remembered him vividly as one of her best and most charming students. In the sixth grade he played the role of Aladdin in a college play put on by college students. But he was not destined to be a thespian, for in junior high school he discovered that he had special talents as a runner and devoted all of his energy to improving his running speed. He was also a good swimmer and became a lifeguard. But because I was a Jewish mother, I insisted on giving him piano lessons. When he was six, I bought him a new piano, and he began taking lessons. But although he originally liked the piano and was quite musical, he preferred athletics. As he grew older, the only bone of contention between us was his practice hour. "Have you practiced your piano?" Like "Bartleby the Scrivener," Eric "preferred not" to play and would often begrudgingly sit down to practice. But he put his heart and soul into running. What would his life have been if he had not developed a hernia by exercising on muscle building equipment at the college? After the hernia operation his running speed was never the same. When he discovered in the first year in high school that he could not be *first,* he gave up the idea that he might someday be an Olympic star. But his preoccupation with running was soon supplanted by a much more compelling concern. For in his second year of high school, he found *love.*

4

First Love

"Love like ours can never die!"
Rudyard Kipling, "The Lover's Litany"

A woman is always a fickle, unstable thing.
Virgil's *Aeneid*

She was a year ahead of him, a junior in Cortland High
School. He was sixteen, sweet sixteen, the perfect age for form-
ing that first deep attachment which the young feel so pas-
sionately, and purely. Nan and Eric rode their bicycles to-
gether in the summer and spent many hours in our house. It
was true that Nan's home was smaller and that it afforded
less privacy, but it seemed to me that Eric was not comfortable
in her house. I suspected that her parents, who were Italian
Catholics, were not pleased that she was seriously involved
with a Jewish boy. At first they might have liked the idea that
Nan had a boyfriend. But when Eric and Nan became in-
separable, her parents must have worried, as we did, about the
intensity of first love and its consequences.

Eric and Nan saw each other every day. When they were
not together, they talked on the phone for hours. They were
deliriously happy, but my husband and I were troubled. I tried
to express some of my fears to Eric. But how do you talk to a
seventeen-year-old boy who is deeply in love and warn him
about the transient nature of emotions? "Eric," I said, groping

39

for the right inoffensive words, "You are both so young and your backgrounds are so different. You have to consider the possibility that things might change between you as you get older."

"You don't understand," he said, annoyed. "We have a relationship that will last. We're really in love. Nothing will change that."

"That may be." I felt sad as he spoke so confidently and so naively. A premonition clutched at my heart. He was so vulnerable, so young, so happy. "But remember Nan's family is Catholic. And we're—"

"Oh, she doesn't care about that," he interrupted me, smiling confidently. "She just goes along with what her family wants her to believe. She has no prejudice."

"But what if her parents object to you?"

"So what if they do?" he replied scornfully. "Remember the time I went to the fair with them? They never spoke one word to me."

"At Christmas time I remember riding by their house, and it was the most lavishly decorated one in the city."

"I know Nan loves me and doesn't give a damn about all that," he said defiantly.

I winced and said no more about this subject. As a philosopher's son, Eric had been brought up to tolerate all religions. He was proud of his Jewish heritage, and was without prejudice. "Different strokes for different folks" was one of his favorite expressions. We were proud of his tolerance but were always concerned about his naiveté and cocky assurance. It was beyond his experience to imagine betrayal in love.

Nan graduated and left Cortland to attend a secretarial school in another city. They seemed to retain their strong affection for each other. In fact, absence seemed to make Nan's heart grow fonder. She visited Eric and wrote passionate love letters. How do I know that? I know because I read the letters. Eric left them on the kitchen table, inviting me to read them. Why? He wanted me to know how much Nan really loved him. That is what she wrote. And when I would see them together, looking at each other with great adoration, I began, despite an intuitive skepticism, to hope that their relationship could survive the pitfalls of youthful infatuation.

I never met Nan's parents. I do not know how much influence they exerted on her. Ultimately, I suppose, she must have made her own decision.

On a Friday before Easter, about two years into their passionate love affair, when Eric was about to graduate from high school, I read a letter Nan had written in which she told him that she loved him and wanted to marry him. I thought as I read this, "I hope you don't talk him into marrying you before he gets to college." A day after Eric received the love letter, he called her and she was not at home. Puzzled at first, he became angry when he was given some information by her roommate. The next Monday Nan called and things were never the same for them again. Eric, for the first time, tasted the acridity of betrayal. Nan had met someone else and was dating him at the time that Eric received the love letter.

I have deliberately avoided describing Nan up to this point because I wanted the reader to imagine the archetypal figure of romance that a young girl is for her young lover. She was a short girl, with long hair and very large black eyes. She always wore blue jeans; in the two years that I knew her, I never once caught a view of her legs. She cut her hair and seemed to my son and others who met her to have a beautiful Italianate face.

What I had feared had come true. The first love which my son believed to be unbreakable shattered into a million pieces. Nan was no longer a high school student. She wanted to marry, and when she met someone who was willing to marry, she could not resist the prize of security. I give her the benefit of the doubt in this matter, for to say that she was in love with Eric on Friday and out of love with him on Monday is to paint a portrait of a typical fickle female. Whatever she felt for Eric she must have sublimated to achieve a secure, safe future. She could not marry Eric, who was planning to go to college. So true love on Friday turned to false love on Monday. Eric was devastated. When Nan came to Cortland to see her family, he spent a last day with her, no doubt trying for a reconciliation. But all that resulted from that effort was a saccharine letter she wrote to him thanking him for the lovely day she had spent with him. But she clearly planned to marry her Italian.

As I watched Eric suffering, I thought of writing a letter to

Nan's parents, listing our assets. Would that have made them forget that Eric was Jewish? But I was not about to bribe Nan's family. This was, after all, the twentieth century, and parents did not meet to discuss dowry arrangements and assure each other of financial worth. Besides, I believed that what I had originally feared was at the root of the betrayal. It was not money. If I had assured Nan that Eric without a job was richer than her fiancé could ever be, I do not think that would have made a difference. I do not believe that Nan was ever comfortable with our Jewishness or our intellectual preoccupations. I saw her several years ago still wearing those blue jeans; she seemed taller, slimmer, more mature. She was with some old Italian women. She asked me to give her regards to Eric.

I did not give her regards to Eric. He never talked to us about her desertion. We tried to make light of it by underplaying our reaction. We were afraid for him; would he do anything rash? We wanted him to think of his sorrow as a normal phenomenon in the lives of young lovers and did not want to exacerbate his grief by dwelling on it. Several years later, when he could talk about his feelings, he complained because we had not been sympathetic enough during the period when he was so sad. But when we explained the reasons for our behavior, he understood. He recalled how I had warned him about the ephemeral nature of young love.

It took Eric a long time to recover. I know he lost his innocence. I suppose one never really forgets the first love affair, and I know he never forgot Nan. About a year before he died he said that he would have liked to see her again. When she learned of Eric's death, she sent me a letter and wrote that I couldn't know what was in her heart. But I think I do know. No matter what she feels for her husband now, she can never forget what she once felt when Eric was a part of her fresh, glorious youth and when they both believed in undying love.

I remember thinking when I read Nan's letter that Eric's life might have been different if they had married. He might be alive today, and I might be a grandmother instead of a grieving mother. For what I feared when they were so close, that Nan would become pregnant and they would have to marry, is what I wish had happened. Another if-then. Another path he might have taken that would have kept him alive. Instead he enrolled at the State University at Binghamton to study music.

5

Never Give Your Children Music Lessons

Eric was a fascinating personality with his overwhelming pre-occupation with music and piano playing and his extremely strong feelings; it was impossible to remain indifferent to him. He was just beginning to come to grips with the need to bring his gifts into focus and to create a discipline capable of dealing with such powerful, almost volcanic emotions. It was a great struggle for him, but he had such tremendous ambitions, and such a vision of what he wanted to be.

Seymour Lipkin, Letter, Dec. 3, 1980

"He was just a wonderful kid. . . . I liked him so much," said SUNY-Binghamton music department chairman Alice L. Mitchell, who had Kaminsky as a student in freshman music theory courses. "I felt so sorry he was transferring, but he just couldn't get away from the lure of New York City. Of course, it wasn't just New York City. He wanted to be in a real school of music, a real conservatory."

Binghamton Evening Press, Sept. 16, 1980

Eric was accepted at Syracuse University. He did not want to attend SUNY-Binghamton because his father was a professor at this college, and Eric had the normal instinct to restrict parental supervision. But when Professor Harry Lincoln in the music department raved about Walter Ponce, a teacher with whom Eric could study, we were all impressed. Ponce had a Ph.D. from Juilliard—no mean achievement—and he was a concert pianist.

Again another if-then. Would Eric's life have been different if he had attended Syracuse University? Perhaps there he would have lost his interest in music. Perhaps he would be alive today.

Music. Music. Everyone who knew Eric talked of his musical promise. One of his piano teachers, Seymour Lipkin, was quoted in *The New York Times*. He said of Eric: "He was a passionate fellow with a tremendous potential. . . . He was just terrific. He loved music and he loved performing. He was in it with his whole self. . . . He was going to burn the world up." (Sept. 16, 1980, B3). But I wish now that I had never bought him a piano or given him his first music lesson. How and why he became *obsessed* with the idea of being a classical pianist I do not know. Perhaps Walter Ponce was primarily responsible for that motivation; I do not know what happened between them. Eric studied with Ponce for one year, and then he studied with Seymour Fink for half a term at Binghamton. Perhaps they know what it was that initiated Eric's insane desire to become a concert performer. I think anyone who wants to be a concert pianist must be touched by a form of madness.

Think of what it means to want to be a concert pianist. It means that you want to be judged in a very special way, not merely as a good performer but as the best performer. It means that you sit alone on a stage playing an expensive piano, trying to join that elite group of great artists. You have been practicing since you were six years old, spending as much as eight hours a day at the piano. You rent a concert hall, fill it with proud family and friends who applaud loudly. But sitting in that audience is one man who has the power only gods are supposed to have. He is a junior critic reviewing your concert for *The New York Times,* and he will decide your fate. Rarely does a music critic with the status of a Harold Schonberg bother to attend the concert recitals of new performers. Instead this work is left to subordinate critics who usually write very brief reviews.

Schonberg has denied that the music critic has any power:

Perhaps the drama critic may have a great deal of power. Not the music critic, though some think they do. . . . There is no case in history where a great piece of music or a great performer has been mortally wounded by a negative or stupid review. Critics don't make careers. Artists make careers. A bad review in the *Times* may set a career back for a season or two; a strongly favorable one may help for a season or two. That is about all. (TSM, Feb. 8, 1981, 41)

Does Schonberg really want us to believe that "artists make careers"? Does he really believe that, despite what critics write, the genius of unfavorably reviewed *unknown* artists will ultimately triumph? To deny that a famous critic has great power is to contradict empirical evidence. Ask the hundreds of aspiring musicians who never received contracts to play for the influential music companies because of reviews like the following one by Bernard Holland:

> Marya Marlowe plays the piano with a coloristic touch and lovely musical instincts, but she does not use these talents wisely. Her recital at Alice Tully Hall Saturday evening frequently crossed the line between freedom of expression and rhythmic misrepresentation—the note values in Chopin's B-flat minor Scherzo and Debussy's great "Hommage à Rameau" too often treated as toys. Miss Marlowe's playing of the Ravel Sonatine was equally strange—its finale slowed to a crawl and the other two movements dismembered by tempo changes.
>
> Much of the evening suffered from bad nerves and bad judgment; but despite the memory lapses and the chaos of the Liszt Sonata, there were frustrating fragments of real beauty. Miss Marlowe's individuality is refreshing, but there is a point where personality in the service of music ends and selfishness begins. (T, Apr. 30, 1981, C18)

Surely no one is so ingenuous as to believe that Marya Marlowe's career was not affected by this review. And yet Schonberg would have us believe that critics are not responsible for making or breaking artists. Does he want us to believe that even *one* small column of ecstatic praise from him does not have inestimable value for a young artist?

There is, of course, another route an artist can take besides the musical debut, and that is the musical competition. Consider the premises underlying both approaches. In the musical debut, an artist performs for the critic on the stage of Carnegie Hall. Usually the critic listens to the sounds of music and hastens to write a review immediately after the concert. It does not matter that he may have heard incorrectly or judged unfairly. It does not matter that such judgment is often the quintessence of subjectivity, for once you have heard a sound in the concert hall it is gone forever. You cannot call the sound back to dispute a critic's review of the sound you made when you hit the piano keys. What ego you must have to survive this ordeal. Wanting to be the best in the concert field is not like wanting to be the best runner, swimmer, or tennis player. Specific objective criteria exist to judge the best runner. But what criteria could be used to judge the best pianist?

Many years ago a musical child prodigy fled from the Nazis in Hungary and came to this country. He spent long arduous hours preparing for his first New York violin recital. I and the rest of the audience gave him a standing ovation after he played. The important critic from *The Times,* however, did not like his performance at that time. Even though my friend went on to receive good and glowing reviews for other concerts, he never attained the status of star performer. Was he as good as Itzhak Perlman or Pinchas Zukerman? Would he have achieved the heights of success if he had had the right connections and *luck?*

Speaking of disputes in music, Donald Henahan claims that it is

> naive and illusory to believe that much more than technical superiority can be proved beyond dispute at these levels of professionalism and artistry. Here we enter the mystic realm of taste, where argument is unending and wonderfully invigorating even though ultimately beyond settlement. It is not by choice that the bitterest disputes in the arts take place not over technical points which can be judged with a fair degree of accuracy to the satisfaction of all, but in the cloudy areas of taste, where distinctions can become so fine that the casual observer may think them foolishly contrived and meaningless.

Henahan, who has himself offered definitive judgments of concert artists and who has condemned the lack of artistry of many musicians, goes on to suggest that we should cheerfully accept the uncertainties and vague limits of taste. "Think, for instance, how drab life would be if we could all agree on what made one Metropolitan opera performer better or worse than another" (T, Jan. 18, 1981, 17).

Many performers would prefer the "drabness" of verifiable objective criteria, since the "uncertainties of taste" usually ruin the careers of many fine musicians. Cecil Licad was the first pianist in ten years to win the Levintritt Award. She was trained by Seymour Lipkin and Rudolph Serkin and judged by Zubin Mehta, Isaac Stern, and many notables in the music world. But she received the following notice from Donald Henahan when she performed with the New York Philharmonic.

Miss Licad, though not the kind of artist who is ever likely to make a listener's hair stand straight up, came across as an appealing combination of fragile grace and fiery power, either of which she could call on when the music required.

She did not really loosen up in the opening movement, taking a rather too regular and marchlike approach to Chopin's Arabesques and ornamented melodies. Even in the slow movement, when Miss Licad's lyrical gifts really began to unfold, she was not free enough with the rhythms or conscious enough of the instrument's coloristic possibilities. Miss Licad's instincts served her well, however, and there were stretches in the movement when she let the piano step into the role of a Belline soprano and sing its heart out.

Technically there was a great deal to admire, of course. Although she stopped short of banging, Miss Licad could lay into the keys and dominate Chopin's famously polite and reticent orchestra. Each of her hands had a mind of its own and what was even better, seemed to be attached to a brain and possibly a soul. Time will tell. (T, Oct. 10, 1981, 14)

Thus, obviously one man's genius is another man's promise. One wonders, was Miss Licad really the only pianist in this country worthy of the Levintritt Award? Did no one in the past ten years deserve this award except Miss Licad? Nonsense. Friends, influence, and luck play as great a role in the musical world as in the world of politics.

There are pianists who attempt to overcome the "uncertainties of taste" by utilizing the competitions in Germany, Chile, England, America, and other countries. Winning first prize in some of these competitions not only involves a financial reward, but is also supposed to guarantee artistic success.

Yet despite the fact that computers and special judges were used in the 1977 Van Cliburn competition in Fort Worth, the audience disagreed with the judges' awarding of first prize to Steven deGroote and raised $10,000 to further the career of Youri Egorov. So far as I know, neither one has obtained the status of Vladimir Horowitz, who abhors the competition route.

Emanuel Ax, who won the first Rubinstein International Competition in 1974, said that

> piano contests are really lotteries. I would stake as much on a bingo game as a piano competition, there are so many variables involved. Suppose you are not feeling well and play poorly—you're out. Suppose you play well and the other ten contestants are all Vladimir Ashkenazys—that's the end of you. Suppose you're in superb form and everyone else is horrible but the jury happens to hate everything you do—you're finished. . . Winning or losing can happen to anyone—it's just the luck of the draw. (T, July 17, 1981, C6)

Eric told me about a pianist who won first prize in an international piano competition. How astonished I was to read a review of his performance several years later; it was dismissed in a sneering one line of criticism. Another pianist told me that he had not achieved either fame or fortune as a result of winning several competitions. Nothing illustrates more clearly the "uncertainties of taste" than the contradictory judgments of established pianists.

Abbey Simon, a famous pianist, was kind enough to invite Eric to his home to judge his musical ability. Simon told me that he had encouraged Eric to continue to strive to become a professional pianist. However, he had a great deal to learn and would need to work unceasingly at the piano. After a year and a half at Binghamton, Eric decided to study music in New York. The day he told us of his plans was one of the saddest we had thus far experienced in our relations with our son. For we both felt that it was wrong for him to leave Binghamton for the dubious career of concert pianist. He had been bitten by the conservatory bug. Professor Harry Lincoln in the music department told us that very often talented students at the university felt that they had to enroll in a conservatory. It didn't matter, he warned us, that facilities for practicing in New York would be unbelievably bad; nothing mattered except that you had to be in the center of musical activity. Eric was warned by a knowledgeable and experienced musician that, in his opinion, the Manhattan School of Music was mediocre. He advised Eric to stay at Binghamton and come in to New York to study with a good teacher, but Eric was obsessed with going to the city. The Manhattan School of Music offered an audition in January. I wanted him to have a successful audition, but I did not want him to live in Manhattan.

Unlike Gertrude Stein and Flannery O'Connor, who did not like music, I loved listening to it. But I was not impressed by my son's desire to make music his profession. I used to read the music reviews every day. What contradictions, sophistry, and negativism they contained. The critics seemed to be motivated by one premise: there isn't enough room at the top for more than a very few; make sure that you stop as many musicians as possible at the very start. Discourage them so that they will leave the field or at the very least give up the mad idea of becoming a concert pianist. From one point of view these critics are correct when they discourage young people from entering a hopelessly limited field. However, I could not stop Eric from pursuing a career he wanted. Despite what he had been told by a professional artist about the insurmountable odds he faced in the music world, he was determined to strive, to seek, and not to yield.

When he was accepted at the Manhattan School of Music, we spent three harrowing days looking for an apartment for him, and finding the most appalling hovels. Finally he rented a room on Ninetieth Street and Riverside Drive in the apartment of an old Jewish woman. (At that time on Eighty-eighth Street a young woman was knifed during a robbery.) The building had a doorman, but the area was so dangerous that Eric usually ran the blocks to his apartment from the subway on Broadway. He boasted that with his speed no mugger could catch him.

What did he find at his music school? Since every student there was majoring in music, he was exposed only to music students, and was completely divorced from the healthy influence of heterogeneity at liberal arts colleges. Since every young person at a conservatory is primarily concerned with excelling, an inevitable and unfortunate competitive climate permeates all activities. Hear me play! is the cry of every performer. Am I not better than I was yesterday? Am I not better than this or that student? What a neurotic existence, to practice eight hours a day, to play and play and play, and then to receive at the end of the year the judgment of a jury of teachers who, like the music critics of *The Times,* pretend to know the objective value of what is essentially subjective. Small wonder that many music majors are neurotic. I worried about Eric's obsession with performance.

Everything Professor Lincoln had predicted about studying music in New York came true. Eric did not have access to a good piano at the Manhattan School of Music beyond the limited assigned time. Often we gave him extra money to study in studios. While at that time it cost no more than $2,500 a year to study at Binghamton, $12,000 a year was required for tuition and living expenses in New York. And the living conditions were deplorable.

After a few months, Eric finally obtained a room at the Ninety-second Street "Y" and we breathed a sigh of relief, for the "Y" had good instruments that the residents could use. However, the "Y" proved to be unsatisfactory because after a year Eric was not allowed to use the pianos. The woman in charge told me that he played too much and too strongly and even broke one of the strings on one of the best pianos. He did not have a gentleman's way of playing. In desperation he moved out of the "Y" and obtained two rooms in a large apartment that his friend rented on 122nd Street and Broadway. To ensure that he would always have money, we gave him an account from which he could draw funds for emergency needs. He withdrew from the account $1,000 to pay for his rooms and for the rental of an old Knabe grand piano: $200 for delivery of the piano, $200 for the monthly rental charge, and $300 for the deposit. The Knabe was old and had poor sound, but it was the typical kind of instrument available in that price range.

When we visited Eric's new home, we were appalled. Several broken bottles of wine and their contents were scattered all over the main floor lobby. Several drunks were leaning against the wall near the elevator. We learned that tenants had been robbed many times. The rooms which Eric's friend rented to students were shabby and dirty. We told Eric that we did not like his apartment or his neighborhood; it seemed unsafe to us. But he was never frightened or nervous in the city; he had visited the place ever since he was a child, and he was convinced that he had "street-smarts." I can still see the grin on his face when he assured us he knew how to protect himself against the muggers.

After a few months he decided that he needed his own apartment. He found one that he liked in Washington Heights on 183rd Street, in a building facing a park, bounded on one side by a synagogue and on the other by a church. The apartment was clean; it had a living room, bedroom, kitchen, and bath, and, most important of all, was so situated that he could practice at any time without disturbing anyone. An old neighbor on his floor referred to him as the Liberace of the Heights, and the janitor of the building told us that on warm evenings the people in the neighborhood would sit in the park and listen to him as he practiced, enjoying the free classical concert. Eric had returned the rented piano just before he moved into his new place. His teacher had assured us that he needed his own instrument. Therefore, we bought him a Baldwin, and Eric set about in earnest to practice, to fill in the gaps in his musical knowledge. Always there was an insatiable desire to find *the* teacher who would really, finally, teach him what he had to learn.

He did not feel that he was learning enough. But he was delighted when he discovered that he could enter the school contest to play with the Manhattan School of Music orchestra as a soloist. Then one of the teachers invited us to visit her apartment and listen to Eric practice a piano concerto.

How pleased I was that, after two years, we would finally meet one of Eric's teachers. We had read Helen Ruttencutter's devastating portrait of the student-teacher relationship at Juilliard, and it left me with very few illusions about the teaching profession in music. But still I was very anxious to meet Mildred Rone. When we entered her apartment and stepped into a living room dominated by two grand pianos, she did not greet us, but sat looking at the score that Eric was playing. The temperature was over ninety degrees, and Eric and the pianist who accompanied him were already performing. For some reason the room was not air-conditioned, and we and the pianists were sweating profusely. After they finished playing, Rone talked to us in desultory fashion about matters having very little to do with Eric. I was so hot, so thirsty. This supposed exemplar of New York sophistication did not do what any hostess in the smallest town would do, offer her guests a glass of water on a hot day. So we left her not one whit wiser as to what she did as a music teacher or what she thought of Eric's musical career. She merely reinforced my negative view of the musical scene in New York.

What I particularly resented was the fact that Eric had to spend so much extra money on private lessons; he never seemed to get enough training at the school where he paid tuition. Like psychiatrists, music teachers insist that an hour of their time is worth at least $50 to $100, no matter what they say or do. I know distinguished physicists, philosophers, logicians, mathematicians, novelists, and poets who spend hours in conference with their students but do not charge them for time spent outside the classroom. When an Einstein works additional hours with a good mathematics or physics student, he does not charge $100 an hour.

When Eric died, we received a letter of condolence from the dean of the Manhattan School of Music. I think he attended the funeral. But the president of the school never wrote to us, not even when he received a donation in Eric's memory from the faculty at Binghamton and other friends at Cortland. The Juilliard String Quartet dedicated a concert to Eric's memory at SUNY-Binghamton. But I did not hear of any memorial concert for Eric at Manhattan, even though I donated his piano to the school. But that's the point, isn't it? If the inaction of the president was representative of the level of insensitivity and decorum in the school, then it would be ridiculous to expect the amenities of civilized behavior from either students or faculty in a conservatory set in the heart of an "open city."

For that is what New York is, an "open city," and if I had known then what I now know about it, I would have shut my son in a cage to keep him from coming to this city. "I love New York," people sing in desperation, trying to convince themselves that they love what they should fear.

In this "open city" my son had one more year to study and earn his degree. He was busy with many plans for his future: auditioning with an orchestra, preparing for admittance to a graduate school, plans for the summer. In my last conversation with him, he said, "I want to go to Marboro this summer, Mom." "Good," I replied, "I'll pay for everything. Just get out of the city." Several days later he talked to my husband on the phone, and the last words he spoke to him were "Give my love to Mom."

Some of my colleagues at Cortland always asked about Eric. They first knew him as a small boy of five and were always interested in his activities and plans. A day before he died, one of them said, "You're lucky you have such a son. He's so motivated, so talented. He doesn't drink or smoke or take drugs, and he hasn't joined one of the religious cults."

Lucky, we thought he was lucky. His music kept him busy, and we could afford to support him in whatever way he wanted us to. He told my brother that he expected to spend the next ten years of his life perfecting his art. But he made the terrible mistake of walking into a subway one night, and all his hopes and plans were destroyed in the second that it takes a knife to pierce through the body, as Stephen Crane noted, "as easily as if it had been a melon."

And now there is no place left in the world for me. When I visit the homes of my relatives, I see Eric sitting in their chairs, eating at their tables. Every room has a memory. When I leave for places where I have never been before to escape memories, I can not escape. If I go to a hotel, I see a young boy who looks so much like Eric that for a moment, an incredible moment, he does not seem to be dead; perhaps some terrible mistake was made; perhaps he ran away, perhaps he was kidnapped, and the body in the morgue was wrongly identified. I spent one afternoon looking at a young man sitting by the pool. His face and build made me, for a second, believe in reincarnation. He was Eric, for a second. Even going to the movies involves pain. Our family loved science fiction films, and even the advertisements for such movies bring back thoughts of happier times. I have not listened to music of any kind since Eric died. No matter where I go, no matter what I do, something reminds me of him, and I feel the anguish of loss as if it had just happened.

6

Before the Trial

Of all the creatures that were made, he [man] is the most detestable. Of the entire brood he is the only one—the solitary one—that possesses malice. That is the basest of all instincts, passions, vices—the most hateful. . . . He is the only creature that inflicts pain for sport, knowing it to be pain.
                                        Mark Twain, *Autobiography*

There is still another kind of anguish that the parents of a murdered child have to endure. If the murder takes place in Manhattan, they have not only the agony of a trial to live through, but also the agony of being involved with one of the most defective systems of criminal justice in the nation. In New York there are too many criminals, too few prosecutors and judges, and too much legal chicanery that benefits the criminal rather than the victim. Anyone who has read the recent books on criminal justice is aware of its appalling deficiencies. Anyone who has had to deal with the Criminal Court in Manhattan will vouch for the accuracy of District Attorney Morganthau's judgment that the "Criminal Court is in terrible shape" (T, June 17, 1985, B2).

A few weeks after my son was murdered, Detectives Martin Gonzalez, Leonard Caruso, and John Bruno arrested Ferman Urena. A month later Gonzalez traveled to Utah where Jose Deltejo had fled, arrested him, and brought him back to New York. That the police were able to apprehend these two criminals was a remarkable feat, since so many murderers are never caught. We expected the trial to begin in a short time.

How naive we were. Awaiting us was a series of interminable delays, the typical ones that make a mockery of the concept of speedy justice and serve to intensify the suffering and despair of the victims.

The police told us that William Greenbaum would be the assistant district attorney in charge of the case. He called us and gave my husband a summary of the procedure that would be followed. Nothing happened for nine months! During that time my husband repeatedly called Greenbaum. He seemed very sympathetic, but harassed, and would give us the only answer he could give us. We had to wait. There were other cases he had to dispose of before he could get to ours. It used to take two years for a criminal case to be heard. We were not to consider it unusual that a year might pass before anything happened.

So we waited, and waited. Every once in a while I would urge my husband to call Greenbaum again, and we always got the same answer. Nothing had happened. He did not give us any details about the case for fear of leakage.

On April 2, the day before my son's birthday, the D.A. informed us that one of the defendants had submitted a plea bargain. He would identify the killer in return for an eight-and-a-half to twenty-five-years sentence. Greenbaum wanted to know what we thought about this possibility. Of course he would not be bound by our decision. He simply wanted to give us the opportunity to express our views. Our view was that we wanted both men to be charged with murder. But since we could not expect this to happen, we wanted the one who actually did the stabbing to receive the worst possible sentence. And if the plea bargain would enable Greenbaum to accomplish this, then we would have to accept the notion of a plea bargain. In fact, we would have to accept whatever he decided to do, since as the victim's parents we were allowed the luxury of mourning but not the advantage of participating in the legal process.

On April 12, 1981, the murderer of Dr. Halberstam was convicted in Washington, D.C., after the jury deliberated for two hours. Yet Halberstam was murdered in December, 1980, four months after my son's death. Unable to control my impatience, my anger, my despair, I called Greenbaum for the first time on April 14. (Until then only my husband had spoken to him.)

After speaking to him, I felt as if I were in the midst of an oppressive nightmare. First there was the unbearable knowledge that instead of talking to my son, I was talking to the D.A. about his murder. Then there was the knowledge that Greenbaum had not been devoting full time to dealing with my tragedy. He had other cases, other horrors he had to deal with. His immediate response to my question was defensive.

"You are," he said, "a teacher. In your world you are used to solving problems in a rational way, demanding the same kind of effort from your students. But in my world we don't always solve problems in a rational, disciplined, and straight-forward fashion." Then I asked him, "What can I do to help?" To give me the feeling that I could do something to help, he asked me a question. "Where is your son's clothing?"

"What clothing?" I asked, puzzled.

"The clothing he wore when he was killed."

"I don't know." Why would he ask such a cruel question? "I suppose the funeral director at the chapel knows what happened to his clothes, or the police or the morgue. It is the custom to bury the dead with fresh clothes."

Recognizing that he had made a mistake, Greenbaum changed the subject. I do not know to this day why he asked me about the clothes, nor do I know what happened to my son's clothes, although I shall remember what he wore when I saw him in the morgue until the day I die.

"Where was your son going that night when he took the subway?" Greenbaum asked.

"I don't know. To see a movie or a friend; to eat at a favorite restaurant. He usually practiced all day, and wanted to relax on Saturday night. Maybe his neighbor or the janitor spoke to him before he left his house."

"You could speak to them if you want to."

"What? You mean go over to his apartment, to where he lived?" I could not speak and handed the phone to my husband. Greenbaum told him that he had tried to make me feel better by involving me in the case and giving me a task. Well intentioned, he had said the cruelest words to me, conjuring up vivid images of Eric's body in the morgue and in his coffin, and images of his lively movements in his apartment. For a moment, as I began to sob wildly, I hated this decent, kind man; I hated him for talking to me from New York *about* my son. I wanted to talk *to* my son who would have been twenty-three on April 3, 1981.

The criminal justice system in the city is designed to torture the victim's family with delays. We waited and we waited and we waited. Greenbaum labored assiduously to bring the case to trial. But my despair intensified on Eric's birthday. For the first time I felt a kinship with Anne Sexton, Sylvia Plath, and those who chose to end the suffering, who chose death over life. Teaching the poetry of Plath and Sexton with the smug attitude of a happy soul, I used to say these women were irrational, uncontrolled, wallowing in their despair, making a mockery of all we value in the educational world: rationality, discipline, control. But this is the kind of platitude we mouth until we confront tragedy. Then we know what it means to want to die.

One night, unable to sleep because the horrific images of how my son died kept me awake, I went into the kitchen and saw a serrated steak knife on the table. I picked it up and pushed it against that part of my body where I imagined the aorta is, the aorta which the murderer cut in my son's body. It seemed to me that Stephen Crane was wrong; the knife does not slice the skin "as easily as if it is a melon." However, Deltejo had the special advantage of the coward. He struck from the back.

In June I finally looked directly at the two faces of evil, and, as Hannah Arendt observed, evil was banal. My husband and I came to New York at the beginning of June, 1981. We met and spoke to William Greenbaum and the three police officers, Bruno, Gonzalez, and Caruso, who had apprehended Urena and Deltejo. We were present in Judge Benjamin Altman's courtroom where he presided over Calendar hearings to determine when trials would begin. The room was filled with criminals, lawyers, victims, and their families. It was there that we first saw Urena and Deltejo. It is difficult for me to describe Urena and Deltejo. My vision blurred when I looked at them, as if my eyes wanted to avoid actually seeing them. However, I remember thinking that they were so slim and so short and so young. This is why the police originally believed that they were thirteen-year-old children. But Urena was seventeen and Deltejo was eighteen when they murdered my son. Deltejo was very short, just a little over five feet, and Urena had a mass of curly hair. They looked like ordinary Hispanics you see everywhere in the city; they were well dressed, calm, and gave no evidence that they had been traumatized by their vicious deeds. How unfortunate it is that the faces of evil are banal; if the faces displayed a message of corruption, we could protect ourselves against them.

It became apparent that Altman would continue to do what he had been doing for several weeks. He gave the defense lawyer, James Moriarty, the opportunity to delay. From the beginning of June until the middle of July, we faced what seemed to me to be judicial procrastination. We would come to the D.A.'s office and sit there and wait for nothing to happen. We would go to Altman's court and discover that still another delay had been mandated. Several times we went back to Cortland. Finally after six weeks Altman decided he had given Moriarty enough time.

No mention has been made thus far of Irwin Klein, Deltejo's privately hired lawyer. He surfaced briefly to demand a plea bargain for his innocent client. He claimed that Urena was lying. Of course, in the eyes of the law, both Urena and Deltejo were equally guilty of the crime, regardless of who actually used the knife. But the D.A. had offered the plea bargain of eight-and-a-half to twenty-five years to Urena because he was convinced that Deltejo was the actual murderer. The first hearing was supposed to deal with Urena's confession and his acceptance of the plea bargain. Altman, preparing to go on vacation, set up a Huntley hearing with Judge E. Torres to serve as the presiding judge. A Huntley hearing in New York is a separate proceeding in a criminal case in which the admissibility of an accused's extra-judicial statements is determined.

The temperature on that day in June was ninety-five degrees. We were, however, hot from more than the heat by the time the day was over. My brother and his wife joined us, and we arrived at the D.A.'s office at 10:00 A.M. We went to Altman's Calendar Court and saw Furman Urena and his lawyer, Moriarty, who once again attempted to delay the proceedings. But Altman assigned the hearing to Judge Torres. We went to Judge Torres's chambers, but never saw him. We waited all afternoon and Judge Torres never appeared. We later learned that he was to go on vacation the next day. I do not know why Judge Altman did not know that Torres would not be present.

Oddly enough, Urena's mother and girlfriend waited with us in the hall outside the judge's chamber. Greenbaum warned us not to talk to them. Probably he feared that I might act irrationally and commit some legal indiscretion. I sat on a bench next to a security guard who had a gun, and I thought of how easy it would be to grab the pistol and shoot the woman who bore Urena. But she was not responsible for her son's acts. She stood quietly, next to the bench, a middle-aged woman, neatly dressed, with a sober, careworn look on her face.

Everyone was disturbed by Judge Torres's failure to appear. The D.A. was so disheartened that he told us he did not think the trial could begin until the beginning of September. But unknown to us, he tried to deal with the Honorable Benjamin Altman on July 10. We did not know about the calendar call that day; perhaps Greenbaum wanted to spare us the agony of another meaningless day at court. When we spoke to him that evening he told us that he had had an unbelievable experience with Altman. When one of the policemen told us what Altman had said, we were incredulous. We could not believe that a judge would make such a statement in court. We decided to send for a transcript of the July 10 proceedings.

The relevant page of the transcript appears at the end of this book so that the reader will not think I have made up the words spoken by Judge Altman. I quote below from page 4. Greenbaum had been pressing Altman to force Moriarty to make a decision about the plea bargain offer. Greenbaum accused Moriarty of using stalling tactics, and wanted to withdraw the plea bargain offer. Altman insisted that Greenbaum had to keep the plea bargain offer open before the Huntley hearing. It was not the defendant's fault that the hearing on July 9 did not materialize.

MR. GREENBAUM: May I respectfully inquire of your Honor as follows? Your Honor has been made aware on the record of the fact that we are now at a point after the People have been answering ready, steadily, since June 3rd, 1981—

JUDGE ALTMAN: *This is only a murder,* Mr. Greenbaum, and I have heard it over, and over, and over again. Only a murder, and we are talking about an 18-year-old. [Italics mine]

I have read this passage again and again. It haunts my dreams. How could a judge make such a remark? "Only a murder." What would Altman have considered to be worse than a murder? Altman seemed to be very concerned about this young defendant, Urena, who robbed my son and pushed him onto the subway tracks. What was wrong with Judge Altman that day? Could anything justify his making such a remark? Was he sick? Did he lose his temper because Greenbaum kept importuning him to set a date for the hearing after so many delays? Had his daily exposure to criminals caused him to lose control? Was he simply, for one moment, irrational; not mean but irrational and incapable of saying what he meant? Perhaps in exasperation, tired, anxious to go on vacation, he vented his irritation at Greenbaum, and the words did not come out quite as he intended. But as a judge, Altman was required to use words more accurately than anyone else in the court.

I sent a transcript of Altman's remarks to the State Commission on Judicial Conduct. On April 7, 1982, the commission informed me that the complaint had been dismissed because there was "insufficient indication of judicial misconduct in the Judge's remark to warrant an investigation."

It was my naive expectation that the commission would reprimand Altman. But evidently some judges can use improper language with impunity. Charlotte M. Hullinger tells the horror story of a woman in Indiana whose four children were lined up in front of her and murdered. She was shot but lived to hear the trial judge casually remark at the sentencing of the murderers of her children, "The dead are dead; now, let us turn our attention to the living," before he brought up the subject of probation for the killers.

Fortunately, Judge Brenda Solof, who took over after Altman went on vacation, decided that the Huntley hearing would begin on July 14. At that hearing Moriarty discussed the plea bargain with Urena. As a court appointed lawyer Moriarty did everything he could to help Urena, and an interpreter was present to explain the meaning of the judge's comments. In the back of the courtroom sat Urena's mother, father, several brothers and sisters, and a girlfriend holding an infant. At first Urena refused to accept the written plea bargain statement. Judge Morris Goldman then ruled that the hearing would begin. Detective Bruno took the stand prepared to give his testimony. At that point Moriarty accused the judge of being intemperate. When Goldman asked Moriarty what he meant by this accusation, Urena suddenly leaned over and told Moriarty that he would accept the plea bargain. For a moment, just a moment, I was relieved, because Urena's admission of guilt meant that he could be the significant witness in the case against Deltejo.

In a deep part of my psyche, I am a Greek, and like Electra and Orestes and all the mythological figures who have the courage to avenge foul murder, I feel this intense desire to destroy those who have destroyed what I love. Unfortunately, I am also like Hamlet, incapacitated by my so-called rational mind. So I think and write, and rage and hate, and I do nothing while the memory of my dead son beckons to me to action, to revenge. And the law moves slowly, and whatever the law does will never relieve me of the conviction that I am a coward. I had plenty of opportunity to kill Deltejo and Urena when they were a few feet away from me during the hearings and the trial. Security was lax enough so that I could have shot them. But I really understood for the first time why Hamlet did not just get to it and kill his murderer uncle. Even to kill Evil is abhorrent to the normal human soul.

So the waiting game began again. From the middle of July to August 24, nothing happened in the courtroom. In our hearts the anguish intensified as we remembered that at the beginning of August, the year before, we had joined our son at the Concord for a holiday and that we would never again be able to share any vacations with him. He would never again enjoy the beauty of summer.

Instead of meeting him in the Catskills and watching him

enjoy himself, eating three fabulous meals and then eating again at midnight, and rowing and playing various games, we were sitting in our house, writing cards for the unveiling. This is a cruel Jewish ceremony which intensifies the grief of the bereaved. After the headstone is placed over the grave of the deceased, about a year after his death, friends and relatives are not only invited to witness a memorial ceremony at the grave but are also invited to the home of the family of the deceased to eat and to drink. I do not know why we had an unveiling. We are not religious; we do not believe in religious rituals. Yet it seemed somehow the only thing left for us to do for our son, and so we followed convention. Perhaps that is what funerals and unveilings are for; they are ways of commemorating the dead so that they, for an illusory moment, seem to be alive. Certainly when I fill out the following card to send to relatives and friends, I cannot believe he is in a coffin. I send out invitations to friends and relatives that begin:

Eric Kaminsky—Unveiling

I used to send out cards that read:

Eric Kaminsky
Invites you to a recital of music by Bach, Beethoven and Chopin
at the Cortland High School
Cocktail buffet at the Kaminsky residence.

The trial of Jose Deltejo was supposed to take place on August 24, 1981. As usual, there was a delay; Klein asked for a postponement until August 27. He asked for a plea bargain like the one Urena obtained. The adversary system doesn't require that Klein should be interested in Truth. It requires only that he defend his client, no matter what he has done, no matter how culpable he is.

At a meeting of 1,500 members of the Association of Trial Lawyers, H. Rothblatt said: "In criminal cases we don't usually love our clients. Some of them are pretty miserable people. But if they've paid the fee, they have a right to be loved for that trial" (T, July 28, 1981, B20). In other words, justice is compromised by economics. Is this not an admirable system that thrives on the employment of men who will defend murderers to earn a living? The system is supposed to work for the benefit of the innocent. But it seems to work for the benefit of the murderer as well; lawyers make a good living out of defending the guilty as well as the innocent.

So Mr. Klein obtained still another extension to delay the trial until August 27. We do not know why Klein was permitted to do this except that the D.A. assured us he had a legitimate reason. On August 25 Greenbaum called to tell us that the trial might be delayed for six weeks, because Klein had requested a psychiatric examination for his client. Greenbaum did not know whether Judge Goldman would grant that request on August 27. If Goldman did not grant it, then the trial would begin on August 27 as planned. On August 26 Greenbaum called to tell us the trial would be delayed until October for a number of reasons: Urena was suddenly uncooperative because he was afraid to talk, afraid that he would be killed by Deltejo in some way; Urena's lawyer, Moriarty, was in Florida, and Greenbaum couldn't talk to Urena unless the lawyer was present. Greenbaum would have to decide on his response to Urena if he refused to testify against Deltejo and reneged on his plea bargain agreement. Then there was the matter of Greenbaum's vacation at the end of September. The trial had been delayed in the summer because a policeman was on vacation. Judge Torres never showed up for a hearing because he was going on vacation. Judge Altman offered his memorable words on the subject of my son's murder before he went on vacation. And now Greenbaum was going on vacation in September.

We did not want to think about the new court schedule, because we did not believe in it. We would believe when we saw the jury members sitting in their seats in the courtroom. Would the trial take place in November, in December, or in January? What new ploy would the defense attorneys dream up that would enable them to delay the proceedings?

We remained in New York until Sunday, August 31, when we attended the unveiling ceremony in the Mount Moriah Cemetery. Mount Moriah is the name of the place where God commanded Abraham to kill his son, Isaac. But Isaac, unlike Eric, did not die. We looked at the stone that had been placed on Eric's grave. It bore a simple inscription:

Eric Kaminsky
Beloved Son
April 3, 1958–September 13, 1980

The rabbi who was supposed to say the necessary words that the ritual demanded never showed up, but fortunately our friend's husband was an ordained rabbi, and another friend, a cab driver, had a Bible with him. So the ceremony proceeded while I fell to the ground, prostrate, weeping uncontrollably, that this vital son I loved should be rotting in his grave. Then everybody went back to Rose Binstock's house, where lunch was served. I had bought the food for that lunch. It is the custom. Can you even begin to imagine what it is like to stand in a supermarket and buy delicious food and drink, not for the usual reason you have always done this, for a dinner party for friends or for a cocktail party for eighty people, but for friends and family who have remembered your son and are, therefore, to be fed while your son lies still in his grave, never to eat again.

These are not events that newspapers or television record—the private agonies that cannot be imagined or described.

After the tragedy of death, of loss, whether it is by accident, illness, or murder, the media lose interest and go on to report new deaths. The reader or viewer is only interested in the event when it is fresh, when it has just happened. Yesterday's news is like stale bread to be discarded. And the public will tolerate one interview, maybe two interviews with John Pius's mother, who describes the horrors of her young son's murder, but after the trial and the incredibly light sentences the murderers of her son receive, her story fades and is forgotten, and the private anguish she will endure for the rest of her life is hardly of interest to anyone but those few who love her. And even they expect her to forget and go on with her life.

After the unveiling, I took a sleeping pill, and the next morning we left for Cortland. In Cortland there is the special kind of pain from feeling Eric's presence in every room in my house. An exceptional kind of sadness comes from giving my neighbor's daughter a gift for her newborn child. I will never have a grandchild.

Then relatives who rarely see us write to invite us to bar mitzvahs and weddings and anniversary parties, while we wait to attend the trial of the murderers of our son. They are the ones who have not come to the unveiling, but want us to attend their joyful celebrations. I feel like the mother in Robert Frost's great poem "Home Burial" who cannot accept the fact that the world goes on while her son is dead. She says:

> The nearest friends can go
> with anyone to death, comes so far short
> They might as well not try to go at all. . . .
> Friends make pretense of following to the grave,
> But before one is in it, their minds are turned
> And making the best of their way back to life
> And living people, and things they understand.
> But the world's evil. I won't have grief so.
> If I can change it. Oh, I won't, I won't! (54)

On September 13, 1981, I lit a Yahrzeit candle in memory of my son. This was a futile act, but the compulsion to perform it was irresistible.

At that time Greenbaum informed us that he had more witnesses. Moriarty attempted to persuade Urena to be cooperative. And Deltejo was to undergo psychiatric tests. Thus nothing would happen until the end of October. If we were lucky my husband and I would receive a Christmas present: Deltejo and Urena would finally know what price they would pay for the murder of my son.

In the middle of October, I decided to visit still another psychiatrist. Thomas Szasz is a literate psychiatrist, the author of many books. The main thrust of his work is to attack the psychiatric establishment and its pretense that it is involved in scientific work. When I called him, he assured me that he did believe in the value of counseling. Because I was impressed by what he had written about the Hinckley case and the strong empathy he revealed for the victims, I decided to see him. In a one-hour session with him in Syracuse, I talked and he listened. He was kind and concerned, expressed his horror at what had happened to my son, and urged me to return because he felt that he could help me. Perhaps if at that time I had read his famous article, "The Ethics of Suicide," I might have become his patient since I was then strongly suicidal. In Szasz's view, suicide is a choice made by an agent. When suicide prevention is used in the case of those who genuinely wish to die, it becomes a form of liberticide. But a few days after I visited Szasz, the trial began, and a Manhattan psychiatrist supplied me with medication that helped me to survive, at least physically, the horrendous ordeal of sitting in the courtroom.

I kept reading the bereavement books, the books on depression, the books that counsel professional psychiatrists on how to deal with grieving patients, and finally the books on death and dying. Philosophers have disagreed about the subject of death as they have disagreed about almost every important concept. Whereas Socrates claimed that death is the only true topic for philosophers, Wittgenstein maintained that death is a non-subject. With the proliferation of courses on death and dying in the university, the subject has become a respectable means of earning points in the academic world. The following announcement is reproduced verbatim as it was sent out to the faculty and students at a large university:

> Associate Professor of Philosophy ——— will be giving an informal discussion for philosophy graduate students and other interested parties on the topic: JOYFUL DYING: REFLECTIONS ON OUR CULTURE'S DISTORTED FEAR OF "FINITUDE."
>
> Our civilization largely takes it for granted that life is "good" and death is "bad". This assumption must be challenged along two fronts. It must be shown (1) that this viewpoint contradicts the fundamentally dialectical structure of human experience; that indeed the deepest human pleasures depend on the glorification of a life-and-death unity; and (2) that the antipathy to death is the product of the deformed individualism of a dying form of culture.

If the professor helped some students at that meeting to overcome their "antipathy to death" as the "product of the deformed individualism of a dying form of culture," he was doing no more or less than other researchers in the death field who try to assure us, like Leibniz, that everything, even death, is for the best in this best of all possible worlds.

The psychiatrist Lisl M. Goodman in her *Death and the Creative Life* urges us to think of death as the culmination of our attempts to achieve completeness. In her view, to accept death is to enhance life. In "Death Does Not Exist" Elisabeth Kübler-Ross states:

> All the hardships that you face in life, all the tests and tribulations, all the nightmares, and all the losses, most people still view as curses, as punishments by God, as something negative. If you would only know that nothing that comes to you is negative. I mean *nothing*. All the trials and the tribulations, and the biggest losses that you ever experience . . . are gifts to you. It's like somebody has to—what do you call that when you make the hot iron into a tool?—you have to temper the iron. It is an opportunity that you are given to grow. That is the sole purpose of existence on this planet Earth. You will not grow if you sit in a beautiful flower garden, and somebody brings you gorgeous food on a silver platter. But you will grow if you are sick, if you are in pain, if you experience losses, and if you do not put your head in the sand, but take the pain and learn to accept it, not as a curse or a punishment, but as a gift to you with a very very specific purpose. (349)

Now, if I understand Kübler-Ross, what she is saying to Mrs. Diane Wood, who e handsome, brilliant husband, Dr. John Wood, a thirty-one-year-old surgeon at Columbia Presbyterian Medical Center, was robbed and murdered by two young boys, is that he was not killed "as a curse or punishment but as a gift to her with a special purpose." The purpose obviously was to make her grow; and the child she was carrying would some day understand that his father's murder helped to make his mother grow, that it was not a negative phenomenon. Elisabeth Kübler-Ross wants to assure all of us and herself that nothing in life is really bad, and that death is a necessary element for growth in life. It is another version of the Garden of Eden myth, and the Fortunate Fall, namely, the view that we had to lose paradise to learn to appreciate it. So nothing is really bad. Drawing Kübler-Ross's simplistic view to its logical conclusion, we should all welcome any form of death because it makes us better people.

This is the kind of talk about death that is an apology for what is patently evil in the universe. Nothing, in my view, can justify the violent, senseless death of a physician who has devoted his life to saving lives. What is growth to Kübler-Ross is regression to me. All that nonsense about growing from the pain of loss is like growing from the loss of an arm. One doesn't grow from the loss of an arm. One shrinks both literally and metaphorically and simply learns to live with the amputation. But make no mistake; loss is the ultimate abomination of existence.

Edwin S. Schneidman understands this when he writes of "The Enemy":

> . . . one should know that cessation is the curse to end all curses, and *then* one can, as he chooses, rage, fight, temporize, bargain, compromise, comply, acquiesce, surrender, welcome or even embrace death. But one should be aware of the dictum: Know thine enemy.
>
> Death is not a tender retirement, a bright autumnal end "as a shock of corn to his season" of man's cycle. That notion, it seems to me, is of the same order of rationalization as romanticizing kidnapping, murder, impressment or rape . . . . All this means that death is a topic for the tough and the bitter . . . . (65-66)

Those who glorify death may be sincere. Perhaps they help some people. But the "Confrontation with Death" books make me hate death more than ever as the ultimate obscenity of life. They do not placate me; they do not reassure me of anything but the finality of my relationship with my son.

On November 2, we spoke to Greenbaum. Once again the trial was postponed. It was supposed to begin on November 9, but Attorney Klein called to say that Deltejo could not get an appointment with his psychiatrist and needed another week. So the judge granted him another delay. There is evidently nothing in the law that takes into consideration the special kind of victimization that parents suffer as a result of such a delay. But since an appeals court might overturn the decision on the grounds that Deltejo was not allowed to see a psychiatrist, the prosecutor has to allow him more time. Now I do not know exactly when the trial will begin. Will it be on November 16, fourteen months after my son was murdered?

Urena's and Deltejo's lawyers are doing what the criminal justice system allows them to do, indeed what it encourages them to do. As I write this, 1,600 people have been awaiting trial in New York City jails for six months or longer. (There are a total of 9,410 inmates.) Three-hundred and thirty-nine have been waiting for more than a year. These include twenty-six who have been in jail since 1979, and one since 1978. The lawyers of defendants cause this delay for a number of reasons: if they know their client is guilty, they hope to gain some advantage in plea bargaining, or they hope for the illness or demise or disappearance of key witnesses. A defense attorney was quoted as saying:

> First, any delay usually works to the benefit of the defendants for a number of reasons. For example, in a lot of street crimes— which is mainly what you see in this court—witnesses will disappear. In narcotic cases, informants or even policemen will be killed or policemen will be transferred. Where there is a tough fact pattern, the more time that lapses, the more witnesses will contradict themselves. (T, Nov. 1, 1981, A1)

Presumably such delays might also cause the district attorney to lose interest in the case. But if that's what motivated Klein, he made a serious mistake, for Greenbaum did not lose interest. The defendants, if they are guilty, are not hurt by postponements. Deltejo and Urena may have preferred to spend as much time as possible in city jails where they could receive visits from family and friends and enjoy a more pleasant existence than they would have in a maximum security prison. Moreover, they probably knew that the months spent awaiting sentencing would be deducted from the total prison sentence.

The Sixth Amendment of the United States Constitution states that "in all criminal prosecutions, the accused shall enjoy the right to a speedy and public trial." Criminal Procedure Law and the New York State Bill of Rights mandates this as well. Prosecutors are required by state law to prepare cases in six months. The defense has no such limitations, and attorneys take advantage of this freedom. Granted that Legal Aid lawyers have heavy caseloads, that there are a limited number of private criminal lawyers, that there are not enough judges, and that the formidable paper work impedes the swift progress of cases. But Justice Jason A. Sandifer correctly recommended that the courts tighten the rules because there are far too many needless adjournments (T. Nov. 1, 1981, 40). And far too many grieving human beings whose lives have been destroyed by these murderers who are protected over-zealously by the American Civil Liberties Union, the Legal Aid Society, and defense attorneys who manipulate the adversary system of justice to favor the dregs of humanity.

There is a passage in John Godwin's *Murder USA* which I have read and reread. I find it hard to believe that it could have been uttered by a lawyer in this country, or in any country for that matter. Godwin quotes William M. Kunstler:

> Although I couldn't pull the trigger myself, I don't disagree with murder sometimes, especially political assassinations, which have been a part of political life since the beginning of recorded history. I'm not entirely upset by the Kennedy assassinations. In many ways two of the most dangerous men in the country were eliminated. (323)

These are the incredible words uttered by a man who does not believe in the death penalty, who does not believe that murderers should ever be executed, no matter how many people they have killed. However, in Kunstler's view, presidents, unlike murderers, can be executed, specifically in the form of an assassination. This is the peculiar logic that sometimes erupts in the legal profession.

Hatred, hatred, hatred—that is what consumes me, what makes it possible to live through each day. Like Yeats, "I study hatred with great diligence/for that's a passion in my own control" ("Ribh Considers Christian Love Insufficient"). And always I get different advice from books and from people. "Trust hatred," says one writer; "Hatred—it will destroy you," says a friend. And I wait to see Urena and Deltejo again. If there is such a thing as killing someone with hatred, they should both be dead by now.

And you, my reader, are you tired of my honesty? Would you rather be reading one of those false, hypocritical, comforting books that give you spiritual uplift, that tell you that despite what happens, like Job you should trust in God, and you will be comforted, and in the end your tragedy will make you stronger and better able to cope with life? I despise such clichés. I despise their inherent dishonesty. Murder destroys whatever is good, hopeful, and meaningful in a human soul. All the well-meaning inanities offered by all the well-meaning spiritualists are lies. The people who write books about how they have learned to live with tragedy say what they are supposed to say, not what they truly feel. No one who has lost someone he truly loves through murder can ever be comforted.

Eric Walbridge of Essex Junction, Vermont, made the following comment concerning the two youths who raped and murdered his twelve-year-old daughter: "I've no hate for them. They're sick. I've prayed for them." And the man whose wife and four children were murdered cried at the funeral: "I forgive the murderer seven times over." These people are incomprehensible to me. Forgiveness under these conditions seems to be an obscenity.

A few weeks before Thanksgiving, we learn that Deltejo has been granted more time to be tested by his psychiatrist. This means we shall call Greenbaum on November 23, after another one of the endless hearings, to learn whether the judge will finally rule that Deltejo and his lawyer have been given enough time and thus the trial must begin. What a Thanksgiving we will have. We will sit home and wait to learn when a jury will be picked, when we will have to come once again to that place of horror called 100 Centre Street where "justice" is dispersed with little regard for the agony of the victim's family. The police arrested Deltejo and Urena a few weeks after the murder. But now, close to fifteen months later, we still do not know when the trial will actually begin. All of this instead of the joyous Thanksgiving when we would join Eric and the rest of the family to celebrate the holiday in New York City.

I think about the psychiatrist who is attempting to judge Deltejo's sanity. Will he give him the same tests Gary Gilmore was given: the Minnesota Multiphastic Personality Inventory, Bipolar Psychological Inventory, Sentence Completion, Shipley Institute for Living, Bender-Gestalt, Graham Kendall and the Roschack? We learn that Deltejo has run out of options. He is judged to be sane. Greenbaum informs us that if Judge

Goldman finishes his current case on time, the trial will start on December 3. This means a jury will have to be chosen. We wait again.

Upstairs in a chest in my bedroom are tape recordings Eric made. I do not have the courage to listen to them. I think of bringing them to the courtroom and forcing Deltejo to listen to the music. Why, I think, didn't you rob him of things instead of his life?

And while I wait, I read what Chief Judge Lawrence H. Cooke of New York State has written of his effort to break the logjam in the courts. As of October 4, 1981, 4,653 felony cases were still pending more than six months after filed indictments—41.5 percent of a total 11,222 felony prosecutions. To dispose of these felony indictments required fifteen Supreme Court appearances. Cooke suggested that, to speed up the judicial process, sanctions be levied against lawyers or prosecutors for their failure to go to trial after a date had been set. He also called for more judges, and for legislation that would enable judges, rather than attorneys, to select the jury.

In the last week of the fall term in December, my husband and I left for New York City. Greenbaum informed us that he was at last picking a jury. We arranged to have our final exams proctored by other teachers and were given an extension to submit our final marks to the registrar after the trial was over. In the Binghamton parking lot, on December 8, as we walked towards our car, I said to my husband, "Why did you agree to teach in a room with the number thirteen?" At that very moment I tripped and broke my leg. The ambulance took me to Lourdes Hospital, where Eric was born on a day of great joy. Now I was there in despair, in pain, desperately hoping that I would be able to leave the hospital to attend the trial. Five hours later I was helped into our car, my leg in a cast and elevated; we drove into the city, arriving late at night during a heavy snowstorm. The next morning I entered room 620 at 100 Centre Street. This trial room was on the thirteenth floor of the building.

7

The Trial

"The law is a ass, a idiot."

Charles Dickens, *Oliver Twist*

Woe to you lawyers also! for you load men with burdens hard to bear . . . .

Luke: 2.46-47

After fifteen months, the trial finally began on December 11. I sat just a few feet away from Jose Deltejo. My husband could not sit in the courtroom because he was a witness for the prosecution. Sitting in front of me was a large woman, wearing a beige mink jacket and mink hat, who was in some way related to Irwin Klein. He would lean over and with his face close to hers talk to her earnestly. She had an enormous gold ring on her finger. I wondered why anyone would come to a murder trial dressed in mink. Irwin Klein wore a cowboy hat. I supposed it was a trademark of some kind.

The first witness was James Urbom, an assistant civil engineer with the New York City Transit Authority who for twenty-one years prepared models and charts for all public presentations of the Transit Authority. He built the model of the 181st Street IND Station in Manhattan used in court. This is a very long station, which requires either an escalator or elevator to enter.

After Urbom stepped down, the jury was asked to leave the courtroom. The following dialogue ensued at the bench.

MR. KLEIN: Your honor, I emphasize my empathy for the family of the victim who, I understand, is in court together with a whole group of vigilantes, a vigilante group or something.

MR. GREENBAUM: They are not a vigilante group.

THE COURT: Gentlemen, let's not have any argument about it. There are people in the courtroom. It's an open court. Anybody is entitled to come in to observe a trial. (Page 39 of the transcript of the trial. All quotes are from the transcript to ensure accuracy.)

The vigilantes Klein was referring to were a group of elderly people from Washington Heights who had formed an organization to protect themselves against crime. They attended the trials of those who had harmed someone in their neighborhood to see to it that justice was done. Both old and young people have been killed in Washington Heights. For example, Margaret Flynn, ninety-one, was robbed and murdered in 1985 in her Washington Heights apartment.

Mr. Klein admitted that they had the right to be there. But, he continued:

My client can't get a fair trial if the people are going to sob audibly. I can hear it and the jury can hear it, and they start to look in the direction from where it's coming from. (40)

The "people" Klein referred to was actually "person"; I was crying. The judge stated that he expected "complete decorum" in the courtroom, complete quiet, and that anyone who disobeyed would be summarily ejected from the courtroom.

The judge had no problem with me after that reprimand, although Klein kept looking back in my direction, hoping perhaps I might break down and cause a disruption. Klein had no difficulty with the mother of Deltejo. She was not present at any time in the courtroom—whether because she was ill, or whether she had refused to sit through the trial, or whether she lacked the stamina to look at a son accused of murder, or whether she had repudiated her son, I do not know. The only members of Deltejo's family that I saw were a stony-faced, expressionless man, presumably his father, and two young girls, presumably his sisters. Every day Deltejo would walk into the courtroom, and with feigned bravado wink at them as if he were participating in some funny play.

Greenbaum was concerned about my emotional reaction. (Did he fear not only that I would weep but also that I would try to attack Urena and Deltejo when I saw them both in the courtroom?) I promised him that I would be quiet. Biting my lips, digging my nails into my flesh, putting a handkerchief to my mouth when I felt I might vomit, I managed to sit through the trial without causing any further disturbance. I was to be a non-person in the courtroom, just as my son was to be what Gaylin calls a "non-presence," the boy without a name, "the boy in the White Shirt."

The first witness who testified to seeing Urena and Deltejo attack my son was Shirley Zwick, a twenty-one-year-old student who had been returning from work. She got off the station, heard a noise, and saw a "boy in a White Shirt" being attacked and being pushed onto the tracks. And what did she do? Listen to her testimony:

> I saw them [Deltejo and Urena] running up the staircase to the overhead passageway, runway, something like that; and I ran over to the end of the platform and ran out. *I don't know why, but I just ran out.* [Italics mine] (55)

Later she was to admit under cross-examination that she did not know at the time that the victim had been stabbed until—

> Well, I was walking down Broadway and a friend of mine read a notice to me about the murder. And at that point, it just hit me, what I saw, you know, it really sunk in, as if I was trying to forget about it. (80)

Notice that she did see my son pushed on the tracks. Why didn't she tell the token clerk about this as she hurriedly left the train? Why didn't she alert a policeman? How could she have pushed into her subconscious the sight of a young man being pushed on to the tracks? Obviously at work here was what I call the Genovese Syndrome—the response which makes some people refuse to get involved in any violent scene because they are afraid. (In 1965 Kitty Genovese was killed as thirty-eight neighbors heard her screams in the street and did nothing to help.) Later their conscience does bother them if they are basically decent, and they do come forward and try to help. Shirley Zwick's testimony was damaging to Urena. She positively identified him in the line-up, and she described certain details of the mugging which were corroborated by other witnesses. She was not a precise witness; she had a speech defect. And because some of her testimony about where Urena and Deltejo were positioned during the mugging was at variance with what other witnesses described, she provided Klein with the opportunity to offer the view that it was not Deltejo but Urena who stabbed my son.

Then Urena took the stand. He was a reluctant witness. He spoke in a low voice and repeatedly had to be reprimanded by the court to speak louder. He stated that both he and Deltejo were Dominicans; he also offered his address, 523 West 160th Street. So twenty-three blocks away from Eric's apartment the face of evil lived to destroy my son. Just twenty-three blocks away. He admitted, as he had in the plea bargaining agreement, that he and Deltejo participated in the robbing and killing of Eric Kaminsky. As he tried to describe what he and Deltejo had done on that terrible day, he asked to speak to his lawyer. As the result of his conference with Moriarty, the court was recessed and Urena was sent back to Greenbaum's office.

What had happened? Was Urena frightened when he saw Deltejo, whom he called Speedy (not because of his intake of drugs but because of the speed with which he could run)? Would we have to become involved in two trials instead of one? Urena remained in Greenbaum's office when the court convened again in the afternoon.

The first witness was Maritza Estrada, age fourteen, who was appropriately called Tiny. She described how she and several of her friends had "sneaked" into the station to go to the park on 189th Street and Amsterdam Avenue. Then she described what she and her friends saw and did.

I was walking down a little more, walking down, when I came

to see, I saw a man on the tracks . . . . I saw him lying there, facing to the uptown side of the train, and his hand hanging through one layer of the track. I called my friend, Polk . . . and I says to come to look, that there's a man there laying on the track. So I told him "Come on help him." So then we went—I jumped on the tracks and Polk says to "jump" . . . . We jumped down. And right then we crossed to see the downtown side through the tracks. And then after that, I said "Polk try his pulse, to see." He was alive, so then we decided to help him up, and we took him—Polk took him through the leg and the arm and through the back, and I took him through one arm and my other friend took him through the other side to help him up. And then I took his head on my hand. And I laid it flat, nice, not to hurt his head. I put it down nice on the platform. (102-103)

When she was asked if the "man" spoke or made any noises, she said:

No, all he was doing was flirting his eyes, going like that. (Blinking) . . . . He was going like that, blinking his eyes a lot.

Then they lifted him on to the platform:

He was still blinking. And then he went, he opened his eyes real wide and then closed them. Right then, he died. (102-103)

As she spoke I died with him.

Maritza then told the court that the ambulance and police arrived about fifteen to twenty minutes after he died. Maritza had no watch, so her conception of the time was based on an assumption. It might have been twenty or even thirty minutes, since the ambulances in New York City are notorious for slow arrival time when they are needed. But as she put it, although the man was alive when she saw him, "he was like coming to dying, really."

Why did Tiny do what she did, and why did Shirley Zwick do what she did? If Maritza and her friends had not pulled Eric from the track, we would not even have had a body to identify. That was why Urena and Deltejo pushed him on the tracks, to remove him as a witness. I thank Maritza and her friends for what they did that night. They tried to help my son and I will never forget that. But I will also always wonder about the ambulance and whether it took too long to arrive. All I have is Maritza's well-meaning conjecture. Later the medical examiner stated that Eric could have lived only if he had received help within four or five minutes, and I continue to think about what might have been if a doctor had arrived in time.

Listening to Maritza intensified my sorrow. But worse was yet to come. Urena had decided to testify. And this time he gave the full version of what had happened on September 13, 1980. Evidently his fear of Deltejo was not as great as his fear of receiving a murder conviction.

He described what happened in faltering English. A court interpreter translated what he did not understand into Spanish. He and Speedy stole a car on 161st Street, a Toyota Celica. Speedy drove; Urena sat next to him. At 173rd Street they picked up Francisco Ortiz; they decided to get money to get high. Speedy drove them to 191st Street to the subway station. Ortiz stayed in the car; they told him they planned to get money from Speedy's relative. What they really wanted to do was rob someone in front of the station. But, Urena said, "We didn't do nothing." They went back to the car, and Speedy drove all three to the 181st Street station. Ortiz stayed inside the car while they both went into the subway. Greenbaum questioned Urena:

Q. How did you get past the booth?
A. We walked through the gate.
Q. Through the gate?
A. Through the gate.

They both saw a man on the platform. Urena turned to see if a train was coming. Urena said:

That's when I turned around and Speedy had the man around his neck . . .
Q. What was his other hand doing, if anything?
A. His other hand was pointing with the knife by his neck, here . . . . That's when he told me to come over and take his money. . . . I brought the man towards me and I took the man's money out of his pocket.

Urena described how he took two dollars from the man's pocket.

Q. Was the man saying anything?
A. He said, "Take my money, but don't kill me."
Q. How many times did he say that?
A. I heard him twice, a couple of times. (120)

Speedy told Urena to look for more money, and Urena looked for more money while Speedy held him around the neck.

Q. What was the man saying, if anything at this point?
A. He was saying, "Take my money, but don't kill me."

Then Urena maintained that "to take him away from Speedy" he pushed him on the tracks.

When I pushed him I saw him on the tracks, he was bleeding from behind. I saw he was bleeding on his back . . . He landed on, like—like in a standing position, but he was bending down. (122-123)

He had taken twenty more dollars from "the man," a grand total of twenty-two dollars, and when he saw that the man was bleeding, he and Speedy ran out of the station. Then he described how they ran to the car, and Speedy drove to 163rd Street "to cop some drugs." They talked to two friends and went to Hamilton House on 139th Street where Urena lived.

He testified that after they got into the car Speedy gave him the knife so he "could clean the blood off."

Several days later Speedy, Douglas Harris, Anthony Bell, and Millie Quinones, Urena's girlfriend, had a conversation in front of Hamilton House about what had happened in the subway. Incredible, isn't it, that these creatures had killed my son and just stood there talking about it to their friends, having a friendly chat, as it were, about an interesting incident in their lives.

Under cross-examination Urena admitted that he and Speedy "used to trip on acid." He denied that they had taken drugs on the day of the murder; instead they had drunk beer. But the day before, they had used cocaine, bacardi, and LSD. They were still high, had a hangover, even though they were "off the acid." Then Klein asked:

Q. Did you put a token in the booth when you went into the
   subway station?
A. No, sir.
Q. You snuck in?
A. We walked in.
Q. Without paying?
A. Yes, sir. (138)

Klein reminded Urena that in a four-page signed statement
(Exhibit B) to the police he had written:

The train change lady said "pay your fare." I turned around
and threw her a kiss. (141)

The token clerk did not call the police. She did nothing.
Nothing. She obviously did not, could not, stop the two cri-
minals who entered the station without paying. There was no
policeman standing nearby who could stop them. Many people
enter the subway illegally. Once in a great while the Transit
Police make an effort to round them up and arrest them, but
the police were nowhere in sight on that ugly night. Urena
admitted that he and Deltejo waited outside the 181st Street
station to rob people to get money for drugs. Many people
came out of the subway, but they didn't attempt to rob them.

Q. Did you ever commit a crime before?
A. Yes, I committed crime.
Q. Did you commit crimes before? Right?
A. Yes, sir. (146)

Urena then stated that he lived with a young woman in a
room at Hamilton House. (This was the same Marie Quinones
who stood next to me during the time Judge Torres did not
appear for a pre-trial hearing. She was carrying a baby—hers,
his, I do not know.) Marie was supported by her parents and
Urena gave her money. After eliciting from Urena the fact
that he robbed the young man of twenty-two dollars, Klein
asked:

Q. At the moment that the man said to you, "take my money,
   don't kill me," did you have your hands on him?
A. No, sir.

Q. Did you put your hands on him after he said that?
A. Yes, sir . . . .
Q. Did you see him after you pushed him to the tracks?
A. Yes, sir, he had his back to us.
Q. What was he doing? Was he moving?
A. Yes, sir.
Q. What was he doing?
A. He was trying to get up.
Q. Did he throw anything up at you, gravel or pebbles or whatever?
A. I heard noises, though . . . .
Q. Let me hear that. You pushed the man to the track?
A. Yes, sir.
Q. He falls on his hands and knees?
A. Yes, sir.
Q. Facing away from you?
A. Yes, sir.
Q. You turn away?
A. Yes, sir.
Q. You hear some noise?
A. Yes, sir.
Q. What does the noise sound like?
A. Like—it sounded like rocks to me.
Q. It sounded like rocks?
A. Yes, sir.
Q. Throwing rocks at you?
A. Yes, or something.
Q. Did he hit you with any of the rocks?
A. No.
Q. Did you see any rocks on the platform?
A. Yes them thin . . . . The thin things.
Q. Did you jump back off to finish him off?
A. No, sir.
Q. Did you throw the rocks back at him?
A. No, sir.
Q. Did you help him get up from the tracks?
A. No, sir.
Q. Did you ever see this man before in your life? . . . .
A. No, sir.
Q. Are you telling us that, out of cold blood, a man you never saw, a stranger, at random, a chance meeting, just that poor man's luck to be there at that time, and that's all you can say about it? (148-151)

Urena insisted that he first saw the man bleeding when he was on the tracks. He first saw the knife in the station, and gave it back to Speedy after he cleaned it in the car. So Urena maintained that he was, after all, only guilty of robbery and of throwing the victim on the track. He was completely innocent of the actual murder—of stabbing him with a knife. What exactly did Urena think would have happened to "White Shirt" if a train pulled in?

Klein referred to Urena's confession on October 3, 1980, on video tape. As a result of the Peter Bartolomeo decision in the Appeals Court on June 16, 1981, the prosecution could not use this confession because there was no attorney present when Urena made it. The trial had been delayed for months because this decision mandated that Urena's attorney had to be present when Urena confessed, since he had a prior arrest. Fearing that the Bartolomeo decision might be retroactive, Greenbaum had to resort to plea bargaining to get Urena's confession a second time in a hearing before Judge Goldman.

Greenbaum advised me not to appear in court on the day the assistant medical examiner, Dr. Darly Jeanty, testified. He did not think that I could control myself if I heard the medical report. Two years later, as I write this, I have for the first time read the trial transcript that describes in medical terms why the boy in the White Shirt died. Since Jeanty had performed about 2,500 autopsies in the last nine years, he was obviously an expert witness on the subject of forensic pathology. He described the autopsy he had performed on Eric Kaminsky. This was the first time in the trial that my son was referred to by name.

Jeanty was wrong about my son's age. He guessed that he was between twenty-five and twenty-eight years old, but he was only twenty-two. How did my son die? He was stabbed.

> Q. The path of the knife went from back to front . . . . And as it entered, what parts of the inside of the body did it pass through?
> A. The lung first and then the aorta.
> Q. Which lung, sir.
> A. The left lung. (169)

Then Jeanty noted that a cut in the aorta, without medical

assistance, will result in death in a matter of minutes. The stab wound was one-third of an inch wide. The wound had "a T-shaped configuration," which meant that the blade was put in vertically and then twisted and removed.

Q. Now, can you tell us, with a reasonable degree of medical certainty . . . what a person who receives this kind of wound can do after he has received the wound, with respect to his ability to move his body and for how long?

A. When someone has a wound of the aorta, it depends on the length of the wound, but for such a wound, this person may live for another three to four, five minutes, and during this time may have some physical activity before staggering and collapsing and fall—and will fall and die without medical attention. (171)

The cause of death, then, "was a stab wound of the posterior chest wall with involvement of the lung and the aorta . . . An acute hemorrhage due to stab wound" (172). In other words, Eric "bled to death internally" (172).

Then there was an argument about whether the two photographs taken of the victim should be shown to the jury. Klein argued that the photograph of the victim lying on his back with his eyes closed would be inflammatory. The judge ruled in his favor, and only the picture of the victim showing the wound on his back was displayed to the jury.

Urena was brought back to the court and described the events leading to his plea bargain. Klein attempted to insinuate that Urena had invented the car, which he did not mention in his first confession, so that he could describe Speedy as sober enough to drive a car, not stoned out of his head. He also contended that Moriarty had convinced him it would be better to plea bargain, because otherwise he would get a second-degree murder sentence. The implication was that Urena was the actual murderer.

The next witness was Anthony Bell, seventeen years old, in the tenth grade, a friend of Urena and Speedy. This witness testified with his attorney, Miss Cody, present, for he had been arrested subsequent to the incident involved in this trial, charged with robbery in the second degree and possession of stolen property. With Klein pressing him to tell more about the nature of the robbery, he used the Fifth Amendment and refused to answer on the grounds that it would incriminate him.

He described how he and Douglas Harris, a friend who is currently an inmate in the Brooklyn House of Detention, were standing in front of the Hamilton House on 138th Street early in the evening on September 14, 1980. Furman, Speedy, and Millie, Furman's girlfriend, walked up, and Millie asked Furman, "Should I tell Mr. Harris?" and Furman said, "I don't care." So Millie said that they had "just stabbed somebody, that Furman had just stabbed somebody . . . ." Klein interrupted and asked:

Q. Who said that?
A. Millie said, "Furman just stabbed somebody."
Q. And Millie is who?
A. Furman's girlfriend.
Q. What happened then?
A. Furman asked Speedy, "Why did you stab him?" Speedy said, "I don't know, he grabbed me." And then Speedy asked Furman, "Why did you throw him to the tracks?" Furman said, "I don't know, I was scared." (211-212)

We are to assume from this contradictory testimony that when Millie first said that "they" had "just stabbed somebody, that Furman had just stabbed somebody," she meant *Furman* and *they* to indicate their complicity in the crime of murder. Klein then elicited from Bell the admission that he knew about the $1,000 reward offered on September 30 for information about the killers of Eric Kaminsky. This was the amount offered by the police who, when asked to offer more of our own money for the reward, assured us that $1,000 in this section of the city would be a large enough sum to tempt someone to talk. But Bell denied he had been promised the money, and under cross-examination insisted that Millie at first had said: "Furman stabbed a fellow" (218).

What a subculture! It seemed to me then that I really understood how social hatred begins. There, clearly defined for me, was evil, embodied in these young people who casually referred to murder as if they were talking about eating an ice cream cone or going to a ball game. Nothing I had done all my life, nothing my son had done, could protect him. For how can we protect ourselves from the banality of evil, from beings who dress and look like ordinary young people, but who have no values except the instinct to rob and to destroy?

Jose Velleard from the Dominican Republic, a nineteen-year-old construction worker who left school in 1976, needed the court interpreter to translate some of the questions for him. His family and Furman's were close friends. He had known Speedy for eight years. His testimony established the fact that there was a car, for he described how he had talked to Speedy and Furman as they got out of their car on 163rd Street and Broadway. Originally three people were in the automobile and Speedy was driving. Speedy said that they had just "made a stew. . ."; they had taken something from somebody. Velleard saw the twenty-dollar bill in the car, but when he learned it had been stolen from the man they stabbed, he backed off and didn't want any part of it, even though Furman had borrowed fifty dollars from him to buy a camera. Then he gave his version of the stabbing.

> They say they grab him in the back, Speedy grabbed him in the back, you know. . . . Speedy say it. (226)

> Later Furman came back to the block by himself and he told me Speedy did the stabbing. (230)

Then Detective Martin Gonzalez (Shield 921) took the stand. I do not deny that I have been demoralized by my encounter with this subculture. But I am rational enough to remember Gonzalez, a decent, sympathetic Transit policeman who worked hard to find the murderers of my son. He traveled to Utah to apprehend Speedy, who fled there after the murder. But Gonzalez was not permitted to tell the court what led him to Salt Lake City. He simply stated that he took Deltejo into custody on October 6, 1980. The jury did not hear any of the damaging information, namely, that Deltejo had committed other crimes. Thus if Deltejo had killed one hundred people before he killed my son, this information would not have been admissible in the trial! None of the reasons for Deltejo's flight to Utah were given to the jury. Gonzalez's testimony takes up one page of the trial transcript. Klein asked Gonzalez if he knew that Deltejo had family in Utah, and Gonzalez said that he did. Klein hoped the jury would concentrate on the fact that Deltejo fled to Utah only because he had family there. Klein did not want to dwell on his flight because he knew that Deltejo, before arriving in Utah, had robbed a bar and fled to Connecticut, where one of his friends raped a woman and was killed by the police. Only the judge was informed of these facts prior to the sentencing of Deltejo; these facts were never given to the jury.

The next witness completed the group portrait of Dominican youth. Francesco Ortiz was a psychiatric patient, and instead of having him testify, Greenbaum and Klein agreed on a stipulation that if Ortiz, the third party in the car, were called to the stand, he would state the following. He was twenty years old, was from the Dominican Republic, had been in the United States for fourteen years, was a passenger in the car, Speedy was the driver, and Urena was the front passenger. Urena left Ortiz to watch the car while they went to Deltejo's brother's house to get some money. No robbery was discussed in the car. They returned, and while Speedy drove the car, Urena was cleaning a knife in the passenger seat. They drove to 163rd Street to buy angel dust. Later that night in Hamilton House, Urena and Deltejo reenacted what took place in the subway.

Ortiz had not worked since 1978, saw a therapist twice a week, was institutionalized in the psychiatric ward for a month in 1979, was in group mental therapy for four days in Santo Domingo, and had hallucinatory dreams. The judge questioned him at length at the bench and agreed that Ortiz's testimony should be given by stipulation. I wonder why. If Ortiz was unstable, would it not have been to Deltejo's advantage to have him testify? Perhaps Deltejo was afraid that the unstable Ortiz might suddenly offer more damaging evidence than he gave in the stipulation.

Nester J. Rivera, the next witness, was the most important one in the case. Greenbaum privately called him a "sweetheart," presumably because he was always available and ready and willing to give his version of the events he witnessed in the subway that night and because he was an intelligent and educated young Puerto Rican. Rivera was twenty-one years old and a political science major at New York University with seventy-six hours of credit. He worked part-time as a ward clerk at the Psychiatric Center of New York Hospital. He had lived in Washington Heights for twenty years. On his way to meet his girlfriend, he entered the station at about the same time as "White Shirt," as my son was to be called throughout his testimony. Rivera arrived at the downtown southbound platform. He said:

> I noticed—I first heard yelling and when I looked up, I saw three guys scuffling and two guys were trying to push the third one on the track. . . . I thought they were just friends fooling around and I kept on walking close to them. He was pushing back and they were pushing him forward. (244)

Rivera pointed to a staircase marked P3 on the map of the subway as the area where he saw the three men. He continued:

> As I got closer, I noticed that they were really trying to push him off and he was pushing back and they were going back and forth. Then finally they went around him and took him by the arm and threw him on the track. (246)

A court officer was used to represent "White Shirt," and Rivera demonstrated the position of the two men during the scuffle.

> Q. What was white shirt doing at this time?
> A. He was just fighting back and just yelling "No," and they kept on pushing him to the front.
> Q. You say fighting back. In what manner?
> A. Pushing back.
> Q. How was he pushing back?
> A. He was like this. (indicating)
> Q. Were his hands extended?
> A. Right.
> Q. And how was his body, arched or straight up?
> A. Like this. (indicating)
> Q. Indicating over slightly?
> A. Yes. (247-248)

White Shirt, White Shirt—this was my son, my son, who extended his hands, no doubt, to protect them from damage.

They were, after all, his most precious possession.

As he got closer Rivera saw

> that they kept on trying to push him off and he was fighting
> back and finally they took him—they moved him over and took
> him by the left arm and threw him onto the tracks. (248-249)

What Rivera did not know was that the only reason they could throw him on the tracks was that one of them stabbed him in the back—the cowardly last resort of an evil being too small to overpower him. Then Rivera described how he had on two separate occasions identified both Urena and Deltejo in a line-up. Once again Rivera was asked to describe exactly what happened as "White Shirt" went off onto the tracks. At that moment I felt as if I had to scream. "Stop calling him White Shirt! He was my son, flesh and blood, handsome, talented, young, so full of desire and hope. He was no "White Shirt." He was a feeling human being.

Once again the court officer was used to represent "White Shirt" to demonstrate where Urena and Speedy were before they threw him off the platform. Then Rivera described how he saw Urena and Deltejo run on to the top mezzanine towards 184th Street. As he chased them, he saw Deltejo put something metallic in his pocket. He saw them as they passed the gate and started to walk a few feet from the turnstile. They turned back to look and then ran out of the subway.

Then Rivera spoke to the token clerk and the following conversation occurred:

> Then I told the clerk that they had thrown this man on the
> track, and she told me to see if he needs an ambulance. And I
> ran back, and there was some kids already helping him up
> from the tracks. (262)

Unbelievable as it may seem, this clerk, who did nothing to report the illegal entrance of Urena and Deltejo, now sent Rivera down to inquire if an ambulance was needed. She received a report that a man had been thrown on the tracks. Why didn't she immediately call the authorities to get help? Any person thrown on the tracks would need *some* kind of help.

Rivera described what happened when he ran back to the tracks. During the rest of his testimony he kept repeating, "I didn't know he was hurt." That statement was Rivera's attempt to extricate himself from the Genovese Syndrome, to excuse his sin of omission, the sin of not doing the right thing at the right time. For Rivera and Rivera alone could have saved my son, and he could have done it simply by opening his mouth and yelling when he saw the three struggling. Klein understood this simple fact. Rivera said:

And I ran back and there was some kids already helping him from the tracks. . . . Two were at the bottom, on the tracks, and two were on the top picking him up. *Apparently, I thought he was okay.* [Italics mine] He got up as soon as they threw him on the tracks.

Q. When you were back on the platform and they had just come up to the upper mezzanine, what did you see "white shirt" do?
A. He landed sitting, a sitting position. . . with his feet extended, with his hand over, covering the third rail, and then he stood up and started to walk downtown. And then I saw like a tear in his back, on his shirt, some kind of a mark.
Q. This is when—
A. That's when I started to run. *I thought he was okay. I didn't know he was dead.* [Italics mine] (262)

Then Rivera described how "White Shirt" was placed near the same staircase from where he was thrown on to the tracks.

Q. And how was he placed down?
A. Lying down, with his feet toward the tracks, and his head toward the wall.
Q. What did you see then?
A. When I ran back, he was having trouble breathing. Then I ran back to the clerk, and told her he needed an ambulance. When I ran back, he was gasping for air, like spasms, trying to breathe.
Q. And then what happened?
A. He just stopped. His eyes closed halfway and he died. (263)

Rivera pointed to the spot on the photograph where Urena and Deltejo kept pushing "White Shirt" and the three of them kept moving back and forth.

> Q. Back and forth?
> A. Right, they were pushing and he was pushing back.
> Q. And during the course of that, did you ever lose sight of them?
> A. At one point they went behind the staircase. They pushed him—he pushed them back right behind. . . one or two times behind the staircase. (268-269)

What did Rivera think they were doing then—just playing games? That misjudgment cost my son his life. "White Shirt" was facing Rivera when he fell off the platform.

> Q. And then he got up, how did he get up?
> A. He got up and started to walk and he was like going side to side.
> Q. And how—what direction was he walking?
> A. Downtown. . . . He didn't know where he was going.
> Q. In other words, he turned around?
> A. Right.
> Q. At what point while you were watching that did the defendant and the other fellow approach you?
> A. As soon as they reached me, I lost sight of him.
> Q. In other words, you turned away.
> A. Right.
> Q. Now—
> A. *I didn't know he was hurt.* [Italics mine] (270)

In his cross-examination Klein asked the questions that have plagued me. It is one thing to hate because evil has destroyed someone you love. But it may be even worse to feel betrayed by someone you are supposed to admire. Klein in his cross-examination of Rivera asked the following questions:

> Q. How old are you?
> A. Twenty-one.
> Q. How tall are you?
> A. Six feet.
> Q. Six feet?
> A. Yes.
> Q. How much do you weigh?
> A. 180 pounds, 85.
> Q. What if anything did you do to prevent this tragedy from being consummated?

A. I didn't know it was. . . .

Q. So you didn't do anything?

A. I didn't know they were mugging him. I thought they were just fooling around.

Q. It's all right to push him like that?

A. I thought they were friends.

Q. Didn't you testify you saw them try to push him off the platform?. . .

A. At first I thought they were friends just trying to scare him. When I got closer is when I noticed. I recognized the victim. (284-285)

Note well that Rivera admitted that he was close enough to see the victim's face. He was close enough to see what was happening.

Q. And then what if anything did you do to prevent it?

A. It was too late, they had already thrown him on the tracks by the time I got close enough.

Q. Did you call for help?

A. I ran for help.

Q. After they left. But I am saying while it was happening, did you yell, "Stop, they are trying to kill him?"

A. There was nobody on the train station.

Q. You were the only one?

A. From what I saw.

Q. Did you see anybody across the platform?

A. No.

Q. Do I understand that after they took off and started running, that you started to run and all you did, you ran to the lady in the booth and said "These two fellows I saw push this fellow on to the track"?

A. *When he got up, I thought he was okay and I ran after them.* [Italics mine]

Q. Who got up?

A. The victim. (286)

Rivera told Klein that the distance between the stairwell and the platform was seven feet. Watching the pushing and shoving only seven feet away, Rivera said nothing. Even a brief "Hey you, what are you doing?" would have alerted the muggers to the fact that someone was watching them, that a witness was present, and that in turn might have kept them from harming the victim. They might have run at the sound of Rivera's voice. Instead he kept silent. Why? His excuse was that he didn't know the victim was hurt. He didn't want to get involved in what he thought was a friendly quarrel. But what was my son doing all this time? He was fighting for his life, trying to protect his hands, trying to keep Urena and Deltejo from pushing him on the track. If Rivera was close enough to see my son's face, he was close enough to see his expression, which must have revealed his fear. Was my son quiet; was he crying out in fear?

I shall never know why Rivera did what he did, or rather what he did not do. His lone presence on the subway at that time might have been fortuitous; he might have saved my son's life. Instead Rivera's value was as a witness to a murder. Yes, he was a "sweetheart" of a witness. He cooperated with the police, gave as much of his time to the investigation as was required, and helped without doubt to convince the jury of Deltejo's guilt. I thank him for what he did. But both he and I will spend our lives with another *if*. For I believe that because Rivera is a good man, he must sometimes wonder about what *might* have happened if he had intervened at the right moment. And I will always wonder. Sometimes I imagine going to City Hall and watching Mayor Koch hand an award to Rivera for saving my son's life. After the ceremony, my son and I take Rivera to the most expensive restaurant in the city, and we give him a free ticket to attend my son's concert at Carnegie Hall.

The last witness was my husband. On the stand he gave his occupation and his address, and informed the court that he had last seen his son on a holiday weekend at the Concord and had spoken to him on the Thursday before his death. For the first time Eric was a presence in the courtroom, a boy with a name, a human being with parents, not a White Shirt, a cipher in a ghoulish tragedy. Greenbaum asked:

Q. When was the next time you saw your son after you saw him in August of 1980?
A. I saw him September 15th, a Monday. September 15th at the New York Morgue. (294)

My husband spoke in a quiet, emotionless voice. But Klein

asked for a mistrial. He said:

> This is no reason to subject this man to this, to put this man on, other than for inflammatory purposes, this is purely inflammatory. It has nothing to do with any of the essential elements of this case. (295)

I began to panic. Would we have to go through another trial? I could not survive it. I knew what it cost my husband to sit there and talk about seeing his son in the morgue. Why didn't my heart stop? How could it take the punishment? The judge ruled that the testimony was admissible for identification purposes.

Deltejo, despite the advice of Klein, did not take the stand. He did not have any witnesses.

In an off-the-record discussion at the bench, which I could not hear but which appears in the trial transcript, Greenbaum informed the court that he had given to Klein everything in the entire file concerning the case, including the names and addresses of people who were involved but were not called as witnesses because either they were not available or their testimony would be cumulative.

Once again Klein called for a dismissal of the indictment on the grounds that the people had failed to prove their case. The judge denied his request and the summation began. Klein argued that everyone was lying except his client. All the testimony was filled with fabrications and inconsistencies. Urena was the real murderer and liar. The three Dominican witnesses were "lying against my Puerto Rican" client. Klein used this tactic to introduce some racial bias into the case, but Greenbaum quickly corrected him and stated that Deltejo had a Dominican background. Klein went too far when he concluded that poor Deltejo was a "victim" and that it was Judge Goldman who bought Urena's "package of garbage" and permitted Urena to plea bargain. Klein warned the jury:

> The guy is going to be out in the street, he'll kill some more. He admitted it, Urena, he admitted killing. He'll be out on the street, it's a revolving door. He is an animal. (324)

(Klein apologized to me after the trial for having defended "an

animal" like Deltejo.) Klein kept describing Urena as an ani-
mal, as a callous robber and murderer, as a liar. But Speedy,
poor Speedy was probably stoned. He didn't know what hap-
pened. Urena and his friends made up the lie about the car so
that it would look as if Speedy were rational enough to drive.
(Probably the car was not mentioned originally for the simple
reason that stealing a car is a crime.) Admitting that Deltejo
was in the subway, Klein concluded his summation with the
following words:

> We can't speculate about what he was doing in the subway.
> Whatever he was doing there, he did not kill that man, he did
> not take any money from the man, he had nothing to do with
> the murder. (351)

The adversary system makes it necessary for a lawyer to
say anything that will help his client obtain a verdict of not
guilty. In defending his client, Klein was approaching the line
of what was not permissible. "We can't speculate about what
he was doing in the subway." Deltejo was just there, an inno-
cent bystander who didn't know Urena? I thought Klein's
summation was unconvincing when I heard it, mainly because
in his zeal to blame Urena for the murder, he tried to absolve
Deltejo of all complicity in the crime. When I read the tran-
script version of the trial, I knew that Klein had gone too far
and stretched the credulity of the jury.

I believe that the ploy of referring to Deltejo as a victim
backfired. Placing the word *victim* in the same context in
which Klein mentioned my son must surely have made the
jurors wince. Klein then made several other comments that
showed his almost desperate inability to defend the indefensi-
ble. He blamed himself for not obtaining a plea bargain as
quickly as Moriarty had, but Greenbaum made him admit that
Deltejo had never been offered a plea bargain. Klein also called
the three witnesses liars. But in the end, nothing he did could
help Deltejo.

Greenbaum began his summation by pointing to the crucial
point of law involved in the case. There was no doubt that Del-
tejo and Urena were involved in the "stew" that resulted in the
robbery and murder of Eric Kaminsky. Greenbaum said:

Throughout this trial, you may have gotten the impression that the question was, did Urena kill Eric or did Deltejo kill Eric, and, now I am going to suggest to you that you needn't find which one, during the course of the robbery, killed Eric, all you need find is that one of them, during the course of the commission of this robbery and in furtherance thereof or in the immediate fight thereof, one of them killed Eric. That's what you have to find, not which one did it. (354)

Even if the jury decided that Urena did the killing, Deltejo would be as guilty as Urena under the provisions of Section 20 of the Penal Code. This was the essence of the charge Judge Goldman made to the jury:

When one person engages in conduct which constitutes an offense, another person is criminally liable for such conduct when, acting with the mental culpability required for the commission thereof, he solicits, requests, commands, importunes, or intentionally aids such person to engage in such conduct. (398)

And this was what defeated Klein and Deltejo. Klein interrupted Judge Goldman during the charge, which prompted him to rebuke Klein:

You committed a gross breach of etiquette and proper procedure in the courtroom, interrupting the Judge's charge. For a lawyer of your experiences it's incredible and I hope it will never happen again. (412-413)

Klein apologized twice. "I have been gracious enough to apologize, I think you should be gracious enough to accept it" (413).

Then the court adjourned for lunch. At 2:30 P.M. the jury reentered the courtroom and asked to hear the Shirley Zwick testimony and to reread the Urena plea bargain. Then the jury retired and in about fifteen minutes reached a verdict. The jury returned and the foreman announced the verdict: Guilty on both counts of robbery and murder. The jurors were then polled individually and each said "guilty." My husband and I clasped each other and wept. Then the courtroom emptied. Klein and the woman who had originally worn a mink jacket but now wore an ordinary coat walked over to us. And once again Klein apologized for defending such an animal.

In any event, that didn't keep him from trying to delay the

sentencing. First set for January 7, the sentencing was to be delayed, presumably by Klein's tactics. A day before the sentencing was to take place, a probation officer called us in Cortland to ask us how we felt about Deltejo. Our answer was simple. He killed our only son; he destroyed the remaining years of our lives just as if he had stabbed us. We both felt that twenty-five years to life, the maximum punishment, was too lenient, and that we were in favor of the death penalty for both murderers.

And so once again, we waited. We had packed and were ready to leave for New York on the morning of January 6 when once again Greenbaum called to tell us the sentencing hearing was delayed. And then the miraculous event happened. The sentencing took place when it was supposed to take place. Even the district attorney was taken aback. On January 7, Judge Goldman refused to tolerate any delays.

Thus what I write here about the sentencing procedure on January 7, 1982, I take from the twenty-nine-page transcript. Klein asked to have the verdict set aside as contrary to the weight of evidence and law. Every point that he made in his summation he repeated again. Then for the first time the judge expressed his opinion:

> My personal opinion that I express now is that this was a very strong case, that the jury verdict was completely justified in every respect. I see no basis for setting this verdict aside. Your motion is denied in toto. (9)

Then Goldman refused Greenbaum's plea for a one day adjournment to allow us to travel in from Cortland. He refused this request because "the presence of the family, while I understand their position, adds nothing in connection with sentencing, it will have no effect one way or the other" (11).

Greenbaum then proceeded to recommend a sentence of twenty-five years to life, and explained why he sought this heavy sentence for Deltejo while Urena received a lighter one. What he proceeded to report had never been mentioned during the trial. In other words, whatever Deltejo might have done in the past only became relevant after the trial, in regard to sentencing. Urena had never been convicted of a prior crime, but he had had a pending burglary charge reduced to a misdemeanor. But Deltejo was convicted in Utah in 1980 of burglary and discharging a gun. The conviction was reduced to a misdemeanor, and he received probation on certain terms, one of which he violated by leaving the state of Utah and coming to New York. On September 19, 1980, Deltejo and two friends used guns to rob a bar on 164th Street and Fort Washington Avenue. The bar was a known drug hang-out. The three fled to Connecticut, where one of them was killed in a shootout with the police concerning a crime with which Deltejo had no involvement.

Deltejo was identified by the owners of the bar, but they refused to prosecute for obvious reasons. Greenbaum said:

> The District Attorney's office was told of this after the time when this case would have been ripe for presentation to the grand jury, we having the subpoena power, the police department not having it. The police department simply closed the case unfortunately and never informed the D.A.'s office. (14)

Incredible, isn't it! This armed robbery enabled Deltejo to travel back to Utah, where he had previously committed a crime. Yet not one word of this was mentioned during the trial.

Deltejo stabbed Eric in the back so that he could buy drugs and have a good time that night. Greenbaum dealt with the family background of Deltejo:

> I would not say that this defendant comes from a bad family. I do not believe this is the case. I have had an opportunity to view the family. They are not terrible people at all, they appear to be decent working class people. . . this defendant, your honor, is clearly a bad seed. (18)

Then Greenbaum described a conversation he had with my husband:

> When he was in my office, your honor, Mr. Kaminsky kept on asking me, and this is true; an individual who is an educated man, he teaches college, philosophy and yet his unfamiliarity with the legal system is probably no greater or less than any other average citizen, and he kept on asking me, I want justice, I want justice, I want justice. Of course, he can't get his son back.

> For the next 25 years Mr. and Mrs. Kaminsky will miss out on the affection and love of their only child. The impact on them is great. As to my own observation, they are people who have suffered perhaps the greatest loss that one can lose, an only child who was the apple of their eye and what an apple, a child who I am informed, your honor, by his friends, would have been a great pianist. It's not simply that Mr. and Mrs. Kaminsky will be denied their only child, it is perhaps that the community will lose out on the beauty of the music that Eric Kaminsky could produce; and he was a great talent, a great talent. (19)

He reminded the judge again of how Eric had resisted Urena and Deltejo by trying to protect his hands, his most precious possession. Noting that both the probation department and the people require the sentence of twenty-five years to life, Greenbaum admitted "that is not the most just result but it's approaching it" (20).

And what was Klein's reaction to all of this? He said:

> Your honor, listening to the prosecutor I am reminded of public hangings and the putting to death of the Christians in the Colosseum. . . . I was wondering here whether we were trying this case in a fit of vengeance, whether the prosecutor was the white knight for the parents and for the community, elderly people in the community who came to court every day. (20)

But what else is a law court but a place of vengeance? It is the only legal resort a civilized human being has for revenge. As for being a white knight, Greenbaum hardly looked like one, but he tried to act like one.

In arguing against the recommendation of a maximum sentence, Klein asserted that Eric's ability to play the piano had no more bearing on the sentence than if he had been a truck driver. Then he made the following unbelievable observation:

> The statute is very vague, it doesn't give the judge any standard at all. Was it done in hot blood; was it done in cold blood; was it a good murder, was it a bad murder; was it a shocking murder, was it a non-shocking murder? There is no standard whatsoever. To take a piece of this man's life, a big piece of 25, even 15 years is a lot when the other fellow is only going to do half as much. (22)

What in the world is a "good murder" to Klein? What is a "non-shocking murder?" And his explanation for Deltejo's refusal to testify was also unconvincing.

> He couldn't take the stand. He didn't know what to say. He didn't recall. But to his credit he didn't get on the stand and commit perjury and lie and come up with some falsified defense or explanation of what he was doing there. He didn't lie. Now there is a trait of character. He refused to get up and perjure himself even though his life is in the balance. There is something good in this man and I ask that your Honor give him the benefit of the doubt. (25)

Klein insisted that the probation report was presumptuous in claiming that Deltejo would commit further crimes if released. When Deltejo was asked if he had anything to say, he replied: "I have nothing else to say right now" (26-27). Nothing, nothing, no plea for mercy, no explanation for the horror he visited on our lives.

Then the judge finally lashed out at Deltejo. The verdict of the jury was "100 percent correct and thoroughly warranted by the evidence in this very strong case":

> This was a wanton killing in the course of a robbery in the subway where the defendant and the other man, Urena, were attempting to get money to purchase drugs. After getting $22 from the victim they finally pushed him on the tracks. This was after stabbing him wantonly, recklessly, needlessly with a knife. I think it's fair to assume that this life was wasted so they could get rid of a potential witness against them. A life was destroyed by two people, one of whom was this defendant. I hesitate to use the word but I think scum applies, the dregs of humanity. (27)

Scum, dregs of humanity—that is an apt characterization. And when Goldman sentenced Deltejo to twenty-five years to life, for the murder, and eight-and-a-third to twenty-five years for robbery in the first degree, both sentences to run concurrently, I was momentarily relieved but not satisfied. I thought again of the woman in Lübeck, Germany, who shot her daughter's murderer in the courtroom six times. How I envied her! Like Antigone, she gave moral law priority over man's law. Antigone disobeyed the king's law and buried her brother because she believed it was the right thing to do. That she would lose her life did not matter to her. I am like Prufrock: "Do I dare to eat a peach?" Incapable of the truly heroic action, I am no Antigone, nor do I have the courage of those who in 1977 revenged the death of Mrs. Santiago when she was shot during the robbery of the family owned grocery store. The next day members of the family killed one of the murderers. A grand jury failed to indict any of them for murder.

What did I think about the trial? I was grateful to the police officers who arrested Deltejo and Urena: Detective Martin Gonzalez of the Transit Police, Retired Shield Number 921, on the Major Cases Squad; Detective John Bruno, retired, formerly with the Manhattan Task Force 3264, now working for the Metropolitan Opera Police Security; and Detective Leonard Caruso in the Thirty-fourth Precinct, Detective Unit, 1626. They were decent, compassionate, caring, hard-working men on whose faces I could see the loathing they felt for the two who had killed my son. Unlike many families who are victimized, we, at least, had the satisfaction of finding the murderers. For that I will always be grateful to these three men. Gonzalez and Caruso were especially kind to us, and gave us their support during the trial.

I also have to thank William Greenbaum for all he did to prosecute the case successfully. He was not a flamboyant type of lawyer. He was perhaps at times too careful, too cautious, but this was because he was aware of the grave deficiencies of the criminal justice system. There are so many examples of criminal injustice at 100 Centre Street that he was justified in being apprehensive about the outcome of the trial. But he had not been hardened by the system, and he showed genuine compassion.

When he called to inform us of the sentence, he was jubilant and relieved. Until the last moment, he did not really believe that he would obtain the twenty-five years to life sentence for Deltejo. He was always accessible to us, always willing to talk to us and give us information about the progress of the case. In that sense he was very different from other district attorneys, who often refuse to inform the victims' families about the legal issues involved.

There is so much I hate about the criminal justice system that it is gratifying to thank four decent, kind men connected with the legal system for what they did to help us. If someone like Gonzalez—and there must be thousands of men like Gonzalez on the Transit Force—had been on duty on the 181st Street station on September 13, 1980, my son would be alive today.

My response to Klein and Moriarty was quite different. For the first time I really understood how the legal adversary system works. My experience did not enhance my respect for that system or for the lawyers who manipulate it. When my brother met Moriarty during one of the hearings, he asked him how he could defend someone like Urena. Moriarty did not answer. Perhaps he would have given the same answer that Professor Alan M. Dershowitz of Harvard gave in *The Best Defense*. The adversary system requires that even the worst criminals deserve the best defense. That is why Dershowitz could write a letter to *The Times* deploring the activities of terrorists in Europe who killed innocent Jews (T, Oct. 17, 1982, E15), at the same time that he himself defended a terrorist and obtained his freedom!

Three members of the Jewish Defense League set off a bomb in Sol Hurok's office and caused the death of a young woman. Dershowitz defended one of these terrorists who was supposed to be a star witness for the prosecution as an informant. In a brilliant maneuver he convinced the Court of Appeals that the authorities had utilized illegal wiretapping and other illegal acts to obtain evidence and deprived the prosecutor of the ability to compel his client to testify. Wasn't it clever of Dershowitz to use the exclusionary rule, which enabled a member of a terrorist organization to go free?

Not every lawyer is impressed with Dershowitz's achievements in defending criminals. For example, the reviewer in *The Times* criticized him so severely that Dershowitz had to answer the attack (TBR, July 4, 1982, 19). His defense of the adversary system is unequivocal even to the point of arguing that the victim *should* remain a non-presence in the courtroom. What I despise about the courtroom procedure is precisely what Dershowitz defends.

The victim and those who love him are non-presences in

the courtroom. The defendant, sitting in the courtroom, has the opportunity to play the part he wants to play to impress the jury, while his lawyer occasionally puts his arm around him. The dead victim is merely "White Shirt." When an attempt is made to describe him, to reveal his personality, it is considered an inflammatory action that might provoke a mistrial.

When Dershowitz reviewed Willard Gaylin's book, he objected to Gaylin's view that the dead Bonnie Garland should have been in the courtroom, and that the jury should have been reminded of what her loss meant. Gaylin wrote: "She should have been brought back to life so they could have appreciated the enormity of her death. . . . The jury should have been made to mourn her" (238-239). But Dershowitz does not agree. He says:

> The temptation to focus on the worth of the murder victim is entirely understandable. . . . But to dwell on her mute presence at the defendant's trial would be a disaster for our legal system. It would make the seriousness of murder—and indeed, the guilt of the murderer—seem to depend on the nature of the victim. That might be true in some ultimate moral sense: The killing of a great musician is, perhaps, deserving of more condemnation than the killing of an unemployed wino. The legal system must, however, resist this temptation to recognize distinctions based on the worth of the victim. (76)

Dershowitz does not want the "seriousness of murder" and "the guilt of the murderer" to depend upon the nature of the victim. He does not want the victim to be known except in terms of the general attributes of the species. Presumably the inclusion of other particular differentiating characteristics might sway the jury's verdict. Yet the perpetrator of a crime is present in the courtroom. He can act innocent, contrite, or insane. He can seek the help of psychiatrists and use all the evidence he can muster to try to convince the jury that he is innocent. Why should not the victim, even if dead, be allowed to plead his case? For example, information about the dead victim is used under certain circumstances when it suits the accused. If the dead victim had attempted to kill the accused before he killed her, that is certainly admissible evidence. If the dead victim was a liar, a cheat, a torturer, a Nazi who repeatedly threatened the life of the accused, that is admissible evidence. Why should not the opposite kind of evidence be admitted: that the dead victim was innocent of wrongdoing, that the dead victim was a talented pianist, that the dead victim had discovered a cure for cancer? The presence of the accused and the non-presence of the victim in the courts is a glaring example of the kind of special pleading which makes society distrust lawyers and the criminal justice system.

Dershowitz staunchly defends the adversary system of justice and his role as a criminal lawyer. He states:

> I do not apologize or feel guilty about helping to let a murderer go free . . . even though I realize that someday one of my clients may go out and kill again. . . . Defending the guilty and despised—even freeing some of them is a small price to pay for our liberties. (T, Mar. 23, 1980, A16)

Is it a small price? Dershowitz does not explain why the price of *liberty* should be eternal vigilance for the criminal. Liberty is a hypostatized term; it has no objective referent, nor is it possible to define the word in an absolute sense. Paradoxically, the concept of liberty always involves restriction. Dershowitz knows that he is not free to yell fire in a crowded place when there is no fire. Yet his defense of the murderer is based on the kind of fallacious reasoning which assumes that liberty is destroyed when we don't guarantee the rights of murderers. If the price of liberty is the freedom of the murderer, then we had better redefine our notions of freedom and rewrite the Constitution.

But many lawyers will not defend the guilty. Our peculiar adversary system sometimes punishes them for such integrity. Thus the lawyer who advised the murderer of the Zwickert boy to confess his crime lost his case. The presiding judge contended that the lawyer should have advised the murderer to plea bargain rather than to confess. Such horrors perpetrated by the adversary system need to be eliminated. Dershowitz attacks the corrupt prosecutors and judges, but surely he knows that criminal lawyers can be as corrupt as any other unprincipled public workers. But he also knows that there are honest judges like Morris Goldman and honest pros-

ecutors like William Greenbaum. The adversary system is
what we have; it is faulty and it should be improved to guar-
antee the rights of the victims.

What is wrong with the legal profession? Simply this: it is
made up of lawyers who know the law but who are not taught
ethics or logic. There is something perverse about a profession
that encourages its members to defend criminals in order to
become famous and wealthy. Harvard President Derek Bok,
formerly Dean of the Harvard Law School, has criticized the
law schools for teaching their students to value the interests
of individual clients rather than the interests of society as a
whole. Robert Reiff has aptly described the cynicism of the
lawyer:

> Lawyers are granted an elite status in our society in return for
> which they are expected to protect the individual—whether
> criminal or victim—from injustice. Some distort this mandate
> to mean their role is to protect the offender from punishment,
> even if that punishment is justifiable on the basis of a fair trial.
> An offender has no right to escape punishment just because he
> can "get away with it." Many lawyers, however, operate on the
> principle that their job is to help the offender get away with it.
> In the fantasies of young law students this is the most exhila-
> rating experience of law practice. What a paradox! The young
> law students learning to be the "guardians of justice" are
> aroused to a high state of excitement by the fantasy of getting
> an acquittal for a person charged with murder. The missionary
> zeal of rescuing someone who is innocent is not what excites
> them—the guilt or innocence of the person charged is imma-
> terial. The thrill lies in the exercise and confirmation of their
> cunning and craftiness. . . . There is probably no other place in
> our society than in the courts, except perhaps in politics, where
> slyness and cunning are rewarded more than straightforward-
> ness and honesty. (105-106)

Reiff is right when he claims that the success of offender
attorneys subverts the social and judicial aims of the criminal
justice system. They contribute to crime in America because
they foster the view that any criminal can be exonerated if
his lawyer is sly, cunning, or deceitful.

James S. Kunen in his *How Can You Defend These Peo-
ple?* contends that everyone involved in criminal court pro-

ceedings lies: attorneys, judges, defendants, police, jury pan-
elists, witnesses, complainants, *"Everybody* lies" (188-189). But
"deception is not deceit. Lawyers and magicians practice de-
ception. Dishonest people practice deceit" (116). In this breezy,
facetious, ironic style, Kunen describes his adventures as a
criminal lawyer. The following comment reveals that Kunen
finds it difficult to answer the question posed by the title of his
book.

It is my job to argue that there is a reasonable doubt . . . it has
to be there, in the evidence. I do my job with pride, believing
that the advocacy system is not only the fairest method of
determining guilt but also the most reliable—reliable *because* it
is fair; each side has the opportunity to negate the distortions
of the other. It is not 100 percent reliable, however.

The foregoing rationale is fine, as far as it goes, but it
sounds like bullshit to me. After all, though it may not have
been my job to decide whether Pepperidge was guilty, I couldn't
help but reach certain conclusions, and I *did* decide that he was
guilty, when his brother told me that he had been in the car.
And though it was indisputably my job as defense attorney to
try to win an acquittal anyway, that doesn't explain why I
should want to undertake that job, or how I could perform it
with such enthusiasm.

It occurs to me that maybe I *like* putting criminals on the
street; that far from being an unfortunate side effect of the
noble enterprise of defending the rights of the individual, may-
be putting criminals on the street is the main point; that, possi-
bly, I am motivated by the sheer joy of thwarting the will of
authority. Maybe I became a defense attorney so that I could *be
bad,* and still be good. I don't know. How would I know? (190)

Kunen's essential honesty and integrity shine through in
the lines quoted below:

It dawned on me that my patriotic rap to the jury about the
United States being different from most of the nations of the
world, because we put the burden of proof on the government,
was *true.* I had thought I was being cynical and manipulative
when I'd said it, but it really was true. And if the government
doesn't prove its case, the accused *should* go free.

I felt proud to be an American.

It was around this stage of my career that the image of someone in my own family being the victim of a violent crime started coming to my mind more and more frequently. I imagined that the criminal would be put on trial, and that I would walk up to him in open court and shoot him dead. (257)

I hated the trial not only because it transformed my son into nothing more than a "boy in a White Shirt," but also because the whole procedure served to reinforce my impression that the criminal justice system in New York City favors the criminal and his lawyer. Our case would have been a simple one if Urena's original confession had not been invalidated by the ruling of the Appeals Court, 4-3, the Bartolomeo ruling, which required an attorney to be present when Urena confessed. This ruling made it difficult for Greenbaum to use the original confession because the police, not knowing that Urena had been arrested in the past, did not insist on the presence of an attorney when he confessed. As a result Greenbaum had to employ a plea bargain, and Urena was given a lenient sentence.

This ruling in the Bartolomeo case is very much like other rulings that have enabled criminals to escape punishment because of legal technicalities. The city of New York freed 613 inmates awaiting trial in Rikers in 1983 because the law required that prisons hold no more than 10,300 prisoners. One-third of those released failed to appear for court dates. More than 40 percent were rearrested for committing new crimes after their release. Even with the recent modification of the exclusionary rule, the Supreme Court will not prevent criminals from escaping punishment because of legal technicalities that zealously protect the rights of the guilty.

Furthermore, New York City is very concerned about the welfare of the people it arrests. It spends $42 million on refurbishing the Tombs to make life more comfortable and pleasant for those who are accused of murder, rape, and robbery. It doesn't like to kill its murderers. It sends them to prisons, which are continually under investigation to determine whether its inmates are treated *humanely*.

I once rode with friends to the Montezuma Wildlife Refuge, and they passed through Auburn, unaware that the murderer of my son, Deltejo, was in the Auburn prison. I could see it as we drove by. How incongruous it was to look at the prison in lovely Auburn with its wide streets lined with tall trees brilliant with the colors of the fall foliage. My son used to eat dinner with us at the Auburn Inn.

The Auburn Correctional Facility is the oldest of the ten maximum security prisons in New York. It is known for the high quality of its educational programs, including a degree program offered by Syracuse University. Inmates are employed in large-scale industries to manufacture wooden furniture for state agencies and license plates for New York and Illinois. As I drove through Auburn, I thought: Is Deltejo receiving a good education? Do my tax dollars help him to live a more pleasant life in prison? Is he learning how to use his knife to make furniture while my son lies stilled forever by the same kind of knife? Does Deltejo enjoy the basketball court, the television viewing area, and the jogging track at Auburn?

The trial also made me think about the probation and parole systems in this country. Those who are released after committing a crime or are paroled after spending only part of their mandated time in jail often become the statistics of recidivism. If Deltejo had been imprisoned in Utah for his robbery instead of being placed on probation, he could not have traveled across the country into New York City to appear on the subway on September 13, 1980. Urena admitted that he had been involved in muggings before he was arrested for my son's murder, yet Urena was also free to appear on the subway and commit another crime.

I remember that Harriet Schiff in *The Bereaved Parents* describes the harrowing experience of parents who recognized their daughter's murderer standing next to them in a store at Christmas time. He was buying holiday gifts! The parents did not know that the murderer had been paroled. I will not let this happen to me. So I call William Greenbaum, and he tells me that Deltejo is now at the Eastern Correctional Facility in Napanoch, New York, while Urena is still in the prison at Elmira.

Every once in a while I watch the ten o'clock news on TV channel 5, and someone begins the program by asking, "Do you know where your children are?" And I answer, yes, in his grave, because New York did not protect him. Nor has it sufficiently punished those who destroyed him. I will never be satisfied with the results of the trial.

In May, 1985, the state of New York enacted into law Bill No. 3033-A concerning the "Victim Impact Statement at the Parole Release Interview." This law requires the Parole Board to consider the views submitted in a written statement by the convict's victim, or the victim's parents, relatives, or friends. Thus neither Urena nor Deltejo should appear before a parole board without my knowledge. Since Urena may be eligible for parole in three and a half years, I have begun to write my "impact statement."

8

The Death Penalty

*One can respect the "reverence for life" that led Dr. Albert
Schweitzer to shrink from treading on a scorpion, without
scorning those who would unhesitatingly crush a tarantula or
shoot off the head of a rattler. To insist that "no killer can be
looked upon with anything but horror, even when that killer is
the state," is to ignore that the bulk of the Americans do in fact
look upon executions of murderers without horror. People like
Lord Justice Denning are not to be consigned to outer darkness
because they consider that "some crimes are so outrageous that
society insists upon adequate punishment, because the wrong-
doer deserves it."*

*The historical evidence demonstrates that the Constitution left
the States free to enact death penalties unencumbered by any
measure of proportionality.*

> Raoul Berger, *Death Penalties: The
> Supreme Court's Obstacle Course*

What do I want? What would make me feel that enough has
been done to Urena and Deltejo? I am not like Norman Felton,
who wrote the following letter to *Time.*

> My daughter, her husband and their baby were stabbed to
> death recently. The bizarre nature of the multiple stabbings
> suggests that the murderer was mentally sick. I cannot believe
> that the execution of the individual responsible for the murder
> of my family is a solution. Rather than retribution, we need to
> support research into mental illness and crime. It is the best

113

way to save lives. As a grieving father, I urge that forgiveness replace anger. (Feb. 14, 1983, 6)

I cannot and will not ever forgive. To do so would mean that I valued my son's life *less* than I value the life of his murderers. I know that some survivors of murdered loved ones are opposed to the death penalty. But I also know that Grace Paruolo, whose son was murdered, collected 10,000 signatures favoring the death penalty and presented them to the state legislature.

For years the subject of capital punishment had been an abstract issue to me. My students wrote term papers on the death penalty. But now an abstraction has become a meaningful topic. Like the mothers who worry about a nuclear war in a haphazard, vacillating, vague fashion, I used to concern myself with capital punishment as a theoretical phenomenon. I was concerned in the way that judges and lawyers are involved if they have never had a relative murdered, or in the way that healthy nurses and doctors and thanatologists not personally involved with death deal with terminally ill patients. You don't have to have cancer to write intelligently about it, and similarly you don't have to have a murdered son to demand justice for the victimized. In fact, personal emotional involvement in a tragedy is supposed to make it well nigh impossible to be objective.

And it is true that shortly after my son was murdered, I could not have written this chapter, which is the result of years of investigation of the arguments used in debating the issue of capital punishment. Four years ago I could not have written this chapter employing the results of scholarship on the subject. I would simply have written what I felt, and what I felt was that I wished that I were a member of another society, where justice is swift and punishment is mandatory.

In China, with a population of one billion and 39,000 crimes a year, there are no appeals, no pretrial motions, no jurors, and the lawyers all work for the state. A judge and two lay people decide the guilt or innocence of the defendant. Someone convicted of rape and murder was tried, convicted, and shot by a firing squad in one day! There is no TV coverage, and murderers can not, like Sirhan or Manson, appear before the public to plead their cases. The prisoners in Chinese jails work hard and eat bad food. In Riyadh, Saudi Arabia, two Filipinos murdered a Lebanese businessman, raped his wife, and stole his possessions. Four thousand people watched as these two murderers were beheaded with a heavy saber in accordance with Islamic law. The Koran states unequivocally that murderers who break the laws of Allah must be killed and thieves must have their arms and legs cut off. In the United Arab Emirates an Indian was flogged and beheaded for raping and murdering two little girls.

These are the people we derogate as Eastern barbarians. We in the West are civilized. We believe that we are especially virtuous because we not only pray to the right God, but we also have a Constitution that guarantees the legal rights of *all* people, including murderers—a view entirely alien to the teachings of the Koran.

In China, on August 30, 1983, one million people were transported to the Peking Worker's Stadium, and they cheered as twenty-nine murderers, rapists, arsonists, and thieves were shot in the back of the head in full view of the audience. The truth is, when my son was murdered, I wished that it had happened in a place like China. As an educated woman I am not supposed to say this. I am supposed to assume the pose of a rational, civilized American who values law above all. But the truth is that I wanted Urena and Deltejo to experience the terror of impending death.

In *The Idiot* Dostoevsky describes an execution which was probably based on his own experience when he faced death in Siberia at the hands of those tyrants who had imprisoned him for political reasons. He believed that there is no greater torture on earth than waiting for the death sentence: the man who is about to be murdered still hopes that he will escape, whereas the man sentenced to die has no hope at all. Albert Camus also took the position that nothing can be as cruel as an execution. In *Reflections on the Guillotine,* Camus tells us that his father watched a murderer being put to death for the killing of an entire family, including children. Although his father had believed the punishment was just, when he returned home he vomited, for "instead of thinking of the murdered children, he could recall only the trembling body he had seen thrown on a board to have its head chopped off" (5). To Camus capital punishment is more repulsive than the crime of murder. He claims that it is "the most premeditated of murders, to which no criminal act, no matter how calculated, can be compared. . . . If there were to be a real equivalence, the death penalty would have to be pronounced upon a criminal who had forewarned his victim of the very moment he would be put to a horrible death, and who, from that time on, had kept him confined at his own discretion for a period of months. It is not in private life that one meets such monsters" (25).

But many such monsters *are* encountered in private life. John Godwin describes their activities in *Murder USA*. The literature of victimology is filled with examples of murderers who kidnap their victims, terrorize them with tales of their impending death, and then ultimately kill them. So horrible were the acts of James Lee Gray that his own mother asked the Mississippi authorities twice to execute him. He had killed his young girlfriend, and when he was paroled after serving seven years of a twenty-year prison term, he kidnapped a three-year-old girl, raped and sodomized her, killed her by holding her head in a ditch, and then threw her body from a bridge into a creek. Did she really suffer less than a murderer who is waiting for an execution?

How absurd it is to talk about equivalency in relation to the victim and the murderer. How revolting it is to read the pages of Camus's *Reflections on the Guillotine,* which are primarily concerned with the feelings of the abused murderer who suffers more than his victim while waiting for death. Camus ignores the fact that by killing, the murderer forfeits *all* rights to be judged as equivalent to the innocent victim. But Dostoevsky and Camus belong to that group of writers who have romanticized the victimizer, headed in the modern era by the most dedicated champion of all, Norman Mailer. In the next chapter I will show how this practice of concentrating on the murderer rather than the victim has led to a literature of empathy with the criminal. Other people and organizations have expressed their objection to the death penalty: Arthur Koestler, Colette, Tolstoy, Hugh Carey, Governor Mario Cuomo, Anthony Amsterdam, American Amnesty International, Henry Schwarzschild and other members of the American Civil Liberties Union, Hugo A. Bedau, John P. Conrad, and *The New York Times.*

When the Supreme Court in the *Furman* vs. *Georgia* decision in 1972 ruled that the death penalty was unconstitutional, it seemed to provide the legal sanction for eliminating capital punishment in this country. But in 1976, in the *Gregg* vs. *Georgia* decision, the Supreme Court denied that the death penalty was necessarily a cruel and unusual punishment proscribed by the Eighth or Fourteenth Amendment. The Court required only that each imposition of the death penalty be separately reviewed to determine whether it meets constitutional standards. As a result thirty-seven states have implemented capital punishment statutes, and as of July 1985, forty-seven murderers have been executed.

Despite the fact that two out of three people in the United States favor the death penalty, despite the fact that the governing bodies of New York have voted for capital punishment, former Governor Hugh Carey vetoed the death penalty bill six times and Governor Cuomo vetoed it three times. Both of these men strongly oppose what the majority of New Yorkers demand.

"Thou shalt not kill," says the Bible. But as Shakespeare observes, the devil can quote Scripture to prove his point. It is possible to use the Bible to argue for or against capital punishment. In Genesis (9.6) we find: "Whoever sheds the blood of man by man shall his blood be shed, for God made man in his own image." God spoke these words to Noah and his sons, clearly giving man the right to kill a murderer. After the commandment "Thou shall not kill" in Exodus the following statement appears:

Whoever strikes a man so that he dies shall be put to death . . . .
If a man willfully attacks another to kill him treacherously, you shall take him from my altar that he may die. (21.12-14)

There is no clearer statement in the Old Testament of God's view. This was a regulation he gave to Moses as he and the Israelites traveled to the Promised Land.

However, John H. Yoder offers "A Christian Perspective" based on the belief in the redemptive power of Christ. Yoder admits that the Old Testament regards life as sacred except for the murderer and the enemy. But in the Sermon on the Mount and in Romans (12.19-21), Jesus' death is a proclamation of forgiveness. God's highest goal was not equivalent injury. Yoder says, "What God always wanted to do with evil, and what he wants us today to do with it, is to swallow it up, to drown it in the bottomless sea of his love" (Bedau, 372). What does this metaphorical rhetoric mean? How exactly does one swallow evil in the bottomless sea of Christ's love? Presumably evil is destroyed simply by the act of accepting Christ's love and his belief that human life is sacred. Christ orders us to forgive sinners and thus commands us to oppose the death penalty. The Mosaic Code is modified by Christ the prophet, priest, teacher, lord, and king who makes no distinction between religious and civil justice.

But if Christ preached forgiveness, his father practiced vengeance. God revenged the sin of disobedience in the Garden of Eden. He threw Adam and Eve out of Paradise and punished them with death and eternal hell if they did not believe in him and obey his commandments. Is that not a worse punishment than the bodily extinction of execution? Furthermore, if we accept the view that God wants to exterminate evil in "the bottomless sea of love," we must first believe in a "bottomless sea of love." But as Freud wisely noted in his "Thoughts for the Times on War and Death": "The very emphasis of the commandment *Thou shalt not kill* makes it certain that we spring from an endless ancestry of murderers, with whom the lust for killing was in the blood, as possibly it is to this day with ourselves" (312).

Some theologians believe that Christ made it very clear that he did not intend to subvert the fundamental principles of law and order established through the Ten Commandments. In Matthew (5.17-18), Jesus says:

> Think not that I have come to abolish the law and the prophets. I have come not to abolish these but to fulfill them. For truly I say to you, till heaven and earth pass away, not an iota, not a dot, will pass from the law until all is accomplished.

Thus the law was sacred to Jesus: he would abide by it and expect everyone to abide by it, "for I tell you unless your righteousness exceeds that of the scribes and Pharisees, you will never enter the kingdom of heaven" (5.20).

Religious leaders have different views on the subject of capital punishment. To them God is either a forgiving or a vengeful being in the Bible. Pope John Paul II visits the man in jail who attempted to kill him and prays for him and forgives him and all murderers, while the Reverend Jerry Falwell in *Time* insists that Jesus Christ favored the death penalty. On the cross Jesus said nothing: "If ever there was a platform for our Lord to condemn capital punishment, that was it; He did not" (Jan. 24, 1983, 36). Five national Jewish organizations approve of the death penalty: the Rabbinical Alliance of America, the Union of Orthodox Rabbis of the U.S. and Canada, the Central Rabbinical Congress of America, the National Committee for the Furtherance of Jewish Education, and the Rabbinical Council of the Syrian, Lebanese and Near Eastern Jewish Community of America.

Then there are the naive, sentimental humanists who are convinced that human life is so sacred that even the most depraved murderer must not be executed. As Professor Elias Schwartz puts it, all of human life is "precious beyond measure" *(Sat. Press,* Mar. 6, 1982, C8). He finds the rationale for this peculiar kind of egalitarianism in the teachings of the pagans and the Christians, in the words of Socrates and Jesus, who tell us that it is worse to do evil than to suffer it. Our knowledge that human life is sacred comes from our love of others. We want those we love to live forever. Having this intuition about the unique person we love, we make it apply to all human beings. Thus even the life of a murderer is precious. When the state takes a man's life, his blood is on all our hands. It harms us more than it does the murderer. The murderer is a human being, and his life is precious beyond measure.

That the murderer is necessarily a human being is questionable. Schwartz, like many academicians, is without real experience of the nature of evil and the foulness of human nature. Is Edmund Kemper, a mass murderer, human? He confessed to killing his mother and grandparents. He shot, knifed, or strangled his female college victims, had intercourse with the dead bodies, and then cooked and ate them. Was

Kemper any longer a member of the human race when he committed these crimes? He himself said that he deserved "death by torture" (Godwin, 316). So unspeakable are the acts of some so-called human beings that we must consider the proposition "all men are sacred beings" to be a falsehood. Surely some of them are perverted forms we would hesitate to call "human."

But no matter how foul the deed of murder, the ACLU regards capital punishment as a worse violation of human rights. Thus even though Stephen Judy himself wanted to die after he murdered a woman and her three children, the ACLU fought to keep him alive. Schwarzschild believes that killing is so horrible a crime that even when the state performs it, it is an intolerable act. Joseph Chuman of Amnesty International also believes that there is something known as a universal declaration of human life, and that the state violates this declaration when it employs capital punishment. An extreme application of this hypostatized notion of the state as a living entity is revealed in Schwartz's argument that if the state can kill for murder, it will eventually kill for parking violations and jaywalking. In such an argument the state as a legal dispenser of justice for its citizens is transformed into a tyrannical thing mechanically extending its power over every facet of human existence. This is a clear example of what the logicians call the "fallacy of extension."

But there really is no universal declaration of human life. If anything, the history of civilization is a denial of this view. Men have been killed in wars for centuries, and it is sheer hypocrisy to assume that human life becomes sacred in relation to the death penalty but is expendable in relation to war. Jonathan Schell in *The Fate of the Earth* has tried to argue that the nuclear holocaust would destroy a special race. Perhaps we are special, but there is nothing sacred about us, and we, like any other species, might vanish from the earth. The law of existence is that each species survives by feeding on another species. We kill to eat, to survive.

But we are "civilized." This presumably differentiates us from the animals. We behave in a civilized fashion, obeying the laws, valuing human life, and punishing those who do not value human life. But the punishment must not involve killing.

As Sydney Schanberg puts it, capital punishment "de-civilizes" us. What is civilized behavior? Schanberg's colleague at *The New York Times,* James Reston, reminds us that this has been the bloodiest century in the history of the human race, with fifty-nine international wars and sixty-four civil wars, with six million casualties as well as untold millions of civilians slaughtered, all in the name of those abstract terms that Hemingway hated: glory, honor, patriotism.

What exactly is civilized about the Holocaust and the atomic bomb? The most primitive savages in their most primitive state did not utilize the grandiose means we now have of killing in the name of God, in the name of nation, in the name of glory, in the name of peace, in the name of brotherhood, in the name of enlightenment. It won't do to use the slogan that the abolitionists use, "It is wrong to kill people to prove that killing is wrong," since this is exactly what civilized people have done for years—only they have used euphemisms such as religious crusades and war against evil. Gil Elliot in *The Twentieth Century Book of the Dead* describes the 110 million murders perpetrated by governments in this century!

There are those who might reply that two wrongs do not make a right, that even though killing has been a normative act for the survival of nations, we should not legalize the approval of such acts by utilizing the death penalty. This is in the abstract a noble ideal based on the assumption that it is heroic and civilized to spare your enemies. But history tells us that this is a dangerous ideal which often results in the destruction of the virtuous. If the social democrats of Germany had taken up arms against the Nazis, the Second World War and the Holocaust might have been averted. To say that killing is *always* wrong is to commit the fallacy of converse accident, the fallacy of believing that all generalizations are true without exception.

I do not think that either the religious argument *or* the view that every human life is sacred is a cogent reason for abolishing capital punishment. However, three important arguments for the death penalty deserve to be examined: revenge, deterrence, and incapacitation.

Revenge used to be a personal act. The right to punish was considered to be the prerogative of the victim or the victim's family, and this punishment entailed the death penalty or a fine or exile. In some cultures, such as those of the Eskimos, the Comanche Indians, the Nuer of Africa, the Ifugao of the Philippines, it was the responsibility of the family of the victim to kill the murderer and his family. The underlying theme of vengeance echoed the biblical words, "life for life, eye for an eye, tooth for tooth, hand for hand, foot for foot, burn for burn, wound for wound, stripe for stripe" (Exodus, 21. 23-25). As J. L. Barkas in *Victims* reminds us, there is no concept of rehabilitation in early practices of restitution in the ancient legal code of Hammurabi in ancient Babylon. According to that code, the victim was always the primary concern and received monetary compensation. If a thief could not compensate his victim, he could be sold as a slave and the proceeds used as compensation. Theft was punished by restitution often involving four or five times the value of what was stolen. But the Greeks and the Romans substituted public law for private law, and society assumed the right to punish, the justification being that a collective force could better protect its citizens than personal revenge. Yet the desire for such revenge has never been extinguished. One of the great eras in history, the Elizabethan age, had an unquenchable thirst for revenge. Not only did people watch executions, but the tortures devised for the criminal were very cruel.

The Elizabethans believed in vengeance and their greatest dramatist believed in revenge. What else is *Hamlet* but a revenge play? Abraham Lincoln, however, claimed that "nothing equals *Macbeth,*" because it teaches us that the commandment "Thou shalt not kill" is a moral imperative.

Walter Berns notes:

> *Macbeth* is a play about ambition, murder, tyranny; about horror, anger, vengeance, and perhaps more than any other of Shakespeare's plays, justice. Because of justice Macbeth has to die, not by his own hand . . . but at the hand of the avenging Macduff. The dramatic necessity of his death would appear to rest on its moral necessity. (Bedau, 337)

Berns goes on to ask whether we can envision a world that does not take revenge on Macbeth, the man who killed

Macduff's wife and children. Can we imagine a civilization that does not hate murderers? The answer is, of course, yes. We can imagine it because we live in such a world; in our world many so-called ritualistic liberals sympathize with the murderer, often excusing his behavior by blaming society for causing him to be a murderer. We make celebrities of murderers; they appear on television and appeal for sympathy. When I watched Sirhan Sirhan and Jack Abbott on prime time television, I knew that there was something very special about this nuclear age. The distinction between good and evil has been blurred—perhaps never to be demarcated again so clearly as it was in *Macbeth*.

Joyce Carol Oates in her novel *Bellefleur* has brilliantly described the feeling that revenge inspires:

> But how exquisite it was really. There was nothing like it. No human experience, not even the experience of passionate erotic love, could match it. For in love . . . there is never . . . anything more than the sense, however compelling, that one is fulfilling oneself, but in revenge there is the sense that one is fulfilling the universe. Justice is being done by one's violent act. Justice is being exacted *against the wishes of mankind*. (496)

That is exactly how I felt when Deltejo sat just a few feet away from me in the courtroom. I wanted to kill him *against the wishes of mankind*, to make him suffer the same pain and terror that my son felt.

Nicholas Gage in *Eleni* tells us how he searched for the communist murderer of his mother in Greece. But when Gage finally confronted this murderer, he could not kill him. The ancient Greeks would have killed Eleni's killer. This might have been *Wild Justice*, the term Susan Jacoby uses in her excellent study of revenge. But is not wild justice better than the kind of sick mercy which makes us free men like Dan White and makes us give brief prison sentences to men like Richard Herrin and Theodore Streleski? As Jacoby astutely notes:

> The anger that proceeds from unredressed suffering can be more terrifying than the original facts of suffering; moreover, the outraged, as distinct from the ostensibly detached, witness

not only expects us to listen but also to *do something* about the wrongs that have been enumerated. If only it were as easy to address the demand for retribution within the constraints of civilization and law as it is to cheer movie avengers who specialize in the shedding of ketchup! We prefer to obscure the nature of these demands by falling back on the formula of "justice, not revenge." We prefer to experience revenge as metaphor, and the survivor who seeks retribution by bearing witness disturbs the peace by demanding that we face the issue in its concrete reality. (355-356)

Survivors who refuse to moderate their anger and continually raise the issue of retribution make everyone uneasy. Revenge is more comfortably viewed as metaphor by those involved in the legal procedure of imposing punishment.

In the name of decency, charity, and compassion, public revenge undertaken by lawyers, judges, and juries often offers the murderer the forgiveness that Christianity favors. The Bonnie Garland case is an example of how this forgiveness doctrine is applied in practice.

Bonnie Garland, a twenty-year-old Yale student, was murdered by her lover, Richard Herrin, when she informed him that she wanted to date other men. He killed her in her bedroom while she was sleeping. With premeditation he went to the garage to obtain the claw hammer which he used to kill her. This Mexican-American Yale graduate, in an interview with Dr. Willard Gaylin, described in detail how he murdered Bonnie Garland. These pages (95-97) in Gaylin's *The Killing of Bonnie Garland* are the horrendous revelations of a vicious murder. Herrin tells us that with both hands he smashed the claw hammer into Bonnie's left temple. This first blow forced Bonnie to turn from the side to her back. When she made an odd guttural noise, and her eyes moved into her head, Herrin once again smashed the hammer down on her forehead. This second blow caused her skull to split wide open, and blood poured out on Herrin's face and bare chest, on to his pants and the walls and the ceiling over her bed. For a third time he raised the hammer and hit it violently against her head. But she continued to gasp for breath. So for a fourth time he smashed the hammer against her neck and chest. Then he tried to kill her by strangling her, but she was still making a strange noise. He grabbed the keys to her car, drove to the rectory of Father Tartaglia, and from then on was financially and spiritually aided by the Catholic community of St. Thomas More Church at Yale.

For this monstrous murder Herrin was convicted of first degree manslaughter and received a minimal sentence of eight-and-a-third to twenty-five years, because in the view of the jury he had suffered a "transient situational reaction." Barry Gray wrote in *Our Town:*

> It is now June 1982. Herrin has been in jail just four years. A few weeks ago, he complained about the uselessness of our system. What good is jail he wanted to know? He should be out working for the good of man—or words like that. As it now stands, he will be on parole in 1986. What do we say to Bonnie's family? What do we say to ourselves? (June 6, 1982, 2)

What we say is that this is how the forgiveness doctrine works. Sister Ramona Pena and the former chaplain at Yale, Peter Fagan, forgave, and their espousal of the cause of Richard Herrin prompted an outpouring of sympathy and money for Herrin. The Yale community contributed to a $30,000 defense fund for Herrin; Herrin, out on bail, was able to attend classes at the State University of New York at Albany; he obtained the best legal counsel and an inexcusably light sentence. Small wonder that the Garlands, the parents of the dead Bonnie, felt betrayed by their church and by Yale, the university they had attended.

In his column on the Herrin case, Jeffrey Hart clearly explained what was wrong with the role of the Catholic clergy:

> The Catholic clergy in and around the Herrin case seemed to lose all grasp of reality and even theology. They "forgave" Herrin almost immediately, and told him that the hardest thing he would have to do is forgive himself. *Several clergy opposed any jail sentence at all.* [Italics mine] But forgiveness in Catholic terms doesn't quite work that way. It requires repentance, confession, absolution and insofar as possible—restitution. (CS, July 8, 1982, 12)

Nothing I read in Herrin's interview with Gaylin indicates

that Herrin has repented in the real sense of the term. Surely the following comments made by Herrin concerning his sentence do not reveal the state of mind that a Christian must have to qualify for forgiveness:

> I feel the sentence was excessive. The judge went overboard .... This being my first arrest, and considering the circumstances I don't think I should have been given eight to twenty-five years .... Well, after a year or two in prison, I felt that was enough. (P, May 15, 1982, 17)

Considering the circumstances? That is exactly what the jury and the judge did not do—consider the circumstances—for if they had, Herrin would have received the death penalty. Dr. Gaylin tells us that Herrin's lawyer, Jack Litman, felt that it was "unjust that he was in prison at all at that point, considering what rejection by Bonnie had meant to Richard and *also that it was a first offense*" [Italics mine] (324-325). Unbelievable as it sounds, an accredited lawyer in this country has stated that if you kill a woman because she informs you that she wants to see other men, you should not go to jail if this was the first time you had killed. Presumably, if you kill a second time, then you might have to go to jail. Litman also reveals his philosophy of law to Gaylin in the following words:

> I think that it's important to have cases where people say things "aren't fair" because of an acquittal. Lord knows if we lived in a society where everybody was convicted right down the line it would be much too repressive. It's important to maintain a balance, to have those cases where people are obviously guilty and get acquitted. That's what gives you faith in the system. (240)

No, Mr. Litman, that is not what gives me faith in the system. It is precisely what makes me lose faith in the system. For a greater philosopher than you, Kant, stated that the moral law demands that "the last murderer" on earth be punished. In a few years Herrin, like the murderer of the Hullinger girl, will be free to lead a normal life, forgiven by those who believe that no matter how heinous the crime, a life should not be taken for a life. Gaylin, who has so eloquently argued for

justice for the lovely, witty, charming, dead Bonnie, only de-
votes about a page and a half to the subject of capital pun-
ishment and concludes: "Practically, I find little in favor of
capital punishment. Theoretically, I find little to oppose in it"
(346). I believe in capital punishment; I believe Herrin by his
act of murder forfeited the right to resume a normal life, to
eat, to love, and to marry while Bonnie lies in her grave.

When we plea bargain with murderers, when we find in-
valid psychological and religious reasons for excusing their
behavior, we alert society to the fact that we don't necessarily
condemn murder. We announce that some courts, some juries,
some lawyers do not have the morality of anger and do not
believe in punishing murder.

Criminals have learned to play the game, to say the right
things to the right judges. How else is it possible to explain the
sentence Judge Peter J. Mcquillan gave to the twenty-year-old
Brooklyn boy who was convicted of stabbing tax specialist
Patrick E. Kehn as he sat with a girlfriend on a bench facing
the east river? The boy said before stabbing Kehn, "I don't like
your face." But after pleading guilty at his trial, he said, "I feel
guilty," and obtained the sentence of eighteen to twenty-five
years. Were Patrick Kehn, Bonnie Garland, and Eric
Kaminsky innocent, decent human beings? If so, why did their
killers receive such disparate sentences? Why should one mur-
derer receive five years, another eight years, another fifteen
years, another twenty-five years, another life, another the
death penalty? The answer is that "justice" in this country is
capricious, and, as Litman indicated above, some lawyers like
it that way.

I believe the forgiveness doctrine in the Herrin case was
evil. There can be no question but that capital punishment is a
legal form of killing people, an act of revenge. To Anthony
Amsterdam such a punishment is the greatest evil, except for
war, that society can commit.

Let us remember what a young murderer said about
stabbing an eighteen-year-old service station attendant:

Simple . . . easy . . . 'cause all's it is is just when you put it in. I
don't know if you ever cut foam rubber or cut your skin with a
razor blade. Once you get through the little skin, and the little

layer that's there as a protective shield there's nothin but just a bunch of blood and intestines—they're soft. It's just like you take your veins and that. It's just like boiled spaghetti . . . He says, "Oh my God, I got a wife." That was his dying words. (Barkas, 63)

Remember Camus and Dostoevsky? Could they really believe that the agony of this young service station attendant—who knew he was going to die and thought of his wife—was less horrific than the pain of the man awaiting execution?

But Anthony Amsterdam also equates execution with murder. Famous for his role in obtaining the *Furman* vs. *Georgia* decision, he was called in to help Gary Gilmore avoid execution. One would, therefore, expect some specially telling arguments from this lawyer. And what do we get? The same old equation: Murderers and executioners are both *equally* ugly and vicious, because they destroy the same sacred and mysterious gift of life which we do not understand and can never restore (Bedau, 348-349). Amsterdam concentrates the full force of his eloquence upon the theme of the ugliness of the execution. He talks about the suffering of the criminal, who is a human being and who, while waiting for his eventual slaughter, undergoes suffering more terrible than death. He also quotes Camus's remark that facing the possibility of execution is more painful than being murdered. He calls our attention to Byron Eshelman's *Death Row Chaplain,* which contains descriptions of the horrors of capital punishment. So extreme and biased is Amsterdam's appeal in favor of the criminal that he points out that Warden Lawes of Sing-Sing and former Governor Wallace of Alabama regularly employed murder convicts as house servants because they were among the safest of prisoners! What an appalling kind of special pleading Amsterdam engages in. Would he recommend that Manson be hired to take care of Polanski's grandchildren?

Amsterdam examines and rejects the two most important arguments for deterrence and incapacitation. He is correct when he notes that all the studies of the past forty years have been unable to prove that capital punishment deters potential criminals from committing crimes. The Supreme Court in 1976 described the evidence for deterrence as inconclusive. As

Charles L. Black wrote in *Capital Punishment:*

> After all possible inquiry, including the probing of all possible
> methods of inquiring, we do not know, and for systematic and
> easily visible reasons cannot know what the truth about this
> "deterrent" effect may be .... A scientific ... conclusion is
> simply impossible, and no methodological path out of the tangle
> suggests itself. (25-26)

Isaac Ehrlich's famous study in 1975 claimed that in the
United States every execution between 1933 and 1969 pre-
vented about eight murders. Since there were a total of 3,411
executions during that period, perhaps 27,000 potential vic-
tims' lives were saved. This study has been criticized by Law-
rence Klein, Peter Passell, Kenneth Avio, and Brian Fort. Still,
others like Ernest van den Haag consider Erhlich's conclu-
sions to be very significant.

We can never count the number of those who did not kill
because they wanted to avoid the death penalty. Perhaps there
are thousands out there who might not have murdered if they
faced capital punishment for their crimes. Were the prisoners
who held seventeen guards hostage at Ossining Prison in
January, 1983, aware that they would be eligible for the death
penalty if they killed the guards? Is this the thought that kept
them from harming the guards? On the other hand, did the
robbers who killed seven people in the Sofitel Hotel in Avig-
non, France, commit their atrocities because they knew that
France had abolished the death penalty a year before?

Sir Thomas More wrote in his famous work *Utopia:*

> How pernicious a thing it is to the public weal that a thief and
> a homicide or murderer should suffer equal and like punish-
> ment. For the thief, seeing that a man who is condemned for
> theft is in no less jeopardy, nor judged to no less a punishment
> than he who is convicted of manslaughter, through this thought
> only he is strongly and forcibly provoked, and in a manner
> constrained to kill him whom else he would have but robbed.
> For the murder once done, he is in less fear, and in more hope
> that the deed shall not be betrayed or known, seeing the party
> is now dead and rid out of the way, who alone might have
> uttered and disclosed it. But if he chance to be discovered and

taken, yet he is in no more jeopardy than if he had committed a
mere theft. (39-40)

Thus, even though we do not have definitive statistics about
the value of deterrence, we cannot ignore the actions of mur-
derers who kill to eliminate a witness. I cannot help but won-
der whether Deltejo knew there was no death penalty in New
York. Did he, therefore, "reason," as Sir Thomas More con-
tends, that he had nothing to lose by killing my son? If he had
regularly seen pictures of those executed for murder on tele-
vision, would he have stabbed my son? Would he have hesi-
tated, if only for a moment? That moment of hesitation might
have saved my son's life.

Amsterdam also deals with another argument for capital
punishment, namely, specific deterrence or incapacitation; in
other words, killing a murderer to prevent him from killing
again. Again Amsterdam uses the "human" argument against
incapacitation. He claims that those who favor incapacitation
do so because they believe that there really is no such pheno-
menon as a life sentence, that it really means parole after
seven, twelve, or twenty-five years, and that guards and other
prisoners are in danger of being hurt or killed by unexecuted
murderers. So, he asks, are we really going to kill people be-
cause we don't trust parole boards? While he himself objects to
life imprisonment without parole (obviously he believes some
murderers should be forgiven and set free), he is willing to
accept this punishment instead of the death penalty because it
is more "humane."

However, parole in relation to incapacitation is not really
the crucial issue. Amsterdam raises a red herring here. In-
capacitation is a form of legal punishment whereby individ-
uals subjected to it are incapacitated, meaning their ability to
commit subsequent offenses is reduced or eliminated by the
punishment. Thus, for example, when the Iranians cut off the
hands of a robber, they are limiting his ability to rob again.
Those who favor the death penalty as a form of incapacitation
do so because the death penalty incapacitates totally, per-
manently, absolutely, irrevocably. Yet, oddly enough, the in-
capacitative function of capital punishment, as Jack P. Gibbs
notes, is seldom emphasized by either revivalists or abolition-

ists. Supreme Court justices and jurists are very much aware of the difference between the concepts of deterrence and incapacitation in relation to capital punishment. For as Gibbs notes, even "the remote possibility that a capital offender may repeat the offense makes the incapacitating effect of the death penalty a central consideration" (Bedau, 107). Thus he finds it surprising that those who favor capital punishment have not emphasized incapacitation more than they have. A woman who killed her first child was placed on probation. She has now been charged with attempting to kill another child. If she had been incapacitated after the first murder, she would not have been able to attempt the second murder—and no guess would have been required about her future actions.

What we must come back to, if we are dealing with incapacitation as a viable concept, is the moral issue of capital punishment. Statistics, surveys, and econometric analyses will not provide the needed answer to the question which lies at the heart of the death penalty controversy: Is it morally defensible to take the life of a human if he has deliberately murdered another human being?

Several centuries ago Cesare Beccaria in his *On Crimes and Punishment* (1764) wrote that the death penalty gives an example of barbarity to men and therefore is not useful. This is known as the "executioner syndrome," which leads individuals to imitate the brutality of executions through lynchings and other acts of murder. But it is equally possible to argue that the death penalty gives an example of morality and is, therefore, eminently useful. Is it not barbaric to permit murderers to live? The Pope has urged that those on death row be granted clemency. He made a special plea for clemency for political prisoners. I would make that same plea for innocent political prisoners. When I talk about murderers, I talk only about those who *deliberately* harm the innocent; I do not talk about those who accidentally or in self-defense take a life.

What the Pope forgets, what Henry Schwarzschild forgets, what Anthony Amsterdam forgets is what Ernest van den Haag remembers:

> Murder differs in quality from other crimes and deserves, therefore, a punishment that differs in quality from other punishments. (Bedau, 331)

This is the crux. Once murder is admitted to be different from any other crime, it is possible to talk about relevant punishment. Very often those who argue against the death penalty seem to ignore or deny this basic point. They argue about how expensive it is to execute a murderer, how it does not deter, how the appeals clog the courts, how it can kill the innocent, particularly the black innocent, how it functions capriciously.

But van den Haag's point in this connection is irrefutable. His attack is against the extreme, fatuous egalitarianism of the abolitionists who claim that all men have the right to live—murderers as well as victims. Van den Haag is oppressed by the thought that such people would argue for the right of Stalin or Hitler to live out their lives. He says:

> Never to execute a wrongdoer, regardless of how depraved his acts, is to proclaim that no act can be so irredeemably vicious as to deserve death—that no human being can be wicked enough to be deprived of life. (Bedau, 332)

Do the murderers in Ogden, Utah, who forced their four victims to drink Drano and then shot them in the head, deserve to have a half-million dollars spent on their appeals to delay their execution? Glen D. King states:

> In the tragedy of human death there are degrees, and . . . it is much more tragic for the innocent to lose his life than for the State to take the life of a criminal convicted of a capital offense. (Bedau, 308)

Not only is it less tragic to take the life of such a criminal; it is the most moral act a society can perform, because by executing a murderer, society says that social justice is achieved if the worst of crimes is punished in the worst way. As van den Haag puts it, "there is no other way for society to affirm its values. To refuse to punish any crime with death, then, is to avow that the negative weight of a crime can never exceed the positive value of the life of the person who committed it" (Bedau, 333). What should have been done to the woman who killed and dismembered her three-year-old daughter in an act that, according to Judge Sybil Hart Kooper, "surpassed all others in brutality" (CS, July 10, 1982, 4)? For this murder she received a twenty-five-years to life sentence. She should have been given the death penalty to show that "the negative weight" of her crime did exceed "the positive value of the life of the person who committed it."

But those who oppose capital punishment are in effect saying: "Kill twenty-five people. Your life, because it is a life, is worth more than the lives of those you killed. It is worth millions of dollars in appeals to save you simply because you are human." It is true that most people who oppose the death penalty oppose it regardless of whether the convicted person is in truth innocent or guilty. For them the question of innocence is not the vital issue it is for those who approve of the death penalty.

For even those who favor the death penalty worry about the possibility that the innocent might be mistakenly executed. They do not want even one miscarriage of justice. But we can never attain absolute justice, no matter how much we may yearn for it. Van den Haag asserts that

> such miscarriages of justice do not warrant abolition of the death penalty. Unless the moral drawbacks of an activity or practice, which include the possible death of innocent bystanders, outweigh the moral advantages, which include the innocent lives that might be saved by it, the activity is warranted. Most human activities—medicine, manufacturing, automobile and air traffic, sports, not to speak of wars and revolutions—cause the death of innocent bystanders. Nevertheless, if the advantages sufficiently outweigh the disadvantages, human activities, including those of the penal system with all its punishments, are morally justified. (Bedau, 325)

Thus for van den Haag unequal justice is still justice. Justice means punishing as many of the guilty as possible. That the innocent being may be wrongly punished does not invalidate the attempt, imperfect as it is, to punish the guilty.

Even the ardent abolitionist Hugo Adam Bedau admits that it is "false sentimentality to argue that the death penalty should be abolished because of the abstract possibility that an innocent person might be executed, when the record fails to disclose that such cases occur" (Isenberg, 145). Bedau here is referring to recent cases. Jack Greenberg, formerly director-counsel of the NAACP Legal Defense and Educational Fund, and an opponent of the death penalty, admitted that since 1976 "the capital convicting and sentencing process has necessarily become extraordinarily careful to avoid executing those who are innocent or who deserve some sentence other than death" (T, Dec. 13, 1984, A18).

The philosopher Sidney Hook claims that

> it is not justice but only compassion that leads us to say that it is better that nine or ninety-nine guilty men escape punishment for their crime than that one innocent man be convicted. For that is certainly not doing justice either to the nine or ninety-nine guilty or to their potential victims. When crime is as rampant as it is today, those who invoke this dictum to justify strengthening the rights of individuals accused of violent crime at the expense of the rights of the potential victims of violent crimes are not even entitled to the self-righteous claim that they are moved by compassion. Compassion, if it is a virtue, must itself be balanced and equitable. Where, we ask, is their compassion for the myriad victims of violent crime? At what point, we ask, do the victims come into the ethical reckoning? (136)

The answer is clear to me. The victims come first in the ethical reckoning, and it is not better that nine or ninety-nine escape punishment rather than that one innocent man should be convicted. This is the bifurcation fallacy, considering only two extreme answers to a question. That an innocent man might possibly be erroneously convicted does not mean that murderers should be set free.

A death row inmate will not be executed until his appeals have reached—
    1. his state's highest court,
    2. a Federal District Court,
    3. a Federal Circuit Court of Appeals, and
    4. the United States Supreme Court.
It often takes three years for a death row case to be heard in the state court system. The convicted murderer John Paul Witt was executed in 1985, *twelve* years after his lawyers first began the appeals process. Contrast this state of affairs with the fact that in 1953 a pair of Missouri kidnappers were executed eleven weeks after they committed their crime; and in

the sixties one-fourth of those who were executed had no recourse to appeals and two-thirds never had their cases examined by any federal court. Even the abolitionist Sanford Kadish, an attorney, says that the chances of an innocent man being put to death are "exceedingly remote." (*Time,* Jan. 24, 1983, 83). The proceedings of the higher courts are designed to guarantee that no innocent person will be executed. Of the 2,000 death sentences imposed since 1972, half have been reversed or vacated by the appeals courts. In a 1981 opinion Justice William H. Rehnquist said that his colleagues had made a mockery of the criminal justice system by approving "endlessly drawn out legal proceedings." Chief Justice Burger, commenting on the Robert Sullivan execution, noted that the justice system had been turned into a "sporting contest" by defense lawyers. Robert Sullivan was on death row for ten years, and to Burger this delay, in and of itself, constitutes a "cruel and unusual punishment." So extreme has been the movement to protect the constitutional rights of offenders that many argue for a constitutional amendment to defend the rights of victims.

Walter Berns has also argued cogently for the morality inherent in the concept of capital punishment. He calls it the morality of anger. His main point is that some crimes are so heinous that if we exclude anger at such crimes and live with self-interest of the meanest sort, we live in a country unfit for human habitation. Berns tells us that Simon Wiesenthal, who has hunted Nazi war criminals for the last thirty years, taught him the simple fact that we want to punish criminals

> in order *to pay them back.* . . . By punishing them we demonstrate that there are laws that bind men across generations as well as across (and within) nations, that we are not simply isolated individuals, each pursuing his selfish interests and connected with others by a mere contract to live and let live. . . . Wiesenthal allows us to see that it is right, morally right, to be angry with criminals and to express that anger publicly, officially, and in an appropriate manner, which may require the worst of them to be executed. (Bedau, 334)

And that is the point, isn't it? The "worst of them to be executed."

To rob someone of money is an offense, but it is not the worst crime. To rob someone of millions of dollars is not as unspeakable a crime as to rob someone of his life. That is why Jesus was partially right. We should forgive our enemies—but not if they have taken a life or destroyed our ability to function normally. But those who oppose the death penalty think only of the way in which it denies the murderer his right to live. They ignore what Berns describes as the relationship between anger and justice and human dignity. Aristotle wrote that anger is accompanied not only by pain inflicted by the one against whom the anger is directed, but also by the expectation of pleasure derived from the possibility of inflicting revenge on someone who is thought to deserve it. Anger cannot be directed against an inanimate object, an animal, or a totally deranged person; it is directed against people who are responsible for their acts. Anger is integrally related to justice. Anger is not self-indulgence; it is an expression of the generous passion of men who care for each other in a community; it is the quality that makes heroes out of men who try to protect the community by demanding punishment for its enemies.

Yet there are those who persist in calling vengeance demeaning. For example, Judith Marciano, former legislative director of the American Civil Liberties Union and a member of the executive committee of the National Coalition Against the Death Penalty, obviously does not approve of the anger that cries out for retribution. Unlike Aristotle, who believed that those who show insufficient anger in relation to evil deeds are morally blameworthy, Marciano argues that the anger that cries out for vengeance is a form of scapegoat justice. But Gilmore, Coppola, Spenkelink, Judy, Brooks, Gray, Bishop, Evans, Sullivan, Williams, Smith, and Antone were murderers; they were not scapegoats. To equate the justice of capital punishment with the justice of the Nazis is to be guilty of the most flagrant kind of distortion.

Henry Schwarzschild of the American Civil Liberties Union castigates those who favor the death penalty by accusing them of sponsoring barbaric and atavistic treatment of criminals. On Sunday, October 9, 1983, on the Brinkley TV news program, Schwarzschild was asked whether he would have opposed the death penalty for Hitler if he were captured alive. Schwarzschild answered that he would not have advocated the execution of Hitler! Another abolitionist, John Conrad, doesn't specify whether he, like Schwarzschild, would have refused to kill Hitler; but in his debate with Ernest van den Haag, Conrad states unequivocally: "I hold that it is wrong to kill anyone, even Gary Gilmore—a ruthless and irresponsible killer—in cold blood, and I will make no distinction as to who is killed" (189). What exactly does Conrad mean by "in cold blood"? Would he approve of killing Gilmore if it were done "in hot blood"? This metaphorical subterfuge does not succeed in obscuring the simple fact that Conrad does not want the state to kill *any* murderers, and that would have to include the Hitlers as well as the Gilmores. Somehow the abolitionists always manage to leave us with the peculiar impression that they view the murderers as the only real victims in our society.

Governor Cuomo wants to use life imprisonment without parole as a substitute for capital punishment. Other well-meaning people have grasped at this straw of a solution. But John Godwin in *Murder USA,* in page after page of lurid documentation, reveals that there is no such phenomenon as life imprisonment without parole in this country. As long as parole boards can offer freedom to murderers for good behavior in prison, as long as lawyers can help murderers discover the technicalities that can result in parole, as long as governors can grant clemency to murderers, the intention of the legal punishment of life imprisonment can be subverted. Finally, who does not know that murderers kill again while in prison and that murderers kill again when they escape from prison.

If it were possible that murderers could be put away for life with no hope of parole, if it were possible to "pay them back" with a lifetime of suffering, then perhaps life imprisonment would be more just than the death penalty. But most criminals prefer the worst food, the worst rooms, the worst living conditions to lying in a grave in the earth. Besides, the tendency now is to build model prisons.

Let us look at the most advanced prison in the country, the Minnesota Correctional Facility in Oak Park Heights. It is secure, clean like a hospital. It has a large gymnasium, a chapel, an educational complex, television, music rooms, indoor exercise and recreation. Each prisoner has a private room with steel toilet, mirror, sink, desk, shelves, a bed with a thick mattress, and windows that can open. The prisoners do not work in the food or laundry departments. The prison is safe and humane. Prisoners only lack Sunday passes to go to brothels!

Of course, not all prisons are as ideal as the Minnesota Correctional Facility. But the public perception, fed by prison riots and the sympathetic columns of media reporters, is that prisoners are entitled to live in ideal prisons, under ideal conditions. Thus one of the prime reasons for the Ossining riot was that the prisoners were unhappy because they did not have enough recreational facilities. Overcrowding is, of course, another complaint. It is assumed that prison life should be comfortable and humane. The Washington State Penitentiary at Walla Walla, Washington, provides three $1,800 trailers to facilitate the conjugal bliss of married prisoners. For example, a former public officeholder convicted of killing his wife was allowed to spend the night at the trailer with his second wife. Then I learned about a mass wedding in San Quentin prison. In December, 1983, eleven women married eleven prisoners on the first Tuesday of the month, when marriages are usually conducted. San Quentin had 123 marriages in 1983. Prisoners are also allowed to have forty-two-hour honeymoons in a trailer on an estate in the prison or in two old Victorian houses in San Francisco Bay. Isn't that wonderful? Conjugal bliss in San Quentin.

On Christmas Day, 1982, convicted murderers in state prisons ate special holiday meals—all the food they could eat. Jean Harris had roast turkey, cornbread stuffing, whipped potatoes, gravy, bread and butter, carrots, cranberry sauce, ice cream, and beverages. In Attica, Mark David Chapman had roast chicken, salad with French dressing, sweet potatoes, corn, rolls, bread and butter, ice cream, and coffee. David Berkowitz and Buddy Jacobsen presumably ate similar meals. My taxes helped to provide them with a holiday feast.

My taxes also helped a prisoner who is serving three consecutive life terms for murder to sue the state of New York in a Manhattan court, for violating his constitutional rights. What was the violation? He had not been served kosher food in jail for three months! It is intolerable to me that my taxes help to defray the cost of such an outrageously absurd trial, and that my taxes help to feed criminals so well and supply them with the so-called necessary forms of healthy recreation. My taxes also help to educate them and supply them with prison libraries.

J. L. Barkas, whose young brother was murdered for a few cents in New York City, wrote the following:

> In March 1977 a photograph of a convicted and confessed murderer rapist appeared in a New York Newspaper. Under the photo was an article describing how this man, who was a prisoner in a maximum security prison, had just been awarded his bachelor of arts degree at the expense of the state and how he was now ready to pursue his master's degree—also on public funds. (177)

Now, it might be argued that we are rehabilitating this murderer, and as an educated man he will eventually be free to contribute to society. That education can transform murderers into virtuous citizens is a dubious premise. Moreover, they often use the prison library solely to find ways to sue the government and cost the taxpayers thousands of dollars. A segment on the TV program "60 Minutes" reported that it cost the state of Oregon $50,000 to deal with a suit brought by a confessed murderer against the son of his dead victim. This son had to spend a total of $15,000 to answer his suit. The prisoner was able to harass the son because the penal code provides for the right of the inmate to have access to a law library and to engage in litigation. He can sue for any reason at the same time that he himself can not be sued.

Thousands of prisoners engage in lawsuits, and those who become lawyers in prison can get an average fee of $2,000 for each case. "60 Minutes" described an inmate who learned the law and sued a hundred times; he sued because the handcuffs were too tight, the guards cursed, and railroads going by his cell were too noisy. He sued judges and lawyers and won 11 cases and was appealing 22. Still another prisoner who became a lawyer in jail participated in 105 cases and won 90 of them. Recently the Supreme Court reversed a lower court decision to eliminate seven prison newspapers. After five years of litigation the American Civil Liberties Union won this case by arguing for the rights of prisoners under the First Amendment. Two articles at Soledad Prison could not be censored, and the $58,000 spent on the salaries of prisoners who wrote the newspapers had to be continued. Some prisoners are clearly better off than our millions of unemployed.

The prison population in New York State is growing at a faster pace than at any other time. Governor Cuomo wants to build seven new prisons at a cost of $600 million, the largest expansion program in the state's history. In view of this penal emergency, why should we tolerate spending any more money on legal fees to deal with the legal chicaneries of prisoners who learn how to manipulate the law? But this is, after all, no more than the expectable result of a climate of opinion that values the civil liberties of prisoners more highly than the needs of people they have cheated, robbed, raped, and killed.

Is anything more indicative of the absurd functioning of the criminal justice system than the following information? John Wayne Gacy, who has been accused of the rape and murder of thirty-three young boys, was ordered to pay one million dollars in damages to the mother of one of the children he was accused of murdering. Mr. Gacy is appealing this award, and of course, millions of dollars will be spent to determine whether Gacy's conviction is warranted.

A clear manifestation of our misplaced sympathies is the argument over the use of lethal injection. While Schwarzschild emotionalizes in *The Times* about how inhumane this injection is, a bereaved parent describes how her sixteen-year-old daughter was raped, strangled, struck over the head at least seven times with a sharp instrument, and thrown into a ditch. This mother asks whether it would have been comforting to her murdered daughter to have received a shot of Valium in the same way that Stephen Judy received one before he was executed (C. Hullinger). Judy murdered a young Indianapolis mother and her three young children. He told the jury that sentenced him: "You better vote for the death penalty 'cause I'm gonna get out one way or another, and it may be one of you next or your families" (Bing. Even. Press, Jan. 30, 1985:D1). But we gave him Valium to make sure that he, unlike his victims, would feel no pain before his death.

Idaho, New Mexico, Oklahoma, and Texas are states that use lethal injections to execute murderers. There are those who want society to guarantee that the lethal injection drugs produce a speedy, humane death for murderers. The question is, how speedy and humane were the deaths of their victims? In what sense are these murderers "human"? Was Dean Corll human when he killed twenty-seven people? Was Paul Knowles human when he killed eighteen people? Was Charles Whitman human when he killed sixteen people?

When Charlie Brooks was given a lethal injection, some writers really worried about the thirty seconds of pain he might have suffered before he died. This is misplaced pity. Let us look at Aristotle's definition of pity in his *Rhetoric:*

> Pity may be defined as a feeling of pain caused by the sight of some evil, destructive or painful, which befalls one who does not deserve it, and which we might expect to befall ourselves or some friend of ours, and moreover to befall us soon . . . In order to feel pity we must also believe in the goodness of at least some people; if you think nobody good, you will believe that everybody deserves evil fortune. And, generally, we feel pity whenever we are in the condition of remembering that similar misfortunes have happened to us or ours, or expecting them to happen in the future . . . More piteous of all is it when, in some times of trial, the victims are persons of noble character: whenever they are so, our pity is especially excited, because their innocence, as well as the setting of their misfortunes before our eyes, makes their misfortunes seem close to ourselves. (Bk II, Chap. 8)

Pity, as Aristotle correctly observed, is for the deserving victims. To pity the murderer is to commit the grossest injustice to the murdered victim.

Those who worry about justice for criminals like to think of themselves as compassionate liberals, men who are devoted to espousing the cause of freedom. But as Sidney Hook noted,

> . . . not all who call themselves liberal understand either themselves or the doctrines they profess. In other contexts, I have referred to "ritualistic liberals" as those who think they can be liberal without being intelligent. A particularly conspicuous species of the genus of ritualistic liberal is found among those writers on crime and law enforcement for whom the victims of crime are only incidental rather than central to the problem of crime prevention. Such writers in their mournful assessment of tragic encounters between lawbreakers and law officers tend to equate with a fine moral impartiality those who are slain while attempting

or committing murder with those who lose their life preventing it. (136)

Such ritualistic liberals utilize their misplaced pity and compassion to argue for the life of the murderer; no matter how despicable his crime, his legitimate rights to life are more important than the life of the victim.

The death penalty issue made the cover of *Time*, January 24, 1983, just as I finished writing this chapter. The authors of the article on this subject quoted the expectable remarks of the abolitionists and retentionists and described the exploits of two prisoners on death row—

On the night of June 3, 1973, a Chevrolet Caprice, driven by a woman, was forced off Interstate 57 in southern Cook County, Ill., by a car carrying four men. One of them pointed a 12 gauge pump shotgun at her, ordered her to strip and then to climb through a barbed-wire fence at the side of the road. As she begged for her life her assailant thrust the shotgun barrel into her vagina and fired. After watching her agonies for several minutes, he finished her off with a blast to the throat. Less than an hour later, the marauding motorists stopped another car and told the man and woman inside it to get out and lie down on the shoulder of the road. The couple pleaded for mercy, saying that they were engaged to be married in six months. The man with the shotgun said, "Kiss your last kiss," then shot both of them in the back, killing them. The total take from three murders and two robberies: $54, two watches, an engagement ring and a wedding band.

The man ultimately convicted of the "I-57 murders" now sits confined in the Menard Condemned Unit, the official name for death row in the Illinois prison system. Yet Henry Brisbon Jr., 28, does not face execution for those three killings nearly ten years ago. Illinois' death penalty was invalidated in 1972 and was not restored until 1977, the year that Brisbon was finally brought to trial. At that time, the judge sentenced him to a term of 1,000 to 3,000 years in prison. It took Brisbon less than one year to kill again, this time stabbing a fellow inmate at Stateville Correctional Center with the sharpened handle of a soup ladle. At the trial for this murder, Will County State's Attorney Edward Petka described Brisbon as "a very, very terrible human being, a walking testimonial for the death penalty." The jury agreed. (30)

Bittaker, 42, is on death row at San Quentin for kidnaping and murdering five teen-age girls. But that is not all. He and a partner raped and sodomized four of them first, for hours and days at a time, sometimes in front of a camera. But that is not all. He tortured some of the girls—pliers on nipples, ice picks in ears—and tape-recorded the screams. But that is not all. The last victim was strangled with a coat hanger, her genitals mutilated and her body tossed on a lawn so that he could watch the horror of its discovery. (39)

These "mutants of hell" led the authors of the article to conclude with the following comments.

Can they be human? Without killers in this league, more of America's logic and instinctive sense of mercy could prevail. There might be more electorates like Michigan's and more Governors like New York's who declare that capital punishment is unworthy of a decent society.

Administration of the death penalty perhaps cannot be made fair enough. As a deterrent, it is probably not necessary. But public passions are inflamed by the inevitable monsters. Civil reason is suspended in the face of what looks like evil incarnate. (39)

Is this not an outlandish observation? The implication is that only those who commit "vile" murders deserve to be executed. Those who commit "ordinary" homicide deserve to live? Who shall stand in judgment that one murder is worse than another? Who shall decide that the woman who was killed by Brisbon suffered more than my son who was thrown on the tracks?

In New Orleans, the Supreme Court overturned the death penalty conviction of Walter Culberth, because, Chief Justice John Dixon claimed, Culberth's crime was not "heinous" enough. Heinousness involved the use of torture or the pitiless infliction of unnecessary pain when killing the victim. In Dixon's view, Culberth did not torture or abuse his victim. Only Justice Walter Marcus on the Court dissented, contending that the victim did not die instantly and suffered until she expired en route to the hospital. This kind of decision reminds me of what Chief Justice Charles Evan Hughes is reported to have said: "You must remember one thing. At the constitutional level where we work, ninety percent of any decision is emotional. The rational part of us supplies the reasons for supporting our predilections" (Hunt, 129).

What is so frightening is that the Culberth case makes us recognize that the higher courts do produce irrational decisions. I can foresee in the rather dark future of our civilization a machine that will be invented to indicate the level of pain a victim suffers to determine if the crime is heinous enough. Below 50 percent on the scale, the murderer goes to a new model prison; between 50 and 75 percent, he goes to an old prison; over 75 percent, he gets executed. Judge Learned Hand of the New York Court of Appeals said to Justice Oliver Wendell Holmes, "Do Justice." Holmes replied, "That is not my job. My job is to play the game according to the rules" (T, Sept. 7, 1982, A23). And that is what is wrong with the law; it can be a game played by men in power according to their individual whims and beliefs.

Nothing illustrates more clearly the phenomenon of game playing in the judicial system than the insanity plea. If it were possible to demonstrate scientifically the difference between sane and insane criminals, it might be justifiable to absolve the criminally insane of moral responsibility for their crimes. If we could determine through objective tests how a murderer's brain malfunctions at the time that he kills, we might accept the view that such a person should be incarcerated in a mental institution. But there is no reliable evidence that psychiatry can make such a diagnosis. George E. Dix wrote in the *American Criminal Law Review* that "the use of mental health professional expert testimony by the state to establish the dangerousness of convicted capital defendants constitutes a significant evidentiary problem. If such testimony is analyzed under traditional evidentiary standards, it might well be held inadmissible as addressing an area not properly the subject of expert or 'scientific' testimony" (47-48).

The contradictory evidence offered by psychiatrists in the Hinckley trial reveals no scientific testimony. The jury could just as easily have found Hinckley to be sane. Hinckley is now in a mental hospital, although we know that he deliberately attempted to kill President Reagan. James Lee Gray was executed on September 2, 1983, after spending seven years on death row, after fifty judges participated in his appeals cases. His lawyer insisted that Gray was insane. But exactly how Hinckley's insanity differed from Gray's sanity no one is able to demonstrate.

The truth is that almost all criminals can be considered insane. Murderers who kill innocent people and disregard the accepted norms of societal behavior are clearly mental deviates. But the present insanity plea permits the criminal to escape prison if he lacks *mens rea,* the consciousness of his guilty purpose. In this view he is not blameworthy even if he kills a hundred people. But a murderer's intention is not fathomable; we can not at this time definitively establish it in a scientific fashion. The insanity plea involves lawyers in a farcical judicial game which often permits the guilty to escape punishment. It should be abolished. But if we have to have an insanity plea, I agree with Harvard Professor Charles Nesson that it should be a "guilty but insane verdict" to show that killing someone unjustifiably is wrong regardless of the mental health of the accused. While all of us might potentially want to kill under terrible circumstances, we control our bad impulses. Hinckley is a prime example of a young man who did not control himself and was not punished for his lack of control. Under a guilty but insane verdict, if Hinckley were released from the mental hospital, he would be sent back to prison to serve the remaining years of a sentence he deserved for attempting to kill the president. He would not be allowed to go free if the psychiatrists decided he was cured.

Governor Cuomo has been quoted in the papers as stating that crime in New York is "disgusting." And he has every right to feel that way. His daughter, son, and wife were assaulted and robbed at various times in the city. His seventy-nine-year-old father-in-law was hospitalized after being severely beaten by muggers. But Cuomo is a Christian who castigates those in public office who do not understand and practice Christ's doctrine of forgiveness.

When Cuomo vetoed the death penalty he wrote "I do not believe that responding to violence with violence or death with death is the answer. It does not undo the loss. It has not proved effective in this State or anywhere else; there is no reason to believe it deters future loss. It does not uplift or ennoble our State. It does nothing more than demean us." In my view, Cuomo's veto of the death penalty demeaned my dead son Eric. His argument reveals that it is possible to care more about the murderer than the victim. Why in the world should the act of killing a murderer "ennoble or uplift the State"? No one who argues for the death penalty uses this kind of irrelevant rhetoric. We kill a murderer to show that the life of an innocent person is worth more than the life of a murderer; we do it to punish him, to prevent him from killing again, and to express our moral outrage. As Herbert Morris says, it is the criminal's *right* to be punished (475).

But politicians do not have to be consistent. On the one hand, Mario Cuomo, who personally opposes abortion, maintains that as governor he has to abide by the law of the land and cannot impose his views on the people he represents. On the other hand, despite the Supreme Court's ruling that the death penalty is constitutional, and despite the fact that the majority of New Yorkers favor the death penalty, Mario Cuomo has imposed his personal views on the people of this state by vetoing the death penalty bill. To answer the charge of inconsistency, he has insisted that he is legally required to accept the abortion law, whereas as governor he is free to approve or disapprove of capital punishment before it is embodied in a law. But this is mere verbal quibbling. As a man of conscience, Cuomo is obligated to argue for or against a principle, regardless of whether it is a law.

In his *Diaries* the governor wrote about how he felt about the person who twice attacked his daughter in Queens, only a block from his home:

> I feel it—and we feel it—the passion. If my son ever got his hands on this guy—forget my son, if I ever did, I cannot predict how I would behave. I'm not a saint and I'm not a God. And if you stood that person in front of me and said, "There he is," I don't know what I would do. (415)

No, Cuomo is not a saint and he is not a God. He is commendably very, very human. In this passage he reveals his outrage at an attack that did not physically harm his daughter. How would he have responded if the attack were fatal? Would he have recommended life imprisonment without parole?

Support for the death penalty is at an all-time high. In 1985 the Gallup Poll reported that 72 percent of Americans approve of the death penalty. The Media General-Associated Press Poll concluded that 84 percent of Americans approve of capital punishment.

French Justice Minister Robert Badinter wrote a book about death by the guillotine called *L'Exécution* (1973) after witnessing the beheading of one of his clients. This official who helped retire the guillotine in France claimed that the sole purpose of capital punishment is to free the anguish, fear, and hatred that exists in the human heart. I see nothing wrong with this "sole purpose." It is the same noble purpose that motivates medical, religious, and other professionals. The next book Badinter writes should be called *The Victim.*

The National Coalition Against the Death Penalty is an association of more than ninety national organizations. I do not know of any National Coalition *For the Victim.*

9

After the Trial

"Well, everyone can master a grief, but he that has it."
Shakespeare, *Much Ado about Nothing*

For a few days after the trial, just for a few days, I had the feeling that perhaps my pain would lessen in the weeks that followed. The trial was over, "justice was done," and now, presumably, I could begin to heal. The bereavement specialists offer contradictory solace. Some maintain that those who suffer a loss begin to recover in two years; others contend that it takes at least four or five years; while still others, like Freud, claim that it is not possible to recover from the loss of a child. Depression engulfed me about a week after the trial. There was no longer anywhere to go to help Eric; there was no longer anyone to talk to about Eric's murderers. Friends and relatives, except for a few, wanted me to forget, not to linger on the past.

Then I began to think again of suicide. I read the books on this subject by Alvarez, Hendin, and Schneidman. Suicide, I discovered, is a respectable topic in philosophy, and books written by philosophers, psychologists, and scientists discuss the right to commit suicide as a serious, profound philosophic issue. One church father, Tertullian, claimed that even Jesus was a suicide! Virginia Woolf, Klaus Mann, Romain Gary, Ernest Hemingway, Arthur Koestler, Sylvia Plath, Anne Sexton, Hart Crane, and John Berryman committed suicide. Arthur Koestler was the head of an organization called Exit, which in a pamphlet teaches its members how to kill themselves painlessly.

149

Montaigne, Voltaire, Kant, Nietzsche, and Dostoevsky believed in the right to suicide. But others, like Albert Camus and Jean Paul Sartre, reject suicide as a viable answer to the nothingness or *nada* of existence. To go on living is to them an act of courage in the face of the void.

Eli Weisel is a famous survivor of two Nazi concentration camps. His father was killed before his eyes, and of his family only he and his two sisters survived. As a young Hasidic Jew in the mountains of Rumania, he had devoted his life and soul to God and the study of the Talmud. In the years following the Holocaust he devoted himself to writing "as a kind of expiation" and also as a way of

> trying to understand something that defies both reason and imagination. It is an existential act . . . an act of defiance in the face of the void . . . out of despair, one creates. What else can one do? There is no good reason to go on living. There is no good reason to bring a child into the world but you must have children to give the world a new innocence; a new reason to aspire towards innocence. As Camus said, in a world of unhappiness, you must create happiness. (T, April 7, 1981, C 11)

Now, if Weisel can not find any real reason for living, if he can not in any way explain the horrors of the Holocaust, why should I even try to explain what the death of one boy means? After all, the Nazis killed 15,000 children in *one* concentration camp. Yet, like Weisel, I try to create out of despair. There is something so terrible, so unforgivable in the loss of the young. It is so because, as Weisel says, we must have children to give the world a new innocence, a new reason to aspire towards innocence. And when the young, the good, the talented are destroyed, we feel as though hope has been destroyed.

The ancient Greeks made a distinction between *Thanatos,* the natural death of old age, and *Ker,* death through violence, disease, and madness. It is hard enough to accept *Thanatos.* But even the most religious thinker finds it difficult to accept *Ker.* And young *Ker* is and remains the most blatant example of existential absurdity.

Yet the latest statistics reveal that suicide is the major cause of death among Americans who are fifteen to twenty-four years old. What does this tell us about our civilization? Something perverse, eerie, frightening is happening when the young who are our future are killing themselves. They are unnatural creatures born into a world they reject. This Shakespeare could not understand. He has Claudio say in *Measure for Measure* (III.i.) what we often think about the gift of life:

> The weariest and most loathed
> worldly life
> That age, ache, penury and
> imprisonment
> Can lay on nature is a paradise
> To what we fear of death.

Goethe, who romanticized suicide in *The Sorrows of Young Werther,* was in actuality so terrified of death that he never visited the room of his mother and wife when they were dying, and he refused to attend the funerals of friends. Yet Jacques Choron reminds us that often it is disgust with life, *anhedonia,* that makes someone commit suicide (68).

I thought of the parents who had killed themselves over the loss of a child, and I thought of those who continued to live— Helen Hayes, Clare Boothe Luce. How did the mother who lost five children in a fire survive? How did the parents of the seven children killed in a bus accident in Paris survive? A soliloquy I have taught for thirty years with objective equanimity now haunts me: "To be or not to be."

Once again my husband tried to find a psychiatrist who could help me. A professor at Harvard recommended Dr. Sanuel Fell. And once again, like a broken record, I began to tell him what had happened. Unlike the other psychiatrists I had dealt with, he spent two hours with me during our first session and made a diagnosis before I left. He said I was suffering from an acute traumatic neurosis. This was, of course, a fancy term for depression. I was surprised that he would offer a diagnosis after one session.

My initial impulse was not to return to him. But I had promised my husband that I would continue to visit Fell for at least six sessions and at least give him the opportunity to perform the miracle that I knew he could not perform. So I visited him and I talked and he listened. At the fourth session he stressed the fact that I did not express my anger. I had revealed my grief but I refused to reveal my anger. Somehow this seemed to him to be very significant. I explained that I had expressed so much anger for nineteen months that I could not at will begin yelling and screaming in his office. I knew that a new controversy had erupted in psychiatric circles over the question of whether it is advisable for depressed people to give vent to their anger or to repress it. (Read Carol Tavris's *Anger: The Misunderstood Emotion.*) Besides, I had spent the day teaching before I saw him, and I was tired. This did not seem to satisfy him, and I left his office feeling worse than when I had entered it. Despite the fact that I repeatedly asked him to help me cope with the terrible images of my son's death, he offered me no help in that connection. The last time I saw him he left me with the following question to ponder: Did I think I was entitled to get better?

Was he right? Was that the crucial question? Even if I really thought I was not entitled to get better, even if I was somehow punishing myself by not wanting to get better, the objective truth was there—it was out there all the time. My son was dead; he had been murdered, and *he was not entitled to that end.*

Fell was a pleasant enough man; he meant well, but he was as impotent as all the other psychiatrists to solve my problem. He could not make the dead live again. As a Freudian analyst he probably believed that if I talked to him a long time I would eventually talk myself out of my depression. I did not feel that he was helping me. However, I had not decided to drop him. I merely told him the truth; I was planning to take a trip to the West after the school term. Shortly after my last session with him, he called our house to discuss a discrepancy in the billing system. My husband spoke to him, and resolved the problem amicably. But Fell did not ask to speak to me. After not seeing me for a few months, he might at the very least have tried to ask me how I was feeling.

But Dr. Fell, like all psychiatrists, had to protect himself against the ravages of emotional involvement with clients. I always had the feeling when I talked to a psychiatrist that I was talking to a businessman. He agreed to listen to my troubles if I paid him. We were involved in a business transaction, and the moment that I did not fulfill my part of the contract, the psychiatrist could turn away, as disinterested in my life and my future as if he had never met me.

In this sense mental health specialists are like some acquaintances you loosely call *friends* when you should not really use that term to describe them. These people you know; you talk to them at work; you see them socially; they inhabit the immediate environment in which you live. They become involved in your tragedy, but not because they are paid to do so, but because at the outset they are genuinely shocked and saddened and feel they should say and do the "acceptable things" at such a time. I also believe some of them experience a form of *Schadenfreude* (malicious enjoyment of the discomfiture of others). They, in some peculiar way, are comforted by the knowledge that *your* misfortune is not theirs. But after a while, they lose interest in your tragedy. There are, after all, so many other calamities. Someone is always dying or dead. Besides, they have their own problems. Those who grieve with you often end up grieving for themselves. Since my son died, at least four couples I know have separated or divorced. They suffered their own kind of personal loss. But not only personal problems make "friends" turn away. They must turn away from death because they have their own fears of mortality which they must sublimate in order to survive. Deep in their hearts they know that even though they are now blessed with healthy children and a good life, someday that will have to end; so that as they mourn for me, they are mourning for themselves as well. And since they are not paid to mourn with me, like the psychiatrist, they cannot and do not have to sustain their interest in me.

Some "friends" abandoned us shortly after the tragedy as if they were afraid of being contaminated. Those friends and relatives who really cared about us showed their concern by spending time with us, listening to us, and trying to console us. They helped me more than the psychiatrists, although I think that if I had been fortunate enough to meet a psychiatrist like the one Judd Hirsch portrays in *Ordinary People,* I might have found him to be invaluable.

The bereavement organizations are valuable precisely because they are not *paid* to care. They try to help others overcome grief, not as professionals, but as fellow suffering human beings. When women like Mrs. Garland, the mother of Bonnie Garland, Mrs. Odile Stern, the president of the New York chapter of Parents of Murdered Children, and Charlotte Hullinger, the founder of POMC, spoke to me, their empathy was spontaneous and genuine. I know a psychologist who sent his mourning sister to the Hope for Bereaved group in Syracuse because he had no faith in his colleagues' ability to deal with the acute grief of loss. My husband brought me to the meetings of this Syracuse organization, though he never attended them. (He never spoke to a psychiatrist either; he had his own very private method of dealing with his sorrow.) Many kind, compassionate people talked about their tragedies and seemed to derive some diminution of their tortured feelings. Most of the participants were Christians. Thus the woman whose daughter was raped and murdered could cope with her anger because she believed in a good God and an afterlife. She believed that she would see her daughter again. But the reason for my unabated grief was that I did not believe that I would ever see my son again.

On April 3, 1982, his twenty-fourth birthday came and went. In the spring of 1982, Mother's Day came and went. Father's Day came and went. Somehow the term ended. And then the running began. We visited the Poconos and the Hamptons to avoid being at home where everything reminded us of the many summers we had spent with Eric. Then we visited his grave. The sun was shining; the grass was green and growing. I knew that I would miss him until I died and I would never be comforted.

Running, running to avoid thinking and remembering, we left for the West at the beginning of August. We drove through Colorado and Utah, and we saw the Rocky Mountains stretching out for miles. Unless the planet is destroyed, they will be here for billions of years. We also saw the Sierra Nevada; miles and miles of rock formations majestically and endlessly looming in the sky. Yet even in this uninhabited innocence there is the ever present history of violence. In Yosemite we were informed that the name meant "There are killers among them." These were the words uttered by the native Indians about the American cavalrymen who had abducted three sons of these Indians. The history of the West is, after all, a history of human predation.

When you take a long trip, the sheer physical energy required to move from place to place is momentarily diverting.

But I was not able to forget my loss. The last long journey we had taken was to Europe when Eric was thirteen; we visited eleven countries, going and returning on the *Queen Elizabeth II.* Wherever we went in the West, we saw parents and their children, and I felt an unbearable pang of envy. Inevitably a young boy looked like Eric. And I hated myself for living and trying to experience pleasure while my son was dead.

One night in San Francisco we went to a movie. The lobby was filled with young people dating on a Saturday night, putting their arms around each other, kissing each other. But Saturday night for me would always be the night my son could not go out on a date because it was the night he was murdered. As I sat there I remembered that he had died exactly twenty-three months ago. I left the theater and cried all the way back to the hotel.

What the trip taught me is that you can never escape what is in your heart and mind, no matter where you go. I traveled 8,114 miles to learn what I knew before I started. No matter where I went, no matter what I saw, I always interpreted everything in terms of my loss. When I looked at Bryce Canyon and saw the spectacular beauty of its carved figures, I thought of the ugliness called Deltejo and Urena, also a part of this world. I thought of the earthquakes that were potential hazards all over the West. What was beautiful could be transformed into destructive ugliness. Just a few feet away from the Ahwahnee Inn in Yosemite, we saw the huge boulders that had fallen during an earthquake. Falling a few hundred feet closer, they would have destroyed the inn. As we passed one of the mountains in Yosemite, our guide pointed to two tiny black spots near the top of the mountain. The two spots, he informed us, were two mountain climbers. Looking at them, two tiny ants, I thought that if the universe is just a second of time in eternity, the loss of one son is hardly significant. But such a philosophical outlook offers only momentary solace. For there is so much beauty, so much to enjoy, so much to learn and experience, that it is impossible to forgive the destruction of a life, even if life is only a second of time in eternity.

After traveling through Illinois, Wyoming, Nebraska, Nevada, Utah, Colorado, and California, we boarded the

Broadway Limited in Chicago. As we entered our sleeper, we saw two policemen with guns pass our door. A few feet away they caught a young man and put handcuffs on him. He had robbed someone at gunpoint at the Union Station and planned to escape as a passenger on the Broadway Limited. The train was delayed for an hour while the police searched for the missing gun. I do not know if they ever found it. But there is no escaping the predators. To travel thousands of miles and walk into the Biltmore in Los Angeles and watch two policemen passing through the lobby with a slovenly young man in handcuffs is to realize that everywhere in this glorious land of ours the criminal lies in wait for the victim.

One night after we returned home, I watched the MacNeil-Lehrer program and heard Senator William T. Smith (New York) discuss the attempts he had made to introduce strict drunk driving laws. His daughter was killed by a drunk driver in 1973. She was a young, beautiful teacher at my college. The day after she died, one of my students who was in her class wept outside my office as I tried to comfort her by uttering all the platitudes: "You must think of her as being at peace now. You must remember her as a wonderful person and teacher. She would not want you to mourn, etc." I did not know Senator Smith's daughter, but as I looked at him speaking ten years after the death of his child, I understood the truth of Solon's observation. Long ago he said that we will achieve justice only when those who are not injured by crime feel as indignant as those who are.

As the autumn began, I waited terrified for the weekend that would bring the second anniversary of Eric's death. I thought of Urena and Deltejo eating, sleeping, watching television, and exercising while my son lay in his grave. I began to keep a diary of curses, utilizing my own peculiar brand of verbal scream therapy. I remembered the School of Wicca, which teaches people how to become witches. Unfortunately they are benevolent witches, and if I were to become involved with demonology, I would at least want to have the power to destroy what I despise. If the reader is shocked by this revelation of intense hatred, I can only answer that I am telling the truth. Most of the books about bereavement seem to be fairy tales with unbelievable happy endings: time heals all wounds, and so on. I know what I think, what I feel, and I have expressed it honestly so that those who read this book will hear the Victim's Song as a song of unadulterated hell. To lose someone you love at the hands of a murderer is to begin a life of unremitting suffering and unremitting hatred.

During the month of September, two years after my son was murdered, the expectable slaughter continued in New York. In a typical weekend about seventeen people would be killed by a bullet, a knife, a baseball bat, a hammer, a rope, or a wire. In Washington Heights, Rose May Jacobs, eighty-four, was robbed and murdered. The vice-president of Con-Edison was stabbed and robbed in his midtown penthouse. At the Waldorf-Astoria, Kathleen Williams, a young and successful executive, was stabbed to death on a stairway in that famous hotel. Hettie Salzman, eighty-two, was killed in an apartment in Washington Square, an area that once served as an elegant setting for one of Henry James's best stories, a lovely place my husband and I used to visit when we attended New York University. The parents of Elizabeth Holtzman, the Brooklyn District Attorney, were robbed. Laura Evelyn, seventeen, was raped, strangled, and thrown off the roof of her apartment house in Queens. A Bronx heroin addict, paroled after serving six years for murder, was arrested for the fatal knifing of a seventy-six-year-old neighbor. Expensive shops on Madison Avenue were burglarized and protective gates were placed on the windows. A young boy was murdered in a subway by a mugger who tried to steal his radio.

Then something happened on Thanksgiving day, twenty-six months after my son died. My brother Hy collapsed and died of a heart attack. But I know that he also died of a broken heart. Hy loved Eric. He was crushed by his death and mourned for him every day. His last two years on earth were so sad that I believe he suffered from *anhedonia*. He refused to see a doctor and willed himself into the kind of inertia which might precipitate from a death wish. Urena and Deltejo destroyed the last years of my brother's life just as surely as if they had put a knife in his back. I loved my brother. He had raised me as if he were my father. We were very close. I shall always miss him, and I shall never stop blaming Urena and Deltejo for his loss as well as for the loss of my son. When a murder is committed, those who love the victim are themselves murdered in different ways. That is why the new law in some states that permits the victim's family to testify about the crime is a fair law. For it recognizes for the first time that a murder has a ripple effect, and that the sentence should take into consideration not only the life of the victim but also the destroyed lives of those who loved the victim.

When my son was murdered, I knew that I could no longer look at the world as I had before. It was no longer possible for me to look at a human being and believe in what I saw. How could one explain the infamous example of human depravity that occurred in a New Bedford, Massachusetts, bar? On March 6, 1983, a twenty-one-year-old woman was sexually assaulted for two hours by four men on a pool table while other men watched and cheered. No one called the police. Nothing, nothing can excuse the behavior of the rapists or the witnesses; they are symbols of how a human animal differs from all other animals in enjoying gratuitous acts of cruelty. Remember the parable of the Good Samaritan in the Gospel of St. Luke: Jesus told us about a man who was robbed, beaten, and left half-dead. Two of the three persons who passed by refused to help the victim. In the New Bedford incident, there was no third person to help. In the famous Kitty Genovese story, thirty-eight neighbors witnessed her anguish and her murder for thirty-five minutes in Kew Gardens, Queens, and not one of them called the police. It is naive to believe that in this crime-infested country good will and good luck will prevent murders.

Now, if that raped woman had walked into that bar with a *gun* in her purse, she could have escaped her two hours of horror. There is a rifle and a registered gun in my house; I have learned how to use the gun and the rifle. I was formerly horrified at the thought that such a phenomenon as a gun exists. But the real world is a dangerous, ugly place, and as long as the Urenas and Deltejos carry instruments of destruction, it is necessary for innocent, good people to protect themselves.

In Kennesaw, Georgia, every citizen is required to own a gun. According to the police chief, Bob Ruble, the town has witnessed a 70 percent drop in crime since 1981 when the gun law was instituted. On the other hand, in Morton Grove, Illinois, shortly after handguns were banned, assaults rose by 30 percent. Even if Police Chief Lorenz Schey is correct in attributing these assaults to domestic incidents, it would still be interesting to know why more violence erupted in families in a town that banned handguns (USA, Mar. 16, 1983, 2A).

Pete Shields, whose son was murdered by a gun, has written definitively in *Guns Don't Die: People Do* about the subject of gun control, arguing that whatever has to be done to curb the use of handguns by criminals should be done. Registration that might in some way limit the freedom of honest, law-abiding people is a small price to pay for saving lives.

At the beginning of 1983 the Koch administration argued for a mandatory five-year addition to all prison sentences for felonies involving the use of a gun. However, no one recommends that this additional sentence be applied to felonies committed with a knife. Rarely does anyone talk about *knife* control! By a vote of seven to two, the Supreme Court ruled on January 19, 1983, that "the use of a dangerous weapon" to commit a crime is a separate armed criminal action and justifies additional punishment. In all the newspaper reports of this decision, which declared that there was no double jeopardy for two punishments for a single act, no reference was made to a knife. The "dangerous weapon" was clearly the gun. Yet people kill each other in many ways, and it is virtually impossible to anticipate whether someone will stick a knife in your back or hit you over the head with a baseball bat. It is not possible to require registration of common household utensils.

I am not particularly sanguine that gun control will necessarily protect the innocent person, since it is possible for the unlawful element to obtain rifles legally in New York State, for example, through the mail from Montgomery Ward and Sears Roebuck. Nor will it be possible to outlaw all devices used to kill people, such as poison, and car assaults. But I think gun control bills should be supported, provided that law-abiding citizens can purchase registered guns and learn how to use them properly. Charles Rivera's father was robbed and murdered with a shotgun in his grocery store in the Bronx in 1965. Rivera himself was robbed fourteen times during the fifteen years he operated a store. Once he was pistol whipped and needed fifty-two stitches on his forehead. Thus when two robbers entered his store on January 16, 1983, and attempted to rob him at gunpoint, Rivera killed them both. He received the "Courageous Citizen's Award" from Jerry Preiser, President of the Federation of N.Y.S. Rifle and Pistol Club, an ovation from a hundred neighbors, and a visit from the brother of one of the dead robbers, who told Rivera he was justified in killing his brother.

Would the handgun control groups approve of what Rivera did? I imagine that if Rivera's gun was registered, they would have no rational reason for objecting to his actions. The moral is clear: if you live in a violent world, you have to have the means to protect yourself against that violence. This is as valid a premise as the one which demands that guns be kept out of the hands of criminals. If my son had carried a gun on the subway, a *registered* gun, he would be alive today. For Pete Shields, whose son was killed by a gun, the answer is gun control. I do not see any contradiction between our two views: control the use of weapons, try to keep them out of the hands of criminals, but do not prevent law-abiding citizens from owning guns under controlled conditions.

A twenty-eight-man contingent of cops, a captain, and a helicopter pilot guard Mayor Koch night and day. That's a larger number of men than the entire police force of many towns in America. The mayor needs this protection, but what does each citizen of New York City need? I believe that more electric shock devices, which do not kill but stop the criminal from acting, and registered guns should be at the disposal of law-abiding citizens in a country in which the homicide rate has doubled in recent years.

No one has written more persuasively and more intelligently on the subject of guns than Chip Elliott. Responding to the lament of Adam Smith in the April, 1981 issue of *Esquire* that fifty million handguns will be used by large numbers of people to defend themselves, Chip Elliott describes how he took up arms in defense of his life and property. He is a novelist, and his wife is a psychiatrist. They left Venice, California, after being robbed of a total of eleven thousand dollars' worth of property on a number of occasions. Chip Elliott was mugged by five men at knife point, and what saved his life was the gun he had purchased and always wore in the streets of Los Angeles after his neighbors had been raped and killed. He shot one of the muggers in the leg, and as he dropped to the ground astonished, the rest of the gang fled. Then Elliott and his wife moved to Culver City, where people were mugged and raped in an elegant condominium, and shot in parking lots and on tennis courts. He and his wife were robbed again and did not even bother to report the robbery to the police. They now live in the Midwest, presumably in a somewhat safer place. But his view is my view. I couldn't express it better. Listen to what he says: The world changed sometime between 1975 and 1980, and because he and his wife adapted, they managed to stay alive. They stayed alive because their adaptation involved owning and always keeping in full sight two guns. Adam Smith thinks owning guns, and being prepared to use them against criminals, is wrong. But Chip Elliott does not think so. He says:

> So you can fuss and bitch, Adam Smith, all you like and you can rail at the hillbillies in the NRA, but the next time someone breaks into your house or your apartment, the next time someone busts the window of your car and rips off your FM radio and your thirty-five millimeter camera, the next time some woman you know gets raped and busted up and you have to visit her in the hospital . . . the next time you are totally freaked out after coming up against a gang halfway between the restaurant and the car, sit yourself down and do some serious considering about who has the right to do what to whom. Often this stuff has to touch people personally before they think about self-protection, and often by then a tragedy of far more epic proportions. . . has occurred. I hope that doesn't happen to you. You have a right to carry on merrily with what you're doing. (37)

As I read Chip Elliott's description of how he had been victimized, I remembered that every member of my family had been mugged. Most recently my sister's car was stolen; previously another car she owned had been stolen in broad daylight in Flatbush. My sister returned home one day to find that a huge hole had been drilled in her door and that her new television set was gone. Yet she does not own a gun—this despite the fact that she lives on a Brooklyn street where criminals rob cars and steal television sets and despite the fact that she had a nephew who was murdered. But she is foolish, like thousands of elderly people in New York who have been victimized, because she does not protect herself. It is not that she is afraid to have a gun. It just never occurs to her that she might someday need a weapon to respond to an assault.

But Chip Elliott gives us the reason why she should carry a gun. He says that if

> we live in a society in which a large constituency thinks it can do whatever it damn pleases—no sense of morality asked for or required—then those of us who have the middle-class work ethic . . . will be seen as potential victims by the flocks of hustlers and lurkers who are out there. It is sometimes tough to get a job. It is also, right now, easier to rob people than it is to work for money. It's easier because it can be gotten away with. These people believe no one will stop them. They're right. No one will. Not the police, not the courts, not the penal system. No one but the growing number of us who have decided we will not be victimized again, ever. (37)

In a very moving passage Elliott describes the death of Dr. Michael Halberstam, who, in the last seconds of his life after he was shot by a burglar, realized that he didn't like being killed and got in his car and ran down the robber. Elliott reminds us that if Halberstam had made this discovery earlier—that he didn't like being killed—he would have bought a gun and he would be alive now.

Elliott doesn't object to gun laws; he would like to have "impossibly tight gun-registration laws." But, he says,

> I secretly scoff. Anyone who's honest can get through any registration process we can come up with. Anyone who's not honest won't bother. The way guns get into the criminal underworld is that they are *stolen*. That makes registration a useless exercise. (36)

I don't think it is a useless exercise. When you mandate a penalty of five years in prison for illegal gun possession, you might deter some criminals from using a gun.

However, they can easily substitute the hammer or the knife. Three juveniles, aged seventeen, eighteen, and nineteen, bashed in the skull of Leon Lifschutz, sixty-seven, during a robbery in Queens. Lifschutz had survived Auschwitz; he had escaped the gas chambers to die in a store in Queens. Where there's a will to kill, even a child can find a way with countless weapons. After viewing a display of knives stained with the blood of victims, the City Council of New York unanimously approved a bill which would forbid the carrying of a knife with a blade four inches long or longer. Presumably a knife with a three-inch blade can't harm anyone.

But weapons alone do not cause murder. As Elliott notes,

> What causes it is that people think they can have the American dream by sticking someone up for it. They think that there ought to be a huge equal society out there. Equal shares for everybody. Forced equal shares if necessary . . . . And any concerted attempt to stop them is viewed as an infringement on civil and constitutional rights. That is, it is a "right" to mug, rape, burglarize, murder, and commit arson for the insurance money. So there you are: a nation of pirates. (36)

Now, if we live in a nation of pirates, it is sheer lunacy to pretend that we live in Disneyland.

On February 13, 1984, three and a half years after my son was murdered, a seventy-three-year-old man was robbed on a New York subway. He pulled out a licensed .38 revolver and shot the robber in the stomach. If all the muggers knew that all the passengers on the subway carried guns, would the miserable, bullying thieves continue to rob? Several years before Eric was murdered, a pickpocket on a train stole fourteen dollars from him. If anyone at that time had suggested to me that Eric should carry a gun to protect himself, I would have recoiled in horror. If someone had suggested to Roberta Kaplan that she should own a licensed gun, she would, no doubt, have recoiled in horror.

Roberta Kaplan, thirty-two, owned a boutique in Greenwich Village and offered her customers champagne and cookies. When someone tried to rob her store, she began to sleep there at night to protect her property. But she was stabbed to death in broad daylight by a thief. Roberta should have armed herself, for she was clearly in the midst of an unending war. Without this awareness she died as my son died, because of her trust and innocence.

Was it possible that the man who killed Roberta Kaplan was a drug addict? Did he need money to sustain his drug addiction? The use of drugs has led to murder. Because of their insatiable need for money to buy drugs, addicts are often driven to commit robberies and murders. If this is so, we need to protect ourselves against them. We need to be ready for them, because there are not enough police in the whole country to protect us against their unexpected assaults.

When Bernhard Goetz used a gun and shot four teenagers on a subway in December, 1984, he was at first acclaimed as a hero in what was perceived to be an act of self-defense. He had acted out the fantasy of every New Yorker who had ever wanted to strike back at the punks who rob, assault, terrorize, and kill. Regardless of what decision the law ultimately makes about the Goetz case, his name will always stand as a symbol of fear of crime in New York City. An ever increasing number of New Yorkers have joined the Manhattan West Side Rifle and Pistol Range. In 1982, 9,268 applications were filed for handgun licenses in New York City, twice the number filed in 1979. How many handguns will exist in the city in the year 2000?

It is now April 3, 1983, the day my son would have been twenty-five years old. But there's no birthday cake, and the only song is the song of the victim.

10

The Rotten Apple

*I wouldn't live in New York City if they gave me the whole
    dang town.
Talk about a bummer, it's the biggest one around.*
    Buck Owens, Song, "I Wouldn't Live in New York City."

"I love New York City," the advertisements tell us. But it is
not worthy of anybody's love, despite the frantic efforts of its
officials to convince us that it is a wonderful place. Most of
the people who live in this city secretly wonder why they con-
tinue to live there, while those outside the city think of it as an
ugly, dirty, expensive, dangerous place which only fools ven-
ture to visit at their own risk.

Ah yes, New York is the cultural center of the world; it has
music, theater, and museums. But the frightening fact is that
those who attend these cultural events are always in danger.
For example, those who are brave enough to visit the theater
district, and foolish enough to pay fifty dollars to see a fifth-
rate musical, might have bricks thrown at them from the
rooftops, or they might be stabbed to death by a mugger as
they leave the theater.

Oh yes, rich people live in New York City. They pay as
much as $50,000 a year to rent an apartment, or $3 million to
buy a three-room apartment. And the middle class lives in
three rooms that rent for $1,500 a month with windowless
bathrooms and kitchens, and walls so thin that they can hear

their neighbors defecating or fornicating. In 1981, Diane Garrison visited model new apartments and wrote: "You wouldn't believe some of the rental studio apartments for $800 [a month] and two bedroom layouts for $2,675 and how bad some of them are. The rooms are getting tinier and tinier. Soon they'll have to shrink the people to get them in" (T, Oct. 15, 1981, C1). In 1984 Deidre Carmody described in *The Times* (July 19, B1:B6) the horrendous housing conditions in the city. Lofts rent for $1,000 a month without heat, with no kitchen and no pipes for a kitchen; studio apartments being sublet require key money in amounts ranging from $2,000 to $50,000; some landlords charge a $10,000 fixture fee; and tenants pay as much as $5,600 to brokers and escrow accounts before they pay their first month's rent.

New Yorkers also have to contend with the ever present rodent. Even the restaurant that the mayor frequents was cited for having rats in the basement. The most fashionable neighborhoods are not immune to the infestation of cockroaches and mice. The largest union of *The Wall Street Journal* asked in its bargaining proposal that a cat be supplied for the editorial room and other rodent infected areas in the building where the paper is produced. I know people who live in expensive buildings who periodically fight the battle against the mice who enter their apartments in endlessly devious ways. A New Yorker, interviewed on Channel 4 on August 17, 1984, suggested that "the mascot of New York should be a roach. The city is its natural habitat."

New York is the cultural center of the world and one of the crime centers of the world, an elegant and foul open city. Its inhabitants live in fear of being mugged, raped, or murdered. This anomalous city has *The New York Times,* magnificent museums, and very rich people who live in luxury. But New York also has many criminals. In four articles in June, 1983, *The Times* described how the Criminal Court of New York City is in chaos and is held in open contempt by those who deal with it. A report issued by the Criminal Court Committee of the City Bar Association on June 23, 1983, denounced the Criminal Court of New York as being "legally dead." The report further noted that the court system is in its "death throes," since it tries only less than one percent of its cases.

Joseph B. Williams, the Administrative Judge of the Criminal Court, said that the "quality of justice is almost nil" in his court (June 26, A1). Judge Jay Gould in 1984 called the Manhattan Criminal Court a "madhouse" (CS, Sept. 28, 9).

Without doubt drugs are responsible for a good deal of the crime in the city. Addicts can purchase heroin, cocaine, and other drugs on the infamous Alphabet Street, on Wall Street, Union Square, Times Square, Eighth Avenue, Fordham Road in the Bronx, and almost anywhere in Harlem. The city has many desperate, poor people; one of every fourth person lives below the officially designated poverty line. Emanuel Tobier, an economist, was widely quoted when he predicted that by 1990 one of every three New Yorkers would be living in poverty. Thousands of homeless, both sane and insane, roam the streets, sometimes sleeping in shelters, and sometimes dying in the streets. The public school system is, in Hunter College President Shalala's words, "a rotten barrel" with a 60 percent drop-out rate for Hispanics and blacks, who constitute two-thirds of the public school population. Youth unemployment is more than 50 percent and rises to 60 percent in some districts. Untold numbers of young people have just given up looking for jobs. It is easy to understand why crime flourishes in a city that is paradise for the rich and hell for the poor. But the poor do not necessarily commit murder.

Poverty cannot be the sole causal explanation for the vicious attacks on the clergy. Poverty doesn't explain why in Harlem a nun should be mugged and raped or why a priest should be beaten and robbed. New York is inhabited by depraved beings who attack the good and the innocent and transform neighborhoods into decaying horrors. The South Bronx, which is known as Fort Apache country, has been described by Sydney H. Schanberg as a

household synonym for abandonment, hellish crime, devastation, terminal urban disease, and in the visual imagery of some of its quarters, saturation bombing. For some time, however, the synonyms have been spreading north and west through the rest of the Bronx—a governmental unit whose population, 1.17 million, is larger than those of Dallas, Milwaukee or Boston. (T, Oct. 6, 1981, A31)

But one does not have to look at the obvious deformities; crime is everywhere: in the best and the worst neighborhoods. New York is a city that deploys more than 420 security guards in its junior high and intermediate schools because the criminals prey on these young children and their teachers just as readily as they do on high school children and their faculty. Many teachers are captives in their classrooms. They merely sit and watch in fear as their hoodlum students play cards. They are afraid because their colleagues have been beaten and killed by students. Bus drivers are killed because of disputes over a transfer; cab drivers are mugged and murdered; the dirty, foul-smelling subways have a rising crime rate. Young punks seem especially fond of strangling and raping the defenseless elderly. Men and women are found murdered in the most expensive apartments.

Even street-wise reporters don't always know the extent of the crime wave, how pervasive it is. Thus at the time that the city was preparing to try two Dominicans from Washington Heights for the robbery and murder of my son, Bill Reel wrote a column in the *Daily News* (Aug. 27, 1981, 62) extolling the Dominican community in Washington Heights. He quoted Father Pat Hennessy, who said that "despite poverty and crime and drugs, our neighborhood is a good neighborhood." Reel was ecstatic about this great neighborhood and the spiritual, religious life of these wonderful Dominicans. Father Hennessy told him: "It's as though every Dominican man studied in a seminary and every woman spent time in a convent." No, Father Hennessy, not every man, for Jose Deltejo and Furman Urena came from your neighborhood. Bill Reel concluded his article by noting that elderly people have never been mugged in this area. If by that he meant only the young are murdered in Washington Heights, he was wrong. Detective Gonzalez told me, when I sat in the notorious Thirty-fourth Precinct in 1980 and asked how such terrible youths could exist in the neighborhood: "There's a hard core of horror out there."

And he was right. Three years later the Washington Heights district, which stretches from 155th Street to the borders of the Bronx, was labeled Dodge City North. In this neighborhood Hispanics fight for control of the heroin and cocaine traffic. The Thirty-fourth Precinct reported 42 homicides in 1982 and 35 homicides in the first three months of 1983. A detective in this precinct said: "Never before has a precinct reported 100 homicides in a year in this city. The way we're going, it's very possible. I'm telling you, it's like a Wild West city up here with all the guns flashing around" (DN, Apr. 21, 1983, 1). The Hispanics who live in Dodge City North include Cubans, Columbians, Mexicans, Ecuadorians, Puerto Ricans, and Dominicans. Among them are many good people who cannot arrest the blight which infects their area.

But a columnist can say different things at different times. Bill Reel later wrote: "The raping of a nun and the ritualistic carving of 27 crosses on her body with a knife is the ultimate sacrilege. Only the Devil—give him his due, use a capital D— could do this. It's a cliché that nothing is sacred in New York, and it's also true. New York is so bad that priests hate to walk around wearing their collars" (DN, Oct. 15, 1981, 16). That is, all priests presumably—except for Father Hennessy, or did Bill Reel forget about Father Hennessy's statement that his part of New York was wonderful and safe? For in still another article on the nun's rape and mutilation, he wrote indignantly about how pervasive crime was in *all* parts of the city: "This crime wave is crushing us. The criminals won't let us live. The constant threat of violence frazzles our nerves and furrows our brows. Every day is a drag. Every night is full of dread . . . . We have lost our liberty. Totalitarianism couldn't be any worse than this. What's the difference if you are stalked in the night by secret police or by street savages. The terror is the same in either case" (DN, Oct. 20, 1981, C16).

Notice the reaction to the rape and robbery of a nun in a city where more than ten rapes occur every day. Mayor Koch calls it "one of the most depraved crimes. . . . I want to see the guy, not figuratively, hung. It makes you wonder how can there be such an animal or animals, walking the streets. [It is a] hideous and horrendous crime" (P. Oct. 16, 1981, 3). Koch offered a $10,000 reward for information leading to the arrest of the rapist of the nun. Supposedly the Mafia had a $25,000 contract out to kill the rapist. Judge Francis X. Egitto said that a homicide in a case like this would have been more charitable. Judge Michael Corriero ordered that the court seal the testimony of the two rapists of the nun, and barred the public and press from the court because of the horrifying facts involved (P. Oct. 29, 1981, 10).

Yet no one offered a $10,000 reward for the apprehension of the killer of the young high school student Allen Spiegel on Forty-first Street and Madison Avenue. Spiegel wasn't even robbed; he was killed for no reason by one of the monsters who roam the streets. Why didn't Mayor Koch offer a $10,000 reward for the apprehension of the killer of Spiegel? Is the crime against this young boy less horrendous, less depraved, than the crime against the nun?

Of course, Koch is first and foremost a politician. There wasn't much propaganda value for him in the death of my son. Thus when Dr. McLeod in Cortland wrote indignantly to Mayor Koch, deploring the senseless, cruel murder of my son, Koch did not answer Dr. McLeod directly, but had one of his aides reply in a form letter. Angered, I wrote to the mayor, rebuking him for not having the time to take an interest in the murder of a young boy in his city and reminding him that he was responsible for pulling out the anti-crime subway police just a few days before my son was killed. Then I received a reply from Koch (Jan. 7, 1981), who wrote to assure me of his deep concern for those murdered in his city. But he did not once refer to the fact that he had, for budgetary reasons, pulled the police out of the New York subway stations. Koch is not responsible for the crime in New York, despite what Jimmy Breslin would have us believe. It is simply that Koch is impotent to do anything about the crime rate in an "open city."

It may be impossible to eliminate crime in New York City, just as it may be impossible to repair its deteriorating infrastructure. The entire physical plant of the city is in desperate need of repair, and it would take billions of dollars to repair New York's bridges, roads, sewers, water mains, highways, and transit system. Vast amounts of money are required to stem the tide of deterioration. The Subway Committee for the Brooklyn Downtown Commercial Crescent solicited $50,000 from private funds to help renovate the oldest IRT subway station at Brooklyn's Borough Hall—these funds merely helped renovate *one* station. But legislative analysts tell us that the state and city need to spend at least $8–10 billion annually to maintain their physical facilities, twice as much as they spend now. The mass transit system alone will need

$14 billion in the next ten years to function adequately. E. B. White once observed that it is a miracle that New York City works at all. Perhaps we face the possibility that the time for miracles has passed, and the city will not work in the future.

The gap between affluence and poverty widens every day to produce the glaring inequities that have transformed New York into a city of extremes—of those who have and those who do not have. A restaurant like the Palace charged as much as $100 to $150 per person for a meal, and Mimi Sheraton tells us that the meal was *bad*. Millionaires donate millions of dollars to improve the Botanical Gardens and the Metropolitan Museum of Art. Athletes are paid millions of dollars for hitting a ball. Is a painting, a flower, a meal, a baseball more important than a human life? Surely a visitor from outer space would find our values and priorities deranged and incomprehensible. For it is true that if those who have the money, and therefore the power, were willing to pool their resources to concentrate on solving what must be the first priority in a civilized society—safety—they might conceivably help to attain the public's safety. Art, flowers, baseball, theaters, movies, and restaurants have no value if people can not safely enjoy them. But the affluent like to be photographed in the newspapers donating money to museums and libraries. They're not interested in crime, especially if they have not been personally troubled by it.

And as a result, the murder rate in New York City in 1980 was up to nearly six a day, more than 1,800 a year. In Tokyo, with a 65 percent larger population, there are 180 murders a year! Small wonder that Jimmy Breslin has suggested that we paint a permanent circle around every murdered body in the streets of New York so that Koch and everyone else will never forget.

Nicholas Pileggi tells us that the brutal truth about crime in New York is that the police, the courts, and the prison system have given up. New York is now an open city for criminals. He quotes Mario Cuomo: "The politicians don't know that crime is New York's biggest single issue. It could turn out to be New York's version of Proposition 13, the kind of issue that turns a whole state around" (26). The most reliably reported crime is murder. There were 390 murders in 1960,

1,117 in 1970, and 1,814 in 1980. This increase occurred despite the fact that one million people left the city in those twenty years. New York has more violent street crime than any other city in the nation. Police make arrests in only about 15 percent of burglary and robbery cases, and they have given up returning personal property after a burglary.

Listed below in the following chart is the Police Department's record of Major Crimes Reported in New York City, 1976-80. According to *The Times,* 1980 was the worst year of crime in New York City history. I am interested in that year because that was the year my son was murdered. Yet the number of cases cleared, though not necessarily resulting in convictions, was 31.5 percent for rape, 13.8 percent for robbery, and 6.5 percent for burglary.

Major Crimes Reported in New York City, 1976-80

Year	Murder	Rape	Robbery	Assault	Burglary	Theft	Auto Theft
1976	1,622	3,400	86,183	42,948	195,243	232,069	96,682
1977	1,557	3,899	74,404	42,056	178,888	214,838	94,420
1978	1,604	3,882	74,029	43,271	164,447	200,110	83,112
1979	1,733	3,875	82,572	44,203	178,162	220,817	89,748
1980	1,814	3,711	100,550	43,476	210,703	249,421	100,478

Source: New York City Police Department

The total number of reported crimes in 1980 was 1,348,000. But the actual number of crimes is not available, because many victims don't report them because of fear or a sense of futility. Moreover, the police and the city's prosecutors use a screening process; as a result of this process many who are arrested either are not indicted or are charged with lesser crimes and misdemeanors. Plea bargaining between the prosecutors and the lawyers is routine. It takes an average of six months and seventeen court appearances to dispose of a felony arrest.

Parole and probation are two practices which often lead critics of the criminal justice system to deride it as a "sick joke." Data from the Department of Correctional Services reveals that 15 percent of parolees are returned to prison after five years as a result of felony convictions, and an additional 20 percent have their parole revoked because of violations of parole, including new crimes. According to figures released by the State Division of Parole in November, 1980, 18,144 prisoners convicted of kidnapping, arson, or armed robbery were paroled in early release programs; of these, 14,000 live in New York City. In 1983, 622,877 major crimes were reported in New York City; 13,500 offenders were convicted and imprisoned. In 1984, 538,878 felonies were reported; less than 2,300 convictions were obtained! In 1985, four men were wrongly accused of participating in the savage East New York Massacre in Brooklyn. In this massacre in 1984, among the ten who were murdered were women and young children. The accused criminals had a total of twenty-nine previous arrests, and yet each one had spent an average of one and a half years in jail as a result of receiving dismissals, conditional discharges, probation, and parole. The Jack Abbott case is a classic example of what happens when you parole a murderer.

In 1981, Nicholas Pileggi called New York an "Open City." In February and April, 1985, the New York State Probation Officers Association made the same charge. Wallace Cheatham, the President of the Association, writes:

> Citizens are unprotected and victimized every day by criminals convicted of murder, rape, robbery, assault and other serious crimes. These convicted offenders sentenced to probation roam the streets unsupervised by the probation department. (2)

The number of current caseloads is 300 percent above State Division of Probation standards. As a result offenders on probation receive little or no supervision, and this accounts for a recidivism rate of more than 50 percent. The Probation Officers of New York City have issued a disclaimer of responsibility: "Because of the department's practice of assigning excessive and unmanageable caseloads we can no longer accept responsibility for any harm which may occur to any person or persons in the community as a result of a criminal act or acts by any individual on probation" (Cheatham, 2).

To the criminals freely moving about in the city add the thousands of derelicts and homeless people and the mentally ill who live on the streets. Is it not inevitable then that New Yorkers would have to confront what Russell Baker aptly describes as the "Menace of the Random"? This is the menace of the slasher, the machete attacker, the crazed motorist, and the cleaver killer. For as Baker notes, "despite the most cunning defenses against the city's menaces, we are suddenly confronted with the possibility of violence at the dinner table. The rage and horror we feel, and which makes the event worth front-page attention, is probably more than rage and horror. Very likely, it is also a form of compassion for ourselves, as we witness the machetes or read about them in the papers, and realize that we have been deceiving ourselves to make city life more bearable, and that we are all at the mercy of happenstance in a society becoming unhinged" (T, July 25, 1981, 23). The point is that we can no longer say that the octogenarian widow in City Island should have known better and kept her door locked and would therefore not have been murdered. It is no longer possible to say that the victim should have known better, for we are *all* subject to violence anywhere at any time.

New York police know that it is a futile endeavor attempting to arrest all the people responsible for aggressive panhandling, smoking in the subway, drunkenness, brawling, urinating on sidewalks and subways, muggings, burglaries, narcotics deals, purse snatchings, car thefts, and larcenies. In 1981, the transit police did issue 100,000 summonses in subways, but most violators never appeared in court. The police were unable to apprehend those who were responsible for 335,775 burglaries in the twenty-one-month period ending September, 1980. More than $600,000 worth of stolen property lies in police warehouses. Only a minimal number of burglaries are investigated. "Today," says Pileggi, "street-savvy crooks and hoolums know they face no prison sentences for burglary, car theft, dope dealing, and comparable illegal and disruptive acts" (22). Pileggi quotes former Police Commissioner Robert McGuire:

There is so much crime in the city today that I know it's having a discernible impact on the quality of life. People are finding they must curtail their normal behavior. They question whether they should go out, where they should park their cars. . . . Mothers give their children stickup money. The old are prisoners in their own homes. But my greatest frustration is the violent street crimes we are finding. I'm disturbed by the random and gratuitous killings and maimings. Robberies have never been higher. . . . There is the sense of violence on the streets—the sense that you stepped on my foot so I'll blow your brains out. (22)

The police department suffered a loss of 9,500 officers in six years. In June, 1984, it had 24,044 policemen, but if the mayor were to add 5,000 cops to the force, he would not be able to eradicate crime, because the criminal knows that if he is arrested, he will have a court appointed lawyer who will plea bargain him to freedom. In May, 1978, 87 percent of the defendants in criminal court cases who plea bargained walked out of court as free men even though they had committed serious crimes and had long criminal records. Plea bargaining is still rampant today and results in either the release of a guilty man or a ridiculously short prison sentence for his misdeeds. Of those in New York State prisons, 64.8 percent have killed or raped or seriously injured their victims. Bronx District Attorney Mario Merola, commenting on this evil and violent population, said: "Given that kind of prison population, do you know that the average individual sentenced to one of these joints serves something like 23 months? Twenty-three months for this kind of convicted felon? Doesn't that tell you something about the system?" (Pileggi, 26).

Two decades of misguided liberalism have produced an ability to see *only* both sides of an issue. In this view, there are no bad or evil people; just those who need to be rehabilitated, who need good conditions in prisons so that they will become literate and moral. They will not kill again, and we are cruel if we do not forgive. But Professor James Q. Wilson, who has written one of the best books on crime and punishment, concludes that the "rehabilitative model" is a historical failure, based on a hypocritical philosophy, and it is inefficacious.

Exposure to TV and film violence has also helped to desensitize us to the horrors of criminality in our society. Over and over again, young children observe on the screen handsome, virile men and beautiful women who commit the most despicable acts, very often with impunity. For example, violence is a subject of fun on the "Barney Miller" TV show. At this precinct inhabited by charming, witty cops, even the most depraved types of criminals are good for a laugh, and the world of pimps, prostitutes, and murderers is depicted sympathetically and with great affection. Manson could walk into the Miller show and get a cup of coffee and a laugh. And if he did shoot Barney Miller, Barney wouldn't die.

According to a psychologist on a documentary on juvenile crime in Los Angeles, aired on CBS television on September 3, 1981, called "Murder Teenage Style," by the time an average boy is sixteen he has watched 18 million violent murders on television! Small wonder then that the teenage hoodlum is indifferent to life. One young boy says on camera, "What's the use of going out fighting. . . getting all dirty sweaty, tearing up your clothes. . . if you can just pull the trigger. Ain't got to worry about the fellow no more. Bang, bang! I got this fool. . . You kinda happy. . . I got him."

One of these teenagers professes to be indifferent to the possibility that he himself will be killed by the same kind of gang members whom he has killed: "It only happens once. You only go down once." I think this teenager does not believe *he* will ever go down, and he doesn't think anything serious will happen to him if he does shoot someone else. He'll just spend some time in a clean juvenile dorm where he'll be able to watch more TV, and if he's only fourteen he can rap with the older boys and have a good time listening to their horror stories. The record shows that in New York City juvenile murderers are not treated as the juvenile offender law intended them to be treated.

Half of the violent crimes in the city are committed by teenagers. The juvenile offenders law mandates that thirteen to fifteen-year-old killers should be prosecuted as adults. But in a twenty-eight-month period, from 1979 to 1981, of 3,208 juveniles arrested, only 503 were dealt with in adult courts. Of these only 215 received a jail sentence, and of these only 111 received the appropriate sentence provided by the law. The 1,223 acts of violence perpetrated by teenagers were dealt with through the Family Court (no public scrutiny is possible in these negotiations) and through plea bargaining, which resulted in minor sentences, probation, family custody, and dismissal.

On September 10, 1981, the *New York Post* headed an article with this sensational headline: "Judge Frees 100 Vicious Juvenile Time Bombs." These 100 time bombs were 100 accused juvenile killers, rapists, and muggers who were freed because of a legal technicality. Judge Robert Carter, a Manhattan federal judge, on April 17 had declared unconstitutional a state preventive detention law that allowed jailing of youths "who were both accused of violent crimes and decreed by a judge to be likely to commit violent crime" (P, 12). Philip Caruso, head of the Policeman's Benevolent Association, bitterly condemned Carter's decision, which since June 1 had made it difficult to jail dozens of accused violent suspects. The Family Court has freed what Caruso calls "monsters who have committed very serious crimes of violence. . . . This judge is actually favoring the rights and privileges of the criminal mind and not looking out for the interests of your average innocent, working, productive citizen." Paul Strausburg, city commissioner of juvenile justice, was quoted as saying that he specifically was required to "release kids even if judges label them dangerous to society. There are time bombs walking around out there. . . . We just don't know what their fuses are."

The Legal Aid Society, which initiated the effort to free thirty of these accused juvenile criminals that resulted in Carter's ruling, hailed it as a great success. Carol Sherman, Legal Aid Society spokesman, said: "It is our position that it is not more likely that a person a judge labels violent will commit a violent crime than your run-of-the-mill person on the street" (P, 12).

Perhaps the *Post* misquoted Carol Sherman. If not, she is equating the criminal with the decent moral human being and makes a mockery of the whole concept of criminal justice. If everyone is equally capable of being violent, why incarcerate a person who has stabbed someone? After all, Carol Sherman is equally capable of stabbing someone at any moment! When she was asked if she would feel concerned that one of the suspects might kill while free, she answered, "No, because there is no way of knowing that a person is going to be violent." *No way of knowing!* Surely a person who has committed a violent crime is more likely to commit another violent act than someone with no history of violence.

Of course, since the records of juvenile criminal offenders are secret, we can not know whether they have killed or raped or mugged while on parole. Judge Carter only had to be concerned with the "legal correctness" of his decision. Vincent Wellman, Carter's law clerk, told the *Post* that Carter was not to be blamed if a juvenile killed after being released: "It is not up to the judge to make this global assessment about the danger to society." But the judge did make a global assessment when he claimed that the preventive detention section "was offensive to a concept of ordered liberty in a free society." This concept is Judge Carter's view; he simply chose to make the legally correct decision in favor of the criminal.

On the other hand, Family Court Judge Richard Huttner of Brooklyn circumvented Judge Carter's decision by ordering two juveniles—one with five previous arrests and the other with fourteen—detained in a state youth detention center. Carter's order applied only to New York City juveniles. The Legal Aid Society filed suit to have the two youths freed, but Supreme Court Justice William Booth ruled in Huttner's favor. Huttner said: "I have to protect society as well as the rights of the individual. That was the State Legislature's intention when it made this law. . . ." (P, Sept. 12, 1981, 2).

Lest we have any misconceptions about the nature of the juvenile mugger, we have only to read about him in the New York newspapers. Claude Brown has described the terrifying, deadly, cynical street teenager in Harlem. This young mugger believes that "murder is the style." It is "fashionable" to kill a robbery victim (TSM, Sept. 16, 1984, 44,54). What should we do about this subculture of cretins who spend their days robbing and killing and who know no other way of life? Judges send them to overcrowded jails, but eventually the criminal system will not be able to control the recidivism rate, which is already very high. About 648 "kiddie" criminals escaped from an unguarded Division for Youth facility in one year. They have robbed and killed new victims, and Frank A. Hall, director of the Division for Youth, said that he had no records of how many of the 648 escapees are still at large (P. Sept. 16, 1981, 9). His Division spokesman, Paul Elija, says it was "almost" impossible to know how many juveniles escaped in 1978, 1979, and 1980. "We don't have very good data capability.... There's stuff in boxes and everything." One of the escapees was charged with slashing the throats of two retarded brothers while their sister watched them bleed to death.

Sydney H. Schanberg interviewed former Police Commissioner McGuire about the "awesome" crime in New York City and about the frightening fact that more and more of it is being committed by children. McGuire said:

> There's no question that so much of the crime now has to do with kids. Not just quality of life crime like senseless vandalism, ripping up park benches, but serious violent crime. It has become a fact in this city that older people are afraid of kids. Sometimes I ask myself, "Are we being hysterical? Wasn't there crime before ...?" No. This isn't the same. The statistics are three, four, five times what they were 20 years ago. And the pathology is much worse. The kids who prey on people have a look in their eyes that says "your life isn't worth anything to me." Whether they injure you is irrelevant to them. Random. Gratuitous. Like pulling wings off butterflies, only the butterflies are people. (T. Oct. 3, 1981, 27)

These fourteen- or fifteen-year-old "kids" have no sense of the value of human life. Most of the violent crime is committed by blacks and Hispanics, but, as McGuire points out, "something is happening to kids across the board. You may not be afraid of the white street kids in Yorkville but they can take your wings off as quickly as anyone." McGuire doesn't believe the police alone can handle the crime problem. "Will we have to bring in the National Guard for emergency patrols? How far behind, then, would the Army be and the Joint Chiefs of Staff?" Unless we have some kind of solution, McGuire believes, "What's ahead is going to be worse than we have now."

A fourteen-year-old defendant in Paterson, New Jersey, crushed a girlfriend's skull with a rock and buried her. The probation department recommended a jail sentence. Judge Carmen Ferrante ignored this recommendation and placed the boy in the care of his parents under probation for three years. This presumably would rehabilitate the boy better than jail. What exactly did Ferrante think about murder? Is it less horrible when committed by a juvenile? And how did the victim's parents feel; did they praise Ferrante for his compassion for the young murderer? What of the fourteen-year-old gang leader who has been arrested ten times for serious crimes, reprimanded, and released? Clearly something is wrong with the juvenile justice system when the American Bar Association and the Institute for Judicial Administration have studied the problem for ten years and produced twenty-three volumes recommending new standards for juvenile justice. But whether the recommendations will ever take effect is doubtful. Too many experts—judges, social workers, psychologists, lawyers, correction officials, police, educators—all have their own pet theories about how to handle juveniles, and to expect them to agree is a Utopian ideal. The incompetent ministration of the Family Court is notorious; somehow reports get written and ignored.

And the judges. How do they function at 100 Centre Street? Arthur Herzog, in an article entitled "My Robe is a Symbol of Mourning," observes: "Criminal Court Judge Murray Mogel's chamber is a place with rats and cockroaches. He judges 120 cases a day, one every four minutes if he can." Mogel describes his court as "the biggest mess in the world. There's no way to make it work" (26). Three hundred of 80,000 cases go to a jury; the rest of the misdemeanor cases are resolved by plea bargaining. Most of these were originally felony charges reduced to misdemeanors despite the strong cases against the defendants, typically male, black or tan, sixteen to twenty-five years old.

Supreme Court Felony Judge Harold Rothwax handles 57 cases a day. Mogel's court has a backlog of 1,100 cases. His judgment of the criminal justice system is that the purposes of the system, efficiency and fairness, are "in tension with each other. As we become more fair, we become less efficient. As we have sought perfect justice, we have come close to having no justice. We ought to be asking if what we gain in fairness is worth the loss of efficiency. The system works better than we have any right to expect but worse than can really be imagined. We are in a state of paralysis" (Herzog, 25).

The State Constitution provides the formula used to determine how many justices should be elected in a judicial district. New York has more than 200 judges in the Criminal Court.

However, the courts use the device of appointing lower court judges as acting Supreme Court judges who often serve for years. A new screening process will require that those aspiring to be acting justices will be interviewed and rated by a screening committee and placed on a rotating list. If one considers the simple statistic that in 1972 there were seventeen state prisons with 12,444 inmates, while there are now fifty state prisons with more than 35,000 inmates, and that approximately 70 percent of the prisoners come from New York City, it is easy to understand why the city needs more judges.

A criminal justice system with a four-billion-dollar budget is very complex, and special interest groups such as police, the district attorney's office, defense lawyers, probation, parole and correction officials, and unionized court officials are constantly in conflict with each other as they attempt to protect and enhance their interests. Therefore, it is not surprising that compromise becomes important and mediocrity prevails. Ideally judges should be intelligent, honest, fair. It is interesting that Supreme Court Justice Sandra O'Connor, when questioned by the Senate Judiciary Committee, made the observation that judges have a great deal to learn and that they, like other people entrusted with important decisions, can go to school to increase their knowledge of their legal duties. But anyone who reads the newspapers even in a cursory fashion reads about judges who are corrupt and prejudiced. They often fall far short of the ideal concept of a judge.

Judges are not sacrosanct, and they are not above criticism from any source. That is why the State Commission on Judicial Conduct was formed in 1975, to discover irregularities committed by the state's 3,500 full- and part-time judges. The commission has held 1,599 investigations and has found 191 judges guilty of some form of ethical misconduct. This commission was given permanent status in 1977 by a state constitutional amendment. (Judicial review groups have also been formed in the forty-nine other states, the District of Columbia, and Puerto Rico.) On the one hand, Supreme Court justices in Manhattan claim that the commission has limited the rights of judges. On the other hand, lawyers contend that the commission has been too lenient, stressing the abuses of 138 part-time judges in small upstate communities concerning such minor infractions as ticket-fixing while ignoring the serious abuse of big city judges with political influence. While federal court justices must file a yearly financial statement, state judges make no such disclosures, and it is impossible to discover conflicts of interests. For example, Charles P. Garvey, a Surrogate and Family Court judge in Essex County, who was found guilty of accepting $11,700 in loans from lawyers who worked in his court and of forging his wife's name on a state license so that he could secretly own a race horse, was merely censured by the commission and remained on the job. In the last six years, 28 judges have been removed, 163 others censured or suspended, but 81 percent of these were only part-time judges. One hundred and nine judges resigned after they learned they were being investigated. Charges of misconduct are usually brought by the public, not by lawyers or judges or prosecutors, and are treated confidentially, so that the public never knows why 260 cases were dismissed by the commission. It only knows that a judge has been found guilty when his case is referred to the Court of Appeals (T, Sept. 16, 1981, B6). If this procedure makes judges uneasy, if it makes them recognize that they are no longer free to do what they want to do, clearly the commission serves a valuable function.

But even Congress sometimes fails to control a judge who for political or ethnic or personal reasons makes an erratic, unwarranted judgment. I am not talking about freaks like the justice who did not open his mail for three and a half years. I am thinking of the judge whose outrageous decision led Senators Frank Padavan and John Marchi to attempt to oust him. However, Congress voted 26-24 in favor of allowing this judge to remain on the bench. The worst offenders are "the bleeding hearts" who have for too long been more influenced by the *rights* of the criminal than of the victim and who have slowly but surely meted out milder and milder punishments. New York does not have the death penalty, and the punishment of the most despicable murders has been incredibly lenient in terms of years of incarceration. Thus acting Judge Richard G. Denzer sentenced Craig S. Crimmins, who brutally murdered the beautiful violinist Helen Hagnes Mintiks in the Metropolitan Opera House, to twenty years instead of twenty-five years to life. Denzer gave the following reason for his decision:

I shall not follow the recommendation of maximum incarceration, which means 25 years to life. In my opinion, that sentence should be reserved for brutal homicides—of which this is surely one—committed by a person whose prior history demonstrates violence and brutality over a period of time. This is not the case here. The nature of the crime, however, does not justify the least severe sentence authorized by law, 15 years to life. (T, Sept. 3, 1981, A1:A4)

In Judge Denzer's "opinion," Crimmins should have committed other murders to deserve five more years of incarceration. I ask Judge Denzer, how many *more* murders should Crimmins have committed—one, two, ten, one hundred? What exactly "demonstrates" violence and brutality over a period of time to Judge Denzer? How cruel his judgment must have seemed to Helen Mintiks's husband, for clearly 1,000 years of incarceration could not make up for her loss, and here was Judge Denzer nit-picking about five years.

To demonstrate further that his sentence was merely the result of a subjective opinion, that nothing in the law prevented him from imposing the twenty-five-year sentence and that other judges impose this sentence for lesser crimes, I offer the following example: For permanently blinding a policeman in one eye, two black militants were given, by Presiding Judge Burton Roberts, twenty-five years to life for attempted murder (P, Oct. 2, 1981, 5). Note the amazing discrepancy here. Pellicano, the policeman, was blinded, but he is alive. Helen Mintiks was brutally murdered, and yet her killer received a lesser sentence. In Texas, Thomas Barefoot was executed for murder; in North Carolina, Velma Barfield was executed for murder; in Florida, Timothy Palmer was executed for murder. The disparity in sentencing in this country is so severe as to make a farce of the criminal justice system. You can kill in one state and manage to be freed on a technicality, you can kill in another state and serve only five or ten years of a twenty-five-year sentence, or you can kill in still another state and, after many years of legal haggling, get the electric chair.

Who is to blame for this peculiar state of affairs? Chief Justice Warren E. Burger, in a speech before the American Bar Association in Houston on February 9, 1981, stated that the fear of crime has created a reign of terror in American cities. They seem to have lost their ability to provide maximum kinds of security in the streets, in the schools, and in the homes. Accused criminals are offered more protection, more massive safeguards, than in any other country in all of history; they are given pretrial freedom for most crimes, defense lawyers paid for by public taxes, trials and retrials and endless appeals. Burger recommended that we reexamine the judicial process and its philosophy with regard to finality of judgment. He argued that the search for justice should not be distorted into an interminable search for technical errors that have no relationship to guilt or innocence. Although Burger had previously criticized lawyers for being professionally inadequate, he appealed to them to provide the necessary leadership for reform.

Speaking at a dinner on November 19, 1982, at the Sheraton Centre Hotel, Burger again warned that the American system of justice might literally break down before the end of the century. He was the seventh member of the Supreme Court to urge a reduction in the Court's case load and to comment on the incredible increase in litigation. In fifteen years Congress and the state legislatures have passed 100 new laws at such a rate that the judicial process cannot cope with them. Burger called for a bi-partisan committee to study federal and state court systems and recommend improvements. For example, they should study the English system, which provides that juries be chosen quickly and which mandates faster trials and judgments.

Speaking for the sixteenth time to the American Bar Association, in February, 1984, in Las Vegas, Burger told his audience:

> The entire legal profession—lawyers, judges, law teachers—has become so mesmerized with the stimulation of the courtroom contest that we tend to forget that we ought to be healers of conflicts. Doctors, in spite of astronomical medical costs, still retain a high degree of public confidence because they are perceived as healers. Should lawyers not be healers? Healers, not warriors? Healers, not procurers? Healers, not hired guns?

Burger predicted that the adversarial system, which has become inefficient and destructive, will disappear eventually just as the old trials by blood and battle were eliminated.

Meanwhile, even when decent, fair, intelligent judges attempt to mete out legitimate punishment, their efforts are subverted by the parole system. Even when justice has been achieved in a murder case, the criminal, through legal loopholes and play acting, can manage to obtain parole. In *Murder USA*, John Godwin documents with frightening detail the way in which parole boards manage to free murderers who will kill again. Two paroled killers murdered two police officers in New York City at the beginning of 1984. In 1983, 1,500 convicted murderers were released in New York State, and 18 percent of these paroled convicts committed murder again.

Not only parole boards but also lawyers strive to free prisoners, and the lawyer's reputation as a "hired gun" has not been diminished by the rules of the American Bar Association. Lawyers, like priests, are required to keep their clients' secrets even at the expense of innocent victims. Confidentiality can be ignored only when the lawyer's self-interest is involved, such as when obvious perjury is committed in his presence or if his own life is in danger. The late Robert Kutok's Commission had recommended that lawyers should be allowed to disobey the confidentiality rule to prevent or correct a client's abuses. The New York State Bar Association is considering a new ethics code for lawyers that specifies when lawyers can act to stop clients from committing crimes. They could ignore the confidentiality rule if the information would prevent death or substantial bodily harm or any other serious consequences.

Why wouldn't a lawyer consider it his legal and moral duty to defend a known criminal, when the American Bar Association encourages its members to value confidentiality above all else? The famous lawyer Edward Bennett Williams said that if he were Nixon's lawyer he would have helped him to "beat the Watergate rap." How? In the Sunday *Times Magazine* section, he describes the strategy he would have used. Like Alan Dershowitz, Williams maintains that everyone, including a known criminal, deserves "the best defense."

> The first thing I would have told him [Nixon] to burn the tapes. I would have advised him, before they were even called for, before they were ever subject to any subpoena, to make a public disposition of these things. (Apr. 17, 1983, 71)

Isn't it remarkable that a lawyer of Williams's stature would publicly make such a statement without being concerned about his reputation? He would have advised a president to burn the evidence and then to inform the country that he burned the papers because they contained state secrets! One conclusion can be drawn from this: so devoid of ethical considerations is a lawyer's relationship to his client that a lawyer is willing to lie, to compromise his own integrity, for the sake of winning a case. Nothing matters—certainly not the truth, not justice—except winning the case. There are thousands of unknown lawyers trying to make their reputations in the same way that the famous lawyers have attained success. They will fight for the rights of their clients to go free, no matter what they really know about their guilt.

A young man was accused of murder, but because of an insignificant technicality concerning the admission of hearsay evidence about his belt, he received a new trial, and his original sentence of fifteen years was reduced when he pleaded guilty. His lawyer won his case. The youth was released from prison in twc months! Three months later he killed a twenty-six-year-old doorman in New York in a dispute over a seventy-five-cent cover charge.

A man was arrested in 1983 for killing a bar owner, Herbert Cummings, in Hollis, Queens. This alleged murderer was picked up in a stolen cab with a gun and Cummings's severed head in a box. The defendant's lawyer asked that a hearing be held to determine whether this evidence was seized illegally. That the law can even contemplate holding such a hearing is another indication of the bizarre nature of criminal proceedings. Let us imagine the kind of questions the lawyer might ask the arresting officer in this case: "Did you know that the severed head was the property of my client? You had no right to deprive him of his property without due process of law. Did you ask the owner for permission to search his car? Did you ask my client if you could remove Cummings's head from the car?" Of course, the defendant did not obtain Mr. Cummings's permission to carry his head in a box!

A forty-three-year-old counselor, Carl Sherman, was murdered in 1970, and his killer received a sentence of zero to fifteen years in 1973. After serving 110 months, the killer was released on October 23, 1980, and on April 14, 1981, he stabbed Olga Rodriquez to death in the lobby of the New York building in which she and her husband conducted a business. She had a husband and two young children. She is buried in the Veterans Administration Cemetery on Long Island, near the grave of Carl Sherman. And always present was the murderer's lawyer, required by law to protect the guilty. For in our system of justice, it doesn't matter whether the lawyer believed that his client was guilty. What matters above all is the adversative contest and the thrill of winning.

Small wonder, then, that a Harris Poll in 1981, dealing with the subject of public confidence in American professions, puts lawyers last in the roll call of public esteem (T, May 4, 1981, A23). Small wonder, then, that a lawyer plaintively writes in a letter to *The Wall Street Journal:* "Was I crazy to spend more than $30,000 and three painful years to become a member of this hated profession?" (Nov. 27, 1984, 28). Speaking at the Fordham University School of Law in Manhattan in October, 1984, Associate Justice of the Supreme Court Sandra Day O'Connor stated that legal education has not focused attention on the ethical and social responsibilities of lawyers. This is attested to by the fact that from 1977 to 1981 there was a 72 percent increase in the number of lawyers who were publicly disciplined in state courts and a 66 percent increase in disciplined lawyers in federal courts. These occurred because of the abuse of moral judgments rather than legal skills.

I turn now to consider one of the special horrors of New York City life: crime in the subway. Talk to someone who has had to sit in the subway when the doors are closed, the train has stopped, the lights are out, the temperature reaches 110 degrees, and someone near you pulls off your gold chain and whispers obscenities. This subway rider will tell you that he has been traveling through a kind of hell. The underground mass transit system is a means of transportation that people use because they have no alternative, but they do so with resentment and fear. What they resent are the filthy, noisy, dangerous trains. Twenty federal inspectors attempted to discover why the subways had 5,000 fires in 1984. On December

18, 1984, they reported that the risk level on the tracks was unacceptable. In their view, the trains were so dangerous that many lines would have been shut down if they were under federal control. What transit riders fear are the criminals who stalk their victims with impunity in enclosed and dark areas of the stations.

As I noted, when I wrote to Mayor Koch about my son's death, he did not in his answer mention the subways. But the day after he was elected to a second term as mayor, he promised that he would play a greater role in seeking improved subway service. In the past he had claimed that he could do very little about the terrible subways, but now he said, "It does me no good or does you no good for me to say that I cannot run the subway system, that the state law gives that responsibility to somebody else. . . . I accept that responsibility" (T, Nov. 5, 1981, B15).

One of the early decisions he made about subway surveillance cost my son his life. Of course, Koch did not want anyone to die, but my son died because he and his officials decided that $350,000 a week in overtime pay for transit police for evening patrols was too much to spend. Sanford D. Garelik, Transit Police Chief, stationed officers in every train and station in 1979. But nine months later Koch ended his anti-crime program, and fewer policemen patrolled the subways in 1980. My son would be alive if at least one policeman had been on duty in the long, empty, cavernous station on 181st Street.

But then even transit cops get killed on subways. In the New York version of Dante's Inferno no one is immune: people have been stabbed with icepicks, swords, cleavers; they have been burned, thrown on the tracks, mutilated. In 1981, Carol Bellamy, the president of the City Council, stated that between the hours of 8:00 P.M. and 4:00 A.M., a subway rider stands a chance of one in forty of being the victim of violent crime, a chance that is three times as great as in 1975 (DN, June 15, 1981, 7). The Citizens Crime Commission reported that 500 criminal recidivists are responsible for 30 percent of subway crime. In a seventy-two-page report the Economic Development Council recommended that the clerical transit police of the Transit Authority be reduced to free officers for patrol on subways. The economic council listed fifty-four problems faced by the transit system, including 10,000 tort claims cases a year, with verdicts totaling one million dollars. It is virtually impossible to pick up a New York newspaper without reading about some new horror in the subways.

I shall never forget a day at the Concord in August, 1980, just a month before Eric was murdered. We were eating in the dining room when Elizabeth Holtzman, who was campaigning for the office of state senator, approached our table. Eric asked her what she was going to do about the terrible subways in New York. She told him that subways were a responsibility of the city, not the state.

Elizabeth Holtzman did not get to be a senator, but she is now a district attorney in Brooklyn fighting crime in her own way. But there's not very much either she or Mayor Koch can do about the criminal element in New York. Koch can't even protect his own cousin, who was robbed of $250,000 worth of furs. Holtzman has admitted, along with the other four district attorneys in New York who attended a Forum on Crime and Punishment at the Sheraton Hotel on March 24, 1983, that the court system in New York is on the verge of collapse. Holtzman, John Santucci of Queens, Mario Merola of the Bronx, Robert Morgenthau of Manhattan, and William Murphy of Staten Island appeared together for the first time, and all of them condemned the criminal justice system. It is a virtual joke to walk into criminal court today. It is overwhelmed by an immense case load. According to Robert Morgenthau, conditions are chaotic; there are 125,000 bench warrants and only 1 percent of the cases have been tried in Manhattan. The rest were dismissed or plea bargained. Merola said that without plea bargaining, which accounts for 90 percent of convictions, the whole judicial system would collapse. Santucci said that in Queens 25 judges each try 20 major cases a year, a total of 500 trials, while 4,000 indictments are made each year. Holtzman noted that there were 36,000 adjournments in Brooklyn last year alone. There are as many as 15 or 20 adjournments on a strong case in a year. The robbery charge is usually lessened to a misdemeanor. Witnesses are not given any special consideration, and the inefficient system usually favors defendants over victims. Small wonder, then, that little can really be done about the criminals in the subway system.

Even when a few hundred are arrested occasionally in an attempt to display that Koch and the Transit Authority are trying to do something, these criminals usually are soon back on the streets again, helped by their very experienced lawyers provided by our taxes. It's a vicious circle.

Sydney H. Schanberg has suggested that the subways be called "The Edward Irving Koch Memorial Subway System." More than a decade ago the Mayor's Task Force on Urban Design described the transit system as "the most squalid public environment in the United States. Since then its decline has been steep. Every straphanger has his own words for it, most of them unprintable" (T, Aug. 20, 1981, A31).

On October 15, 1981, the New York Public Interest Group and the Institute for Public Transportation issued a report on the subways. Based on six months of observation of 3,300 trains at midtown stations between March and August, 1981, the report stated that its observers rarely saw a transit cop. The appearance of uniformed policemen was judged to be one tenth of one percent of the time (P, Oct. 15, 1981, 9).

Mayor Koch said that the New York transit system is

basically one of the safest in the country and I suppose in the world. (DN, Jan. 16, 1982, C17)

At about the same time, Transit Police President James B. Meehan said that crime rose six times faster in subways than in the city. Other officials have observed that it is more dangerous in the subways than on the streets because the subways are a closed system that provides criminals with the opportunity to harm people with impunity.

Richard Ravitch, the former Chairman of the MTA, told the Association for a Better New York that he would not permit his two children to ride the subway at night (P, Jan. 21, 1982, 30). After Senator D'Amato's daughter was sexually assaulted on the subway, he said:

When I go on the subway I don't feel safe. . . . Unless we deal with the problem of crime the subway system is bound to wither away. . . . If I ran the subways I'd take the state police and flood the system. (P, Nov. 21, 1983, 14; Nov. 29, 1983, 14)

At the end of January, 1982, on the very weekend that Paul Theroux's article "Subway Odyssey" was published in the Sunday *Times,* 100 violent crimes were reported in the subways, including murders, stabbings, robberies, and assaults against passengers. What Theroux tries to do in his essay is to provide a true picture of the New York subway. What he ends up doing inadvertently is romanticizing the system. On the one hand, "the subway has the most macabre crimes." It is a nightmare, a madhouse. Crime rose a record 80 percent in August, 1980 (a month before my son was murdered). But Theroux still admires the subway: "It is New York City's best hope." He admires the architecture and the different stations, but he does hate the people who misuse the subway, "the way you hate kids who tear the branches off saplings" (Jan. 31, 1982, 20). This last analogy reveals what is wrong with Theroux's essay. When kids tear the branches off saplings, the trees might survive or might be replanted. No one can replant a human life that has been cut apart by a knife. Theroux's metaphor does not evoke the real horror of what happens on the subway. In the end one is left with the sad feeling that Theroux is a writer who finds beauty in what is essentially ugly. Why else would he call the subway New York's "best hope"? To most New Yorkers this would seem to be "the fatuous remark of the year."

James S. Kunen describes the sordid environment of the subway in uncompromising terms:

> Heading back to school, I squeezed onto a subway car and saw there were seats in the next car. I bravely walked, while the train was in motion, from one car to the next. My foot slid— shit! Shit on the floor of the IRT car. Under the knowing and sympathetic gazes of my fellow riders, I scraped my foot ineffectually, sat down in the stench, and rode in the stench the next ten minutes, my woolen suit absorbing the odor, I knew. The car was filthy, scarcely an inch not smeared with ugly, indecipherable graffiti, sprayed scars over seats, windows, maps, everything, the floor thick with dirt, the car thick with people breathing one another's breath, and breathing dogshit, too, this time. I told myself the ride was an experience. (10-11)

The New York papers often print discussions about how to

improve the subways and eliminate crime. Different figures are always forthcoming to explain how many police are patrolling the 6,150 subway cars. The Transit Authority planned to enlarge the transit police force from a low of 2,650 cops to 3,600. Presumably by 1982 there would be one transit officer for every three trains, and the 75 percent rise in crime in December, 1981, would not be repeated in 1982.

On April 11, 1982, a twenty-two-year-old woman was sodomized and raped on the IRT subway at 2:30 A.M. The rapist cleared the train of passengers by brandishing a card that made him seem to be a police officer. From 125th Street to Fourteenth Street, this so-called human being repeatedly raped the woman. Not a single officer appeared on the subway during that time. Finally at the Fourteenth Street station a police officer spotted the attacker (P, Apr. 12, 1982, 13).

The *New York Post* suggested that cops should be placed on every train, in every station. This would require the hiring of 6,792 transit police. But what would it really take to rid the subways of the vermin, 75,000 or 100,000? In 1984, MTA Chairman Robert R. Kiley stated that the subway system is plagued by so many difficulties that it is having "a nervous breakdown." Filthy stations, vandalism, antiquated tracks, derailments, fires, faulty equipment and needed repairs, labor and management problems, decreased ridership, and a rising crime rate are all signs of a system in radical decline (T, July 30, 1984, A1). The late Senator Caemmerer and Mayor Koch recommended that a special subway court should try subway offenders. Assemblyman Vincent Marchiselli of the Bronx introduced legislation that would require judges to add twenty years to a sentence for felony crimes committed on buses and subways.

But not everyone shares these people's view that the subway is a special kind of nightmare and deserves special justice. For example, on the subject of compensating victims in the subway the Appellate Court and State Supreme Court disagreed. While private transit systems are responsible for damage to victims, city systems have enjoyed immunity. Two women who had been raped and robbed and maimed on the subway sued the MTA. They won damages against the MTA because the Appellate Division of the Manhattan Supreme

Court ruled that "a subway straphanger deserves more protection than a citizen walking the streets, and a crime on a transit facility is different from one committed in the streets." However, this decision was unanimously reversed by the State Supreme Court. Judge Bernard S. Meyer gave as a reason for the ruling the court's judgment that the Transit Authority and the transit police are immune to standards of care required by private railroad lines.

The attorneys for the plaintiffs contended that the decision was made to protect the city because of its financial straits and inability to deal with crime. I believe this to be true. If the Supreme Court had upheld the decision, the MTA would have been inundated with thousands of lawsuits and would have been forced to shut down. One of the plaintiffs, Ann G. Weiner, sixty-nine, is justifiably bitter. In the eight years since she was attacked and her right hand paralyzed, she has never used a subway for fear of going into psychic shock. "I was once a free soul, and now I'm locked in," she said. "New York was once a Garden of Eden for me and now I absolutely hate the city" (T, Feb. 19, 1982, B3).

Why was the *Daily News* so overjoyed that subway victims could not sue the Transit Authority? The editorial in that newspaper on February 20, 1982, stated: "The idea that the Transit Authority must compensate riders who suffer injury or loss at the hands of subway criminals is ridiculous" (C13). Victims of such crime deserve sympathy but not money, for the Transit Authority and the city would go bankrupt if the victims received compensation. The *Daily News,* like the Supreme Court judges, obviously believes that there's a difference between being stabbed to death on the subway and being stabbed on a private bus. The city abrogates its responsibility; it doesn't have to worry about paying victims of crime.

In Beaumont, Texas, Mrs. McWhorter and her daughter were killed by a truck on April 17, 1981. Their survivors received $26.5 million from the trucking company that owned the truck. Ann G. Weiner, who was robbed and injured on the Twenty-third Street station of the Eighth Avenue Independent Subway Line, was only one of thirteen people who had been robbed on that subway between January 13 and October 23, 1973. Wasn't the Appellate Division correct in assuming that the Transit Authority was negligent for failing to remedy a situation it knew was dangerous? In truth the Transit Authority was more culpable in relation to the death of my son and other victims of subway crime than the truck company that hired the driver who killed the McWhorters. In that case an individual was to blame. In my son's case, and in the cases of all the maimed and murdered subway victims, the city and its officials and the Transit Authority are to blame.

In April, 1982, the City Housing Authority paid $225,000 to the father of a Chinese schoolgirl, Irene Hsieh, who was raped and murdered at an East Side housing project which had broken locks and no police protection. Why was the City Housing Authority responsible for the safety of the tenants in its buildings, while the Transit Authority was absolved of all responsibility to protect its tenants in the subway? Why? The answer is obvious. Judges often make political, not legal, decisions.

In the view of the State Supreme Court's decision, my son's dead body was different from Barbara McWhorter's dead body or Irene Hsieh's dead body, because he died in a subway. The moral is clear. You don't want to die in a subway. That doesn't count. Imagine what might have happened if the Transit Authority had been forced to reimburse all of the victimized people in the subway. The transit system might have been forced into bankruptcy, and then perhaps reform might have been initiated. The city originally owned and ran the subway until 1966, when the MTA assumed control. Four of the fourteen members of the MTA are appointed by the mayor, six by the governor, and four by the county executives. In reality the mayor still controls the transit cops because the city budget pays for them and the city police chief commands them.

There isn't a day that goes by without some observation in the newspaper about the transit mess, about deals that fall through to raise new money for the subway system, about the inflated salaries of executives and their inflated pensions, about dirty, unsafe cars and stations. On February 8, 1982, Koch said: "We're going to do as much as we can as quickly as we can to deal with subway crime" (T, Feb. 9, 1982, B4). On April 17, 1982, a protest meeting of 500 subway riders was held at Public School 87. Sixty community organizations were involved in this second annual accountability session known as the Straphanger's Campaign. At this meeting Alexander Staber bestowed the Second Fiddler Burner Award for the second year in a row to Mayor Koch, who is Transit Enemy Number One in New York City, "because the Koch Administration is fiddling while the Transit System burns" (T, Apr. 18, 1982, 42). Because in 1982 subway ridership fell to its lowest level since World War II, Koch was anxious to demonstrate that he had done something by adding 500 transit police, many of whom were assigned to nighttime patrol.

When my son was murdered in the New York subway in 1980, the city had reduced its transit police force from 3,500 in 1975 to 2,500. In 1983 there were more than 3,500 transit policemen. This did not prevent twenty-three-year-old Pablo Ramales, on January 20, 1984, from being robbed and stabbed to death in a Brooklyn station near the transit policemen's headquarters. (He died in full view of a token booth clerk.) This did not prevent Lawrence E. Papino, a post office supervisor, from being stabbed to death by a mugger on the 155th Street and St. Nicholas Avenue station. This did not prevent 13,624 crimes from being committed on the subway.

By contrast, the Japanese seem not only to know how to make saleable products, but they also know how to handle crime. In 1983 the Tokyo violent crime rate was twenty-two times lower than the New York City crime rate. In Tokyo, which has the fourth largest subway system in the world, only two cases of police handled incidents in the cars were reported in the last three years. Moreover, the Japanese pay a fare of fifty cents to ride in clean, safe, and efficient trains. New Yorkers pay ninety cents for an unsafe, unclean, and inefficient ride.

New York subways are dangerous even when police are present. Riders have to contend not only with criminals but also with sexual deviates and homicidal maniacs. On April 24, 1984, Kate Milford described in *The Times* (19) how she cried after her daily experience with the "subway lecher" in the crowded, filthy, smelly subway. In that same month, twenty-five transit policemen were used to subdue twenty-two hoodlums between the ages of thirteen and twenty, who robbed and terrorized passengers on an F train. On that very same day some people on a J train were beaten by a group of eleven- to sixteen-year-old youths. On March 1, 1984, a deranged man shoved a young bride, Li Yung Cheung, under an IRT train, and she was decapitated. On April 3, 1985, a twenty-two-year-old woman, Marie La Fortune, died after she was shoved under the wheels of a train by a madman. This tragedy occurred despite the fact that the system was manned by 3,800 officers, the largest police force in its history.

Statistics released in April, 1984, revealed that subway crime had risen more than 13 percent in the previous months and that April had seen a whopping 15.9 percent increase. Blah-blah-blah, said all the newspapers. We must do something about the transit system. Blah-blah-blah, said all the city officials and crime committees. We must do something about the forty daily felonies in the subway. No one seems to agree about who should take complete charge of the Transit Authority. Mayor Koch? Blah-blah-blah, the discussions continue, and so does the crime. Governor Cuomo says that subway trains are "worse now than they have ever been. It has never been so bad" (P, Feb. 14, 1985, 3). Felix Rohatyn, head of the Municipal Assistance Corporation, in an address at the Waldorf-Astoria on February 11, 1985, described the transit system in New York City as a "social threat, an operating nightmare, and a financial disaster." He predicts that this system faces "physical and financial catastrophe."

Listed below are only a few of the typical incidents on the subway that Koch once had the temerity to call the safest in the world. I do not list the many derailments, equipment failures, fires, and other hazards that make riding a New York train a truly unforgettable experience.

Even though extra police were assigned to guard the subway stations after the Bernhard Goetz incident, a "wolf pack" of six young muggers savagely beat an eighteen-year-old woman and assaulted other passengers and crew on a Brooklyn BMT line.

A subway passenger was robbed and murdered on the Twenty-second Street and Broadway station. He was a musician.

A thirty-seven-year-old man was pushed to his death under the wheels of a train on the Flushing Seventy-fourth Street station.

A postal inspector who rode the subway to work for many years was robbed and stabbed to death on an IND subway at 155th Street.

Transit Authority Police Officer Irma Lozada was shot to death by a mugger who ran out of the subway with a stolen necklace.

A seventy-year-old Brooklyn man was shot and killed in a robbery carried out in a subway passage at Thirty-eighth Street and Sixth Avenue.

Detective Glen Whelpley of the Thirty-fourth Precinct in Washington Heights was shot in a lower Manhattan station.

A gang of teenagers attacked a man and his son on the 138th Street and Grand Concourse station and threw them on the tracks. The son was electrocuted.

An emotionally disturbed man pushed a passenger to his death in front of a subway train at Times Square.

A young woman was thrown on the tracks and her arm was severed. She was a musician.

Three Brooklyn teenagers robbed five people at knife point on four Manhattan subway trains.

TA Officer Robert Marks was stabbed in the back by two teenagers before he shot them as they tried to steal his wedding ring.

Four youths chained a token booth clerk to a turnstile and robbed him of $2,500 in tokens and cash at the 174th Street Bronx IRT station.

In a thirty-minute period, there were three incidents involving knives. One youth kept brandishing the knife at a Forty-second Street station even after he was shot.

Four muggers who netted three dollars laughed and hammed it up on their way to jail. One boasted, "I'll be out on the streets by noon." They had terrorized a lone passenger in the station until he was saved by two transit policemen who came into the station.

Mrs. Lorraine Koppell, the wife of State Assemblyman Koppell who heads a watchdog committee over the Transit Authority, was mugged at high noon on the IRT Broadway-Seventh Avenue Line. This was the second time she was victimized on the subway.

Twenty-five youths went on a rampage on an upper IND Manhattan station; they harassed passengers, kicked out windows, and stabbed two men who tried to stop them.

Twelve youths armed with guns and a sawed-off shotgun robbed and terrorized passengers on a Lexington Avenue IRT express and shot a passenger at point-blank range.

A token booth clerk was stabbed fourteen times by a deranged Hispanic man in a Brooklyn subway station as he emptied the turnstile. The nearest cop was three stations away.

The left leg of a twenty-year-old Brooklyn woman had to be amputated after two young muggers pushed her between a departing train and the station platform.

On December 12, 1981, three gunmen robbed twenty passengers at a 125th Street Broadway local, netting $10,000 in cash and jewelry.

In the early part of 1983, three transit cops were shot and almost died at the hands of subway muggers. In February, 1983, the Transit Authority reported that a $1.2 million television surveillance system would go into effect. This would happen even though, in a year-long experiment with a $500,000 system of seventy-six television screens monitored round the clock at the Fifty-ninth Street Columbus Circle station, the crime rate rose 30 percent at the station.

At the 170th Street Concourse station a token booth clerk said after he stabbed Darrell Primo in the chest when he jumped the turnstiles, "I've taken all the crap from people and I couldn't stand it anymore."

"Thank God," Mayor Koch said, "you're living in the city of New York. That for all of its problems, of which we have many, that when you compare the city with other cities in the country, this city is the place to live, the place to be."

Of course it is if you don't care about murder, especially the murder of young people. For it is not only people in the subway who are victims but also people in the city as a whole, and especially *young people*. Dr. Sol Blumenthal, the head of the statistics section in the Health Department, said that homicide is the leading cause of death among young people fifteen to twenty-four years old in New York City! Think of what this means. New York is the capital city of culture and early death. It is the place where the most expert medical care in the world can do nothing to save the lives of its murdered young people.

But you don't have to be in the subway to die. The beautiful model Marie de St. Antoine was killed on June 20, 1982, in the hallway of her apartment house in downtown New York. Her cousin said she was "scared to death of Manhattan. She lived there because of her work but she rarely left her apartment at night and never took the subways and was very security conscious. She wanted to move back to Montreal with her parents and lead a normal life" (P, June 21, 1982, 3).

Forty-four Cambodians fled from the horrors of their homeland to live in Brooklyn. There they were mugged and beaten. Fearing the violence they suffered in Brooklyn, they fled the city. These are examples of reported crimes. However, thousands of crimes are never reported. As John Godwin has said:

> In a country positively inundated with statistics, there is no such thing as a dependable nationwide crime index. Umpteen governmental and private organizations spew out reams of documentation on the subject, but since they apply different yardsticks and use different sources, they seldom arrive at the same totals. Even the FBI's *Uniform Crime Report,* quoted reverently by every newspaper, offers no more than approximations. These annual reports are based on figures supplied by local police chiefs, most of whom are deeply concerned with not rocking political boats. They therefore tend to understate crime in their territories by anything up to 100 percent. (6)

To vouch for this fact, former Police Superintendent Richard J. Brzeczak of Chicago admitted, after a ten-month internal audit, that at least 40 percent of the city's serious crimes had been dismissed as "unfounded" (*USA,* Apr. 28, 1983, 3A). Thus, if the crime rate is reported to have declined in the subways in the first three months of 1983, even if it has declined 30 or 40 percent according to the latest statistics, always add the figures that are not counted, the hundreds of crimes that are not reported for many reasons: politics, fear, laziness, or the strong pessimistic conviction that nothing will be done about the act of violence.

After interviewing tens of thousands of people, the Justice Department surveys produced a study in the mid-seventies revealing that a third of all violent crimes and an even greater percentage of property crimes were not reported to the police and thus were never used by the FBI for the compilation of the Crime Index. *The New York Times,* in listing the following FBI Crime Index figures for the Northeast, mentioned this fact (April 20, 1984, A17).

City	1982	1983
Bridgeport, Conn.	17,504	17,121
Buffalo	28,592	25,990
Elizabeth, N.J.	9,066	8,749
Jersey City, N.J.	18,583	17,267
Hartford	23,512	18,794
Newark	36,172	33,281
New Haven	13,839	13,550
New York	688,567	622,877
Paterson, N.J.	13,571	11,456
Philadelphia	94,641	89,764
Rochester	26,821	25,192
Stamford, Comm.	7,664	7,165
Syracuse, N.Y.	13,194	11,669
Waterbury, Conn.	7,809	6,703
Yonkers	10,492	9,216

While most newspapers rejoiced in the fact that for the first time since 1980, crime decreased by 7 percent in 1984, the chart reveals a shocking fact about New York City crime. Despite the decrease, New York has more crimes per capita than any other city on the chart. According to the annual FBI report for 1983, New Yorkers have a greater than average chance of being victims of crime. The rate of crime in the city, 9,819 per 100,000 people, is very much greater than the national average. Add to these statistics the unreported crimes that do not appear in the FBI Crime Index, and we can understand why the 2,000 members of the Federation of New York State Judges recommended on April 22, 1984, that all convicted criminals be sent to prison and that new prisons be built. The federation's president, Justice Frances T. Murphy of the Appellate Division, stated that the fear that exists in New York City now would have been unbelievable to New Yorkers a generation ago. They would have considered it insane to have apartment windows covered with gates and security guards patrolling all apartment buildings. Murphy said:

> Criminals have taken the city . . . crime has beaten government to its knees, the moral passion for justice has been drained out of society and, in its place, there is an overwhelming sense of helplessness. (T, Apr. 23,1984, A1)

Two movies were made recently about the Bronx: *Fort Apache, The Bronx* and *1990: The Bronx Warriors.* The latter film is loosely based on the experiences of Fabrizio De Angelis from Rome, who visited the Bronx by mistake when he missed his stop on a subway to Manhattan. He said that he feared for his life when he was chased by a group of hoods wielding switchblades. He compared the area near Yankee Stadium to Dante's Inferno. "It is a modern day hell. While I was running for my life, I decided to make a movie" (P, Apr. 19, 1983, 17). The officials of the Bronx would not approve of these two films that describe the Bronx as a wasteland ruled by savages. A third, futuristic movie, *Escape from New York,* depicts the city as a maximum security prison inhabited only by convicts. Obviously these three films are not good for the tourist industry of New York. Obviously they are sensational exploitations of violence. But the very fact that they have been produced reveals a pervasive and persistent view of the city as an archetype of the Evil City, the beautiful red shiny apple rotten at the core. And it deserves that reputation.

Admittedly, many places in this country have violent crimes. Murder can happen anywhere in the world. But I write about what I know, about the city in which I was born, the city in which I grew up, the city in which I was married, the city in which my son was murdered.

At Pratt Institute, where a student was murdered on campus, the list of daily muggings is reported on a bulletin board. Senator Christopher Dodd and his companion were mugged on the block where the mayor's mansion sits in splendor. While Robert Wagner, Jr. was dining with Mayor Koch, Wagner's apartment was robbed of $4,000 worth of household and electronic materials. The worst mass slaughter in this city's history occurred on October 15, 1984, when ten people were shot to death in their home in Brooklyn.

Sydney H. Schanberg, in his column in *The New York Times,* contends that Mayor Koch's stewardship has not improved the quality of life in the city, and in some areas it has grown worse with the

> cratered roads, the dangerous subways, the littered streets, the rule-breaking behavior everywhere. . . . Citizens who would be thoroughly shocked to be identified publicly as part of the criminal element have nonetheless been breezily breaking all sorts of laws in public—traffic laws, drug laws, littering laws. Citizens who are less easily shocked have turned rowdiness, vandalism, and graffiti-scrawling into a special New York life style.
>
> This city is as close as one can get to every-man-for-himself without being in a declared state of anarchy. (Apr. 21, 1984, 19)

Roger Starr has given his book the apt title *The Rise and Fall of New York City.* Lewis Mumford writes in his *Sketches from Life:*

> More than once lately in New York I have felt as Petrarch reports himself feeling in the Fourteenth Century, when he compared the desolate, wolfish, robber-infested Provence of his maturity in the wake of the Black Plague, with the safe, prosperous region of his youth. . . . The city I once knew so intimately has been wrecked; most of what remains will soon vanish. . . . (5, 21)

The city Mumford knew and loved, the city I knew and loved, has vanished.

11

Literature And Murder (Norman Mailer)

Popular entertainment—movies, television, and novels—are
frequently, and correctly, accused of glorifying the criminal,
making his violence appear acceptable and encouraging imita-
tion of criminal acts.

J. L. Barkas, *Victims*

After my son died I resumed my duties as a teacher of English
at SUNY-Cortland. I taught a course entitled *Introduction to*
Fiction. In this course my students read the following stories:
Stephen Crane's "The Blue Hotel," Yukio Mishima's "Patrio-
tism," Richard Wright's "The Man Who Was Almost a Man,"
and Flannery O'Connor's "A Good Man is Hard to Find."
But as I taught them after my tragedy, I was unable to control
my revulsion. In "The Blue Hotel" the main character kills
someone with a knife; in "Patriotism" a Japanese couple
commit *seppuku* by disembowelment. In "The Man Who Was
Almost a Man" a young boy runs off with a gun to prove that
he is a man, while in the O'Connor story a grandmother, her
son, her daughter-in-law, and her two grandchildren are mur-
dered by an escaped convict.

What had happened? These were the same stories I had
read before. They are all judged to be of superior quality. What
had happened was the simple phenomenon that anyone expe-
riences who has been personally involved with or affected by
violence. It no longer is possible to read about violence or crime
or murder, even in the greatest classics, without being en-
gulfed by an overwhelming feeling of repugnance. A knife can

203

no longer ever be a knife for me. Every time I see or read about a knife it has only one association and one symbolization.

Still it is absurd to think that art can exist without dealing with violence and murder, for man, who is the subject of art, and is perpetually the provocateur of evil acts, provides the artist with his one enduring theme—the theme of evil. Great writers through the ages have used violent stories to offer meaningful commentary. The Greek plays and Shakespeare's dramas are replete with ugly violence and murder, but they are used to offer moral truths about human relationships. Shakespeare never glorified the criminal or the murderer.

However, some of the greatest writers have harbored the most inane views of the criminal. Freud maintained that Dostoevsky regarded the criminal as a Christ-like figure who takes on himself the guilt which must be borne by others. Still another kind of drivel is used to excuse the criminal activity of a writer. Jean Genet was an avowed thief, pimp, homosexual prostitute, Nazi, police informer, and "professional masturbator." He believed in the "beauty of crime." But Sartre, Gide, Cocteau, Mauriac, and Claudel successfully petitioned President Auriol to annul Genet's life sentence on the grounds that Genet was a genius. In recent times the Abbott-Mailer relationship reminds us that the concept of genius is still being used to exonerate evil.

But the attempt to exculpate and glamorize the life of the murderer is not restricted to literary genius. Many writers are like scavengers who run like wild dogs to the garbage cans of sensational murders and who try to extract perfume from what is essentially foul. Shana Alexander and Diana Trilling both have written books about Jean Harris and Dr. Tarnower, her murdered lover. I do not know why Shana Alexander, who wrote *Very Much a Lady,* called Diana Trilling's book "a piece of s——" (*USA,* Mar. 16, 1983, 2D). It is, of course, possible to make the same judgment of Alexander's book.

A long list of works have been produced by writers who are guaranteed an audience with an insatiable interest in murder. I was a member of that audience, along with presidents and intellectuals, who read murder mysteries to relax, to be entertained. Murder sells newspapers, articles, books, movies, and TV programs. *Who Killed the Robins Family?* was a best seller, and the reader who answered the question in the title received a $10,000 reward. At the Rocking Horse Ranch in Highland Park, on March 9, 1984, guests paid $350 for a weekend of fun centered around solving a murder mystery. But murder takes on sinister significance when it occurs to "me," not to the "other," and then what might have seemed like a harmless pastime takes on the stench of what Geoffrey Gorer calls "the pornography of death."

Truman Capote's *In Cold Blood* belongs to that group of *fraction* novels that purport to tell the truth, nothing but the truth, about the criminal and his murders. To achieve this admirable end, Capote transforms the murderer into a fascinating personality and demeans the life of the victim.

In my opinion the most famous example in this century of the writer who glamorizes violence is Norman Mailer. He is the paradigm case. For that reason I have devoted a special section to a study of his work and influence. Anyone who is interested in Mailer's personal life, in his marital, political, and legal escapades, can read his biography written by Hilary Mills or any of the other writings that concentrate on Mailer as a personality. I propose to deal with him as a literary phenomenon.

The Naked and the Dead is Mailer's first and best novel. But *Barbary Shore, The Deer Park,* and *An American Dream* were, as Tom Wolfe put it, "tenderized by the critics" (Lucid, 152). Elizabeth Hardwick, Stanley Edgar Hyman, Philip Rahv, and Tom Wolfe wrote negative reviews that "pulverized" *An American Dream* (Merrill, 67). Then Mailer won the National Book Award and the Pulitzer Prize for his *Armies of the Night* in 1968. Criticism of his work is characterized by an extreme polarity. No one seems to be capable of a moderate reaction. Mailer is either condemned for his beliefs, his personality, his actions, his mediocrity, or he is lauded as one of the great American writers fighting the battle of good versus evil. He is either a bad prose stylist or a great innovator. He is a profound thinker or a blithering idiot. As Calder Willingham observes, Mailer has been a "philosophical leaner," moving from elementary Marxism to the anarchism of Jean Malaquais, to neo-Freudian psychology, to the Beatnik movement, to a peculiar form of Zen Buddhism, to odd recurring thirsts for God and Christ, to the philosophy of the hipster, his peculiar brand of existentialism (Lucid, 241). Most controversial of all has been Mailer's stance towards the criminal and violence.

There seemed to be some kind of inevitability about the events that propelled him into playing the role of God to Jack Henry Abbott's devil; as if his whole life, his beliefs, and his writings were merely a preparation for that one real moment when his theoretical playing with fire would ultimately lead him to the pyre of tragedy on which his literary ashes would be burnt.

Some critics who have been sympathetic to Mailer's love affair with violence have not attempted to excuse it as an aberration of a sick mind but have justified it as a metaphysical, philosophic, moral means of combatting evil. Thus Raymond A. Schroth considers Mailer a moralist, Max F. Schulz refers to him as a metaphysician and philosopher who has written his Divine Comedy, and Richard M. Levine states that Mailer is working out his salvation in novels as devotional exercises dealing with the Manichean conflict between God and the Devil, saints and sinners. What Mailer believes, says Levine, is that we must "learn the Devil's stratagems in order to do service for the Lord" (L. Adams, 29).

Doing service for the Lord, Mailer writes in *The Presidential Papers*: "The characters for whom I had the most secret admiration . . . were violent people" (136). There was nothing secret about this admiration in "The White Negro," and he made the following explicit remark about violence in an interview he gave in *Mademoiselle* in February, 1961. He said of a gratuitous, brutal murder:

Let's use our imagination. It means that one human being has determined to extinguish the life of another human being. It means that two people are engaging in a dialogue with eternity. Now if the brute does it and at the last moment likes the man he is extinguishing then perhaps the victim did not die in vain. If there is an eternity with souls in that eternity, if one is able to be born again, the victim may get his reward. At least it seems possible that the quality of one being passes into the other, and this altogether hate-filled human, grinding his boot into the face of someone . . . in the act of killing, in this terribly

private moment, the brute feels a moment of tenderness, for the
first time perhaps in all of his existence. What has happened is
that the killer is becoming a little more possible, a little bit
more ready to love someone. (161-162)

These terrible, infamous words reveal the depths of Mailer's
perverse empathy for the criminal mentality. He has inspired
normally intelligent critics to comment on his views on vio-
lence in the following way:

That Mailer's own personal rebellion is futile could not be more
eloquently revealed than in the stabbing of his wife. Mailer not
only loved his wife, but it was probably for that reason that he
stabbed her. (Braudy, 90)

But nothing that Mailer has written about violence can com-
pete with the sordid story of his relationship with two real
criminals: Gary Gilmore and Jack Henry Abbott.

In a sense it might be argued that Abbott was as much the
result of Mailer's fantasizing as Rojack in *An America:1
Dream*. "Let's use our imagination," Mailer wrote, and that
was what he used when he transformed Abbott into a cause
célèbre. Writing in 1973, Nathan S. Scott had predicted that
Mailer, "a great primary force in American cultural life,"
would, as "spokesman for the American conscience," give us a
theory defending "the simple separate person" against totali-
tarianism in a doctrine similar to Walt Whitman's "personal-
ism" (97). But the leader in the struggle against totalitarian-
ism in the sixties turned out to be in the eighties the defender
of the personalism of a murderer.

Jack Henry Abbott, thirty-five years old, was an unknown
criminal serving twenty-five years in prison for robbery and
murder. He wrote letters to Norman Mailer in 1978 about the
horrors of prison life. Mailer, who at that time was busy writ-
ing about another murderer, Gary Gilmore, was so impressed
that he used his influence to have Abbott's *In the Belly of the
Beast* published by Random House. For this book Mailer also
wrote a laudatory introduction, which the *New York Review
of Books* printed to announce the emergence of a great talent.
In this introduction Mailer wrote:

> Not only the worst of the young are sent to prison but the best—that is, the proudest, the bravest, the most daring, the most enterprising, and the most undefeated of the poor. . . . Those juvenile delinquents . . . are drawn to crime . . . as a positive experience—because it is more exciting, more meaningful, more mysterious, more transcendental, more religious than any other experience they have known. (June 11, 1981, 15)

Presumably, in Mailer's judgment, Abbott was one of these best young men.

It is to Joyce Carol Oates's credit that she recognized what Abbott had done in *In the Belly of the Beast*. She said, "To me *In the Belly of the Beast* was more a literary book than an authentic book. It showed he'd read a lot of Genet and other writers" (TSB, Sept. 20, 1981, 36). It showed that Abbott had learned to do in prison what others before him had done to impress parole boards and influential people with their intelligence and capacity for rehabilitation. Either they sought release from incarceration through their study of law, or they developed literary talent to attract influential writers. Eldridge Cleaver, Edgar H. Smith, and Tommy Tantrino are examples of former prisoners who sought help in this way. Not only Mailer, but also William F. Buckley and others have tried to help convicts. Roger Knobelspiess, a writer, served only part of a five-year sentence for a 1977 robbery because President François Mitterand pardoned him. Knobelspiess wrote two books on his terrible life in prison, which earned him the admiration and support of such French intellectuals as Michel Foucault, Claude Manceron, Yves Montand, and Simone Signoret. Manceron, arguing for Knobelspiess's release, said: "France should not deprive itself of this natural resource." But after being paroled, Knobelspiess embarrassed his staunch supporters when he was arrested again and accused of armed robbery. At least he, unlike Jack Abbott, was not accused of murder (TBS, July 24, 1983, 27).

Abbott did not spend all of his time in prison eating cockroaches or being beaten by guards. Obviously he had time to read and write. According to *The Times,* he had agreed to become a prison informer before he was released, and this is why Barry Gray predicts that Abbott will be killed in prison (2). In any event, Abbott impressed Mailer and others sufficiently for them to write glowing letters of praise for Abbott to the Utah State Board of Pardons. As a result, a dangerously violent man was paroled.

Eight years before, Abbott had failed to impress Jerzy Kosinski. When he attempted to correspond with Kosinski, Kosinski rebuffed the prisoner, objecting to Abbott's use of Marxism as an apology for his life of crime:

> Don't tell me that you know the truth of life and society—the industrial, American society, that is—because at the age of 12 it had turned you into a criminal. Hundreds of thousands of young Poles, Russians, Jews, Ukranians, Germans, Greeks, and others survived World War II when they were 12—and in 1945 I was one of them. The war was western society at its most barbaric. It was a hell of hells, a terror of terrors . . . and when the war ended and we were like you once were, all 12 years old, none became criminals. The war taught us that society must be defended from men like you, Jack Abbott, who claim that because they were once hurt in "capitalist" kindergarten, they can now go on and hurt and kill and molest and torture others in the name of that once felt pain and rage. And they have no such right. And you have none, and with every fiber of my being . . . I will make certain that . . . I can keep myself away from you. So stay away Abbott. You have killed a man already. You can't kill a man in me. (TSM, Sept. 20, 1981, 38)

This is what Mailer should have written to Abbott. Yet even Kosinski joined in the accolades for Abbott and toasted him at a party on July 9, 1981. Later Kosinski blamed himself for becoming part of the "radical chic." He should have recognized that Abbott was not simply an intellectual but an "emotionally unbalanced just-freed prisoner" (T, July 26, 1981, 26).

But Mailer and Abbott were greeted as celebrities on the "Good Morning America" show, and reviewers Anatole Broyard, Barry Jacobs, Sue M. Halperin, James Boatwright, and Terrence des Près lavished great praise on *In the Belly of the Beast*. What does Terrence des Près, a Colgate University professor, think these days when he remembers that he said that Abbott's book is "awesome, brilliant," and "we must be grate-

ful to [Mailer] . . . for helping to get Abbott out on parole"
(TSB, June 20, 1981, 15). This review was on the newsstands
July 18, 1981, the day Abbott plunged a large knife into the
chest of Richard Adan outside the Binibon restaurant, where
Adan, a promising young playwright, worked as a waiter.
Abbott escaped but was captured in Louisiana.

I believed that Abbott would be found guilty of the charge
of second-degree murder. He was, after all, a recidivist. He had
committed a horrible murder and admitted his guilt. Assistant
District Attorney Fogel had been introduced to my husband
as one of the best prosecutors in Manhattan. The man who
witnessed the crime, Wayne Larsen, testified that the knife
plunging into Adan's heart "made a resounding impact," a
noise still ringing in Larsen's ears as he spoke. "It was as
loud as if I had struck myself and I was 70 feet away" (P.,
Jan. 14, 1982, 7).

But I should have known better. My brother, who had
served on jury trials, told horror stories of illiterate, amoral
juries and incompetent judges. Furthermore, had not Mailer
proved that men of influence are able to change the opinions
of parole boards? Why then could they not influence jurors
and judges? I do not know why Judge Irving Lang allowed
the jury to consider the charges of first- and second-degree
manslaughter. But he did. And Mailer played the role of loyal
friend to the bitter end.

In 1970, William F. Buckley, Jr. helped a convict, Edgar H.
Smith, Jr., obtain his release from prison, believing that Smith
was innocent of the murder of a fifteen-year-old girl in New
Jersey. Smith had studied law in prison and wrote a book pro-
testing his innocence. But when Buckley discovered that Smith
was guilty of the murder, he admitted that Smith should never
have been released from prison (Godwin, 301-302).

Defense lawyer Ivan Fisher said that Mailer gave Abbott
moral support before he testified in his own defense. Mailer
had written in his introduction: "I love Jack Abbott for surviv-
ing and for having learned to write as well as he does. His
letters revealed an intellectual, a radical, a potential leader, a
man obsessed with a vision of more elevated human relations
in a better world." That vision turned out to be no more than
the sordid vision of the murderer. For Abbott had written

about the act of murder in *In the Belly of the Beast:*

> You've slipped out a knife (eight- to ten-inch blade, double-edged). You are holding it beside your leg so he can't see it. The enemy is smiling and chattering away about something. . . . A light pivot toward him and the world turns upside down: you have sunk the knife to its hilt into the middle of his chest. Slowly he begins to struggle for his life. As he sinks you have to kill him fast or get caught. He will say "Why?" or "No!" Nothing else. You can feel his life trembling through the knife in your hand. It almost overcomes you, the gentleness of the feeling at the center of a coarse act of murder. You've pumped the knife in several times without even being aware of it. . . it is like cutting hot butter, no resistance at all. They always whisper one thing at the end: "Please." (89-90)

When the following words from *The Belly* were read in court, "Killing of aggressors is necessary in prison to retain manhood," Abbott said: "It's good, isn't it?"

Crying, screaming, smiling, Abbott put on the performance of his life, trying to convince the jury that he had worn a knife and killed Adan because of a "tragic misunderstanding." Abbott felt Adan planned to kill him because of an argument about using the Binibon toilet. Of course, in the end, prison was to blame for what he had done.

On January 18, 1982, Mailer became a major actor in the Abbott trial. On that day he testified on behalf of Abbott, and then at 4:30 P.M. he held a news conference with thirty-five hostile reporters. A few days later he also had an interview with the press in his agent's home. Listed below are some of his choice bits of wisdom as reported in the New York newspapers and in Hilary Mills's biography.

Mailer said that he hoped Abbott would not get a major sentence because "it would destroy him" (Mills, 17). He hoped that Abbott would, at most, receive a sentence "of ten years or so" (Mills, 16). The only ones who benefited from "this mess" were the law and order people, because "more law and order means moving this country toward a fascist state" (Mills, 16-17). He admitted that "Adan's family have a right to hate me and revile me. . . . I had an immense responsibility in the entire affair" (DN, Jan. 23, 1982, C9). But Mailer stressed the fact that he was unsympathetic to the view that the victim's family have "the right to demand blood atonement of a criminal" (Mills, 17).

Responding angrily to the jibes of antagonistic reporters, he defended himself against the charge of taking an unwarranted risk with Abbott.

> Society is taking risks all the time. What did you do that was so righteous? What did you do to make it a better world? The fact of the matter is that in this country the rich are getting richer and the poor getting poorer. The wave of law will make a fascist state. Adan has already been destroyed; let's not destroy Abbott. Abbott will either grow or deteriorate in prison. If he grows and develops, and changes, I feel he has a chance on the street again, then I will help him. . . . If society is willing to invest in nuclear weapons, we should be willing to invest in people like Jack Abbott. Society is built on risk. We've been living on the edge of a major conflagration for 30 years. (DN, Jan. 23, 1982, C9)

To compare the Abbott case to the danger of a nuclear holocaust is indeed a misused analogy. Equally outrageous is Mailer's attempt to equate the worth of Adan's life with the value of Abbott's literary talent.

Abbott, unlike Adan, is alive. He won't be executed. And if he is paroled, Mailer will be out there waiting to help him. Abbott received a sentence of fifteen years to life for manslaughter instead of twenty-five years to life for murder. He will also have to serve eight additional years for breaking parole. Mailer said that this is too long a sentence; it is a "killing sentence." He insists that he is willing "to gamble with a portion of society to save this man's talent" because "culture is worth a little risk" (Mills, 17).

In Mailer's *Pieces and Pontifications,* which contains what Stefan Kanfer has correctly described as an amalgam of "adrenaline, mysticism, and flapdoodle" (*Time,* June 28, 1982, 73), Mailer makes the following inimitable and notorious statements about violence:

> If a boy beats up an old woman, he may be protecting himself by discharging a rage which would destroy his body if it were left to work on the cells, so he takes it out on the old woman. (29)

Mailer . . . would sit by himself . . . when . . . The Star Spangled
Banner would be played . . . . It sounded like the first martial
strains of that cancer he was convinced was coming on him
and who knows? If he had not stabbed his wife, he might have
been dead in a few years himself—the horror of violence is its
unspoken logic. (22)

In other words, Abbott had to kill Adan to protect himself
from getting cancer. Violence as therapy may have its unspo-
ken logic, but it is the logic of sick and demented minds.

What can be said about the Abbott-Mailer relationship has
been stated unequivocally by Niel R. Ayer in a letter to *Time:*

Jack Henry Abbott's release from prison is living proof that a
criminal's lot can sometimes depend upon the wealth and im-
portance of the people he knows. It would be entirely fitting for
Norman Mailer to be tried as an accessory in the murder of
Richard Adan and for the parole personnel to serve the balance
of Abbott's term. (Aug. 24, 1981, 3)

As for Mailer's defense of Abbott, Ira Edelson has expressed
the following opinion:

Mailer's plea for leniency on behalf of Jack Abbott is further
proof that a literary genius(?) can also be a stupid, anti-social
idiot. (DN, Jan. 25, 1972, C17)

When Mailer won the Pulitzer Prize for *Armies of the
Night,* he was supposedly rewarded for writing what George
Levine called one of his devotional journalistic exercises deal-
ing with God, truth, peace, and the devil. But when he was
awarded the Pulitzer Prize for *The Executioner's Song,* I was
puzzled. I know that literary prizes do not necessarily go to the
best writers; publicity, influence, and prevailing cultural atti-
tudes often result in the strangest decisions. When in 1941 the
Pulitzer Prize Advisory Board recommended that *For Whom
the Bell Tolls* should receive the Pulitzer Prize, Columbia Uni-
versity President Nicholas Murray Butler, to his everlasting
shame, said: "I hope that you will reconsider before you ask
the University to be associated with an Award of this nature."
There was no Pulitzer Prize awarded for fiction for 1940, and

the Post Office declared *For Whom the Bell Tolls* to be non-mailable. Today we deplore such narrow-minded puritanism. But the Pulitzer Prize, which was not awarded to the Hemingway novel, a romantic, idealistic work with impeccable moral values, was awarded to *The Executioner's Song,* which is in the worst sense of the word a "dirty book," not because it contains foul language, which it does, but because it glamorizes and sentimentalizes murder and violence.

How odd that I should be making this judgment about *The Executioner's Song* when almost all the reviewers have responded with the same robotlike drone of adulation. The *Los Angeles Times* calls Mailer the best journalist in America. Mailer's style and language are "impeccable." The *New Republic* calls it a "masterpiece." The *Village Voice* says that it is "absorbing, scary and startlingly funny." The *Nation* refers to its "near flawless craft," and the *Boston Phoenix* lavishes praise in the most hyperbolic language: It "takes on a quiet grandeur that's close to Tolstoyan. . . . It's his whole vision of America, high and low, damned and saved. . . . there is more compassion, understanding and sense of truth here than in any recent American novel you can name."

Tolstoyan? More truth than any other recent novel? These are grandiose claims even for hyperbolic book blurbs. When *The Executioner's Song* was published, I asked the same question Anthony Burgess asked, "Why devote 1,050 pages to the last days of an executed murderer?" Now, I know that the non-fiction fiction form has attained respectability in critical circles. But like Aristotle and Rebecca West, I like my genres uncontaminated. Despite the oxymoronic nature of the fraction novel, that is, despite the fact that it mixes fact and fantasy, writers of such works seem to seduce their readers into believing that *truth* is being disseminated, objective truth. As Tony Tanner shrewdly observed, Capote's *In Cold Blood* was full of lies (L. Adams, 119), and, as Diane Johnson wrote, after reading *The Executioner's Song,* "one can only wish to know how it really was" (NYRB, Dec. 6, 1979, 6). Every murder case is potentially a financial bonanza for writers and publishers. The public's avid interest in the lawless elements of our society is unquenchable, and our capacity for idealizing the worst criminals in our history has been amply documented by John Godwin in his *Murder USA*. He has shown how we have made despicable murderers like Billy the Kid, Doc Holliday, and the James and Younger brothers into great heroes of the West.

I was not planning to read *The Executioner's Song*, but I changed my mind when it won the Pulitzer Prize. Perhaps it was, after all, Mailer's *chef-d'oeuvre*. Perhaps it was more than the usual crime novel written for the sole purpose of titillating the basest instincts of man. Perhaps Mailer had finally invested his veneration of violence with a Tolstoyan grandeur.

Mailer has sometimes soared as a writer and sometimes sunk so low and flat that his style has received a gamut of contradictory judgments from critics: some think he is a bad stylist and some think he has, through the use of obscenity and outlandish tropes, raised language to new heights never before imagined. In *The Executioner's Song* Mailer uses a flat, reportorial style enlivened by obscenities in the speech of his characters. Every love letter written by Gary Gilmore and Nicole Baker is essentially a model of sexual obscenity. Gilmore has the foulest mouth of any character Mailer ever imagined.

The following are examples of Mailer's "impeccable style" when he speaks in his own voice:

1. "That was when he got scared shitless" (1,008).
2. "seemed pissed off about the whole deal" (276).
3. "That teed Earl off personally" (662).
4. "He had to be reciting out of his hind end" (27).
5. "Of course, he was probably worried the FCC would go all over ABC's ass" (793).
6. "The risk of media exposure went deeper than Gilmore being able to shoot off his mouth" (665).
7. "Prison was wanting to breathe when somebody else had a finger up your nose. Soon as they took it out, the air got you crazy" (100).

For the most part, the writing in *The Executioner's Song* consists of mediocre, trite, slang idiom. It is journalistic only in the worst sense of the term, journalistic in the sense that the late Bernstein of *The Times* would have repudiated. Short paragraphs, separated by spaces; dialogues reprinted from transcripts, letters, and interviews; quotes from newspapers; and imaginary dialogue interspersed with authorial intrusions are Mailer's structural devices. As for the humor in the work, the following is a sample:

> "God they were crude. Gary would tell an awfully gross story. It seems there was this old boy Skeezix, who would perform fellatio on himself. He was proud of that. Nobody else in OSP could."
> "OSP?" asked Brenda.
> "Oregon State Penitentiary." (48-49)

In an afterword of three pages, Mailer describes how he wrote these "factual accounts of the activities of Gary Gilmore and the men and women associated with him in the period from April 9, 1976, when he was released from the United States Penitentiary at Marion, Illinois, until his execution a little more than nine months later." Mailer claims the story is as "accurate" as one can make it in view of the "interviews, documents, records of court proceedings, telephone conversations which would approach 14 thousand pages" (1,020). Mailer had to select, and it is his point of view that gives meaning and shape to the book. True or not, it is *his* version of the Gary Gilmore story, because it is what he chose to include and emphasize in *The Executioner's Song* that gives the book Mailer's truth. Mailer said his "treatment of Gary Gilmore was fair and did not romanticize him" (T, Aug. 17, 1981, B4). I disagree. Mailer's treatment did romanticize Gilmore. It ignored the victims of the murder, and made Lawrence Schiller and Norman Mailer two important subsidiary characters in the novel.

When Mailer wrote his book about the gratuitous murders of two decent young men, he had a preconception that shaped the tone, point of view, and characterizations in *The Executioner's Song*. Never timid or inhibited about his unconventional sympathy for the criminal, Mailer at the outset makes clear his view of Gary Gilmore:

> In the mountains, the snow was iron gray and purple in the hollows, and glowed like gold on every slope that faced the sun.

The clouds over the mountains were lifting with the light. Brenda took a good look into . . . [Gilmore's] eyes and felt full of sadness again. His eyes had the expression of rabbits she had flushed, scared-rabbit was the common expression, but she had looked into those eyes of scared rabbits and they were calm and tender and kind of curious. They did not know what would happen next. (28)

This is clearly a *romanticizing* posture. The effect is ineradicable. If you begin by comparing a murderer to a monster, to a snake, you produce a very different effect from when you compare him to a "tender, kind, scared rabbit." In this passage, one of the few times in the book when Mailer writes a descriptive sentence, perhaps consciously imitating Hemingway, Mailer is full of empathy for his scared rabbit.

Over and over again Mailer tells us that Gilmore was intelligent, that he read books, that he impressed most people as being intelligent. Yet there is no evidence either in Gilmore's actions or in his speech of this intelligence. Indeed, Gilmore more often than not comes across as a muddled, mentally impaired character with the sophomoric, immature responses of an illiterate adolescent. Besides, Mailer knows that intelligence alone won't gain sympathy for his hero. He knows, as we all know, that in the age of the Holocaust, culture and bestiality are compatible. So he tries to arouse interest in Gary's character from another vantage point. He tries to make a mystery out of the motivations for the murder and thereby keep us in suspense for 1,000 pages "until the real Gary Gilmore stands up."

At first Gary states that he doesn't know why he killed Max Jensen and Ben Bushnell (293). Then when Jensen's friend tries to get into jail to kill Gary, Gary says, "You know, this is the first time I've ever had any feelings for either of those two guys I killed" (386). In fact when Gilmore cries, "I hope they execute me for it, I ought to die for what I did," he has made the ultimate judgment and the book should end at that point (296). But Mailer needed to give Gary the "hipster's" stance, the glorified pose of the rebel against society, even though at times even those who are most sympathetic to Gary say things like: "That man [Gilmore] could stick his knife in you and keep a smile while doing it" (604), or "He could kill you because you gave him coffee in a paper cup" (659).

Now, why was this intelligent man a killer? Noall Wootton, the prosecutor, gives the classic *post hoc* explanation: "Jesus Almighty . . . the system has really failed with the man, just miserably failed" (442). It never occurs to Mailer to suggest that Gilmore has failed the system. At one point Gilmore says he murdered the two men because he didn't want to kill Nicole, that he would have killed more men if he had lost Nicole (672). Nor did he kill because of hatred of his mother (826). Near the end of the book Mailer finally offers us his explanation of Gilmore's turmoil. Gilmore's sex life was deranged as a result of prison life. He was not a "situational homosexual." But he did like to read books with photographs of children. In a letter to Nicole, Gary described how he kissed a beautiful young boy of thirteen who looked like a girl (853-854). What Gilmore really feared to acknowledge was the urge to be a child molester. Mailer speculates: "Nothing might have been more intolerable to Gilmore's idea of himself. Why, the man would have done anything, even murder, before he'd commit that other kind of transgression" (855). Thus even in a true account of a murder, Mailer cannot avoid using his typical, simplistic equation of violence and sex. At this point I think, "Is this why I have read more than 1,000 pages, to find the answer is just another worn-out cliché—to find out that if Gilmore had been locked up as a potential child molester, he might not have killed Bushnell and Jensen?"

To be fair to Mailer, he does quote what Kathryne, Nicole's mother, says to April, who has spent the night with Gilmore after he kills Jensen: "Were you with that dirty crumb all night" (241)? And we can only ask why we, as readers, are staying with the "dirty crumb." Kathryne would say:

> "He's nothing but a damned killer and he deserves the death penalty. No . . . that's too good for him."
> "You don't understand him," Nicole would say. "No," Kathryne said, "I don't, but why don't you try to understand those two poor women who have to raise those kids who don't have a father now, while you are running up every cockeyed day to see that damn killer." (469)

Mailer doesn't care about the victims in this murder story. He is only interested in the murderer, and he wants to leave us with a sympathetic view of Gilmore, as an almost Christlike figure. So it is not surprising that Nicole Baker, Gilmore's weird Juliet, would be totally uninterested in the men Gilmore shot.

Mailer portrays Nicole Baker as a passive, pathetic character. If Nicole is as Mailer describes her in *The Executioner's Song,* then she wouldn't be disturbed by her characterization in the novel. She wouldn't understand what he has done to her. For Nicole is the kind of "woman-thing" monstrosity that Mailer creates in his novels. She belongs to his gallery of such demented grotesques as Guinevere, Deborah, Lannie, Elena, Lulu, and Cherry.

Nicole, who was in an insane asylum at the age of thirteen, ends up in the insane asylum again after she attempts to commit suicide at Gary's instigation. She has been passively promiscuous during her young life, and when she breaks with Gary before he commits the murders, it is hard to believe that she will care about him once he is imprisoned. But for some inexplicable, sick reason she seems to fall passionately in love with the image of Gary, the soon-to-be-executed killer. Her transformation into a despairing Juliet who cannot face the "horrible loss" of her Romeo is about as moving as the obscene, tasteless, illiterate letters she and her lover exchange. Gilmore is disturbed by the fact that Nicole is always writing and telling him about "getting fucked, getting fucked, getting fucked, getting fucked. Everybody fucks Nicole. Everybody" (403). Gary's description of how he would fuck Nicole is a model of the kind of obscenity that Mailer himself loves to use (471).

Nicole answers Gary's request that they commit suicide by collecting fifty Seconals and twenty Dalmane pills. She reserves half of each kind to take herself and puts the other thirty-five pills in two yellow balloons inside her vagina. When she visits Gary in prison and sits on his lap, he has to make a terrible effort to get it out of her vagina, and then he pushes the balloon up his rectum (553-554). But the suicide attempt of these lovers fails. Nicole is hospitalized, and Gary Gilmore survives because he hasn't taken enough pills to kill him. According to Larry Schiller, this is not a sordid romance. It is an interesting relationship (1,006). Interesting indeed! Gilmore makes her try suicide so that she won't be with any men after he dies. And she, poor fool, receives, for all this, brain damage. It is, therefore, easy enough for Schiller to befriend her and manipulate her to obtain the interviews Mailer uses.

But enough about poor Nicole and vicious Gary. After the suicide attempt, Mailer turns his attention to a critique of the media's involvement in the Gilmore story. At this point Mailer's chutzpah becomes offensive. It is one thing to attempt to record the motivations of people involved in a murder; but to write the following passage as a critique of the media is an example of Mailer's questionable stance throughout the work. "The moment that suicide attempt hit the media, not only was Larry Schiller on the plane, but everybody was heading for Salt Lake, ready to check into the Hilton, where each of the media monkeys could watch all the other monkeys. There were going to be a lot of monkeys in that zoo" (580-581).

Including, of course, the most famous monkey of all in that zoo, Mailer himself, not literally there then, but there for ambitious, financial reasons in a 1,050-page book. At one point Mailer says of Lawrence Schiller, "[He] gets in when people are dying" (546). Elsewhere he calls Schiller, a former photographer for *Time* magazine and producer of theater and television programs, "the journalist who dealt in death." Mailer implies that everyone else involved in trying to make money out of the Gilmore story is guilty of sin. But although Mailer seems to place himself above the "carrion-birds," he has received, in the end, the biggest piece of meat to digest with the greatest profits.

At a meeting at Brigham Young University, students asked Lawrence Schiller, "Why don't you do the story about Ben Bushnell rather than Gary Gilmore?" Schiller answered that "at this point in the realm of the United States, Gary Gilmore was making history. . . . Fair or not, Benny Bushnell and his death never would"(850). This is also Mailer's justification for making short schrift of the Jensen-Bushnell tragedy and dramatizing at length Gilmore's actions, feelings, and writings. He devotes about nine pages to the Jensen murder and nine pages to the Bushnell murder. Brief references to the widows and the father of one of the victims appear in no more than three pages. So in a book of 1,050 pages, there are a total of about eighteen pages dealing with the victims.

The description of the courtship and marriage of Colleen and Max Jensen involves a tonal shift: "Now they were marrying each other. Forever" (216). Mailer writes condescendingly about the conventional virtues of the young couple; their religious and moral values are made to seem self-righteous. By comparison, Nicole and Gilmore, flawed as they are, have passion, and that makes them more human.

But Mailer isn't really interested in the Jensens. Nor is he interested in Ben and Debbie Bushnell. He offers a perfunctory description of the Bushnell murder and moves on quickly to involve us in Gilmore's problems after he commits the two murders. It's almost as if Mailer senses that if he writes even one page about the real torment of widows, he would not be able to sustain any audience sympathy for Gilmore in the pages that follow. He gives us a detailed, very sympathetic portrait of Bessie Smith, but the mothers of Bushnell and Jensen are never mentioned. In a brief excerpt from the *Desert News,* Jensen's father, a religious man, states that he wouldn't want to trade places with Gilmore's parents (578). A brother of Shirley Pedler, executive director of the ACLU, asks, "What about the victims and the families?" (753). And the reader asks, What about them? and receives no answer from either the ACLU or Mailer or any of the organizations frenetically involved in trying to save Gilmore from dying.

That is what interests Mailer most: the attempt to save Gilmore's life and what he construes as the sensationalizing of that attempt by Lawrence Schiller and the circus media. His basic premise is that despite what Gilmore has done, he doesn't deserve to die. Capital punishment is horrible, monstrous; and with an inversion of values that Mailer has been using for years, he contends that those who attempt to kill Gilmore are evil, while those who attempt to save him are good. Mailer doesn't offer a single rational discussion of the death penalty issue. The people of Provo who support the death penalty are satirized as stupid Mormons. Mailer and Schiller, who want to save Gilmore, are the righteous ones, despite the fact that they both make money out of the subject of death and violence.

Over and over again Mailer quotes disparaging remarks about Schiller which are applicable to himself. "The man was something of a carrion bird: already he'd done business with Susan Atkins, Marina Oswald, Jack Ruby, Madame Nhu, and Lenny Bruce's widow" (698). Now he is doing business with Gilmore, but, the reader thinks, so is Mailer. So far as I know, he hasn't given the proceeds of *The Executioner's Song* to the widows of Bushnell and Jensen.

Mailer himself tells us in the novel that thousands of dollars were offered by the *New York Post,* the *Daily News,* Jimmy Breslin, and others who wanted Schiller to get them tickets for the execution. ABC had spent $70,000 on the assumption that it would buy Schiller's story. But ABC pulled out of the agreement, presumably because the wife of a top executive at ABC, studying at the Columbia School of Journalism, convinced her husband that the network should not do Gilmore as entertainment (793). David Susskind originally offered as much as $20,000 for the rights to Gary's story to Boaz, Gilmore's lawyer. Schiller offered even more money for the rights. Susskind, however, retracted the offer because he considered the Gilmore affair to be a "sensational, malodorous, exploitative mess." But Schiller stayed with the story to the bitter end. Mailer tries to modify the portrait of Schiller as a scavenger by having Schiller refuse to take money from those who wanted to attend the execution. He has Schiller say, "They might call him a carrion bird, but he knew from deep inside that he could live with Gilmore's life. He did not have to profit from this death" (802). Of course not, because he also thinks, "With Gilmore alive, the story would not be as obviously dramatic, but it could be good" (801). Alive or dead, Gary would be great entertainment. Schiller knew it and Mailer knew it, and together they collaborated on this great entertainment which appeared in hardcover and paperback versions, and they collaborated on the Gilmore TV mini-series. Dead or alive, Gilmore has been a source of income for both men.

But oh, how they sobbed when it appeared that Gilmore might die. The ACLU and the NAACP fought to save Gilmore. (Ironically, he had a pathological hatred for those two organizations.) Bill Moyers did not want Gilmore to die. Schiller did not want Gilmore to die. Breslin was "cursing up a streak, How dare they shoot the fucking guy, these fucking people? Breslin was even more furious at Gilmore for wanting to be offed" (867). (This is the same Breslin who screams about foul murderers in his *Daily News* column.) Bob Moody, a lawyer, wept when Gilmore told him he didn't fear dying. Anthony Amsterdam, a professor of law at Stanford who won the landmark case against capital punishment in the Supreme Court, tried to save Gilmore (681). The crescendo of protest rose. "Of course, by now, everybody was liking him [Gilmore]. Even the people that didn't like him, liked him" (867).

So the Gary in the transcripts, with twenty-seven different poses—"racist, Country and Western, poetic, artist manqué, macho, suicidal, Karma County, Texas, Killer Irishman, movie-star, and awfully shit-kicking, large-minded aw-shucks"— Gary turns out to be a humane figure. Barry Farrell, who was Schiller's assistant, asks, "By God, was Gary like Harry Truman, mediocrity enlarged by history?" (All of this prompted by the fact that Gilmore donated his eyes to a young man.) Gilmore was really a decent man (805-806). But, appearing with a cast of about 200 forgettable characters, the real Gary Gilmore never stands up. He is a figment of Mailer's imagination based on Mailer's view of the world.

When Gary desperately tries to stop the legal attempts to keep him alive, Schiller says to him:

> Gary . . . maybe you're not meant to die. Maybe there's something so phenomenal, so deep, in the depths of your story, that maybe you're not meant to die right now. Maybe there are things left to do. We may not know what they are. Maybe by not dying you may be doing a hell of a lot for the whole fucking world. Maybe the suffering that you're doing now is the way you're giving back those two lives. Maybe you're laying a foundation for the way society and our civilization should proceed in the future. Maybe the punishment you're going through now is a greater punishment than death, and maybe a lot of fucking good's gonna come from it. (907-908)

Like Christ, Gilmore undergoes his apotheosis. But instead

of a crucifixion, his gift to mankind would be his refusal to die. And at the memorial service, Gary is practically canonized by those who speak. Vern Damico says: ". . . I've seen the inner side of Gary, and he is human, tender, and yes, understanding, very capable of love. Gary is on his way to a new life with God" (993).

Mailer selects material that will make the reader hate the Mormons and the state of Utah for killing this wonderfully tender Gary Gilmore. He lists how much it cost to execute Gilmore. He offers a detailed description of Gilmore's death, obviously designed to horrify the reader. Note that he does not describe in detail what Gilmore did to the bodies of Jensen and Bushnell. He quotes Barry Farrell's comments on Gilmore's integrity and dignity in meeting his death.

> Barry couldn't imagine what Gilmore might have done better. That helped to relieve him of his own doubts about his own involvement in these last days. This whole obscene, niggling business of translating the best thoughts of one's soul and conscience into one more rotten question, one more probe into the private parts of a man as protected from self-revelation as a clamshell from the knowledge of a caress. (978)

So Gilmore's behavior excuses the circus, "the obscene, niggling business of probing the private parts of a killer." And presumably it excuses Mailer's probing into the private parts of Gary Gilmore. Furthermore, Mailer's condemnation of "blood, lust and atonement" is his moral justification for treating the Gilmore story as he does. (Remember that in the Abbott case Mailer objected to the concept of blood atonement.) Mailer has the ACLU lawyer Judith Walbach express his hatred for the Mormons who believed in blood lust:

> This business of living for eternity certainly contributed to capital punishment, brutality, and war. Why, Brigham Young with his countless wives pining on the vine had the guile to state that if you discovered one of your women in adultery, it would behoove you as a good and Christian act to hold her on your lap and run a knife through her breast. That way she'd have her whack at the hereafter. (924-925)

This is peculiar satire from a man who wrote the following poem, "Rainy Afternoon with the Wife," in *Deaths for the Ladies:*

> So long
>   as
>   you
>   use
>   a knife,
>
> there's
>   some
>   love
>   left. (n.p.)

Presumably a knife in the name of love is necessary; in the name of the Mormon God it is proscribed.

At the beginning of *The Executioner's Song* Lieutenant Nielson says, "There's got to be forgiveness somewhere along the line" (297). Mailer not only forgives, but he also perpetuates the myth of the saintly criminal. He writes about the people of Provo as if they were evil for sympathizing with the victims. Henry Schwarzschild, the New York Coordinator of the National Coalition Against the Death Penalty and director of the Capital Punishment Project of the American Civil Liberties Union, condemned the execution of Gary Gilmore as a "judicial homicide with Mr. Hansen as an accomplice." Utah Attorney General Robert B. Hansen replied: "No death can be elevating and there is much sadness when anyone dies . . . but I am infinitely more sorrowful about the two victims' families than the fact Mr. Gilmore is no longer alive" (995-996).

And that says it all. Mailer is primarily interested in the murderer. I kept hearing the guns that shot Jensen and Bushnell.

In his writing Mailer fantasized about the role of Satan in modern life. John W. Aldridge has described Mailer's notion of the apocalyptic orgasm of the hipster as "a means of attaining oneness with God. But for this to become possible, the Devil in us must first be vanquished. Hence, behind every apocalyptic orgasm is an apocalyptic defecation. From one exit we ejaculate toward divinity. From the other we evacuate the Devil's work. The route to salvation is thus from anus to phallus, from organic excretion to orgasmic ecstasy. If there is in fact a Great Chain of Being, Mailer's advice would be obviously to pull it" (Lucid, 189). And he has pulled that chain with vengeance, and the result is *The Executioner's Song*.

But Mailer has not finished this task of "evacuating the Devil's work," and "ejaculating towards divinity." Dealing with scatology, buggery, incest, and violence is a very remunerative activity for him. Hilary Mills tells us in *Norman Mailer: A Biography* that Mailer will receive $4 million for a trilogy that includes *Ancient Evenings*. In this novel Mailer shifts the scene to Egypt, but he is still working with the same obsessions that led him to glamorize the meaning of Gilmore's and Abbott's murders. It comes as no surprise that Mailer has written a murder mystery, *Tough Guys Don't Dance*. "Certain themes," he says, "I go back to over and over and over . . . sex and violence, excrement, death, guilt, murder, and incest" (USA, Sept. 12, 1984, 1D). Mailer's love affair with violence is always in full bloom.

I can think of no better way to end this chapter than to quote from the words of Alfred Kazin, one of the best critics in America:

> The biggest thing in my life is the Holocaust, and the basic fact about it is that a great many people killed without having any interest in whom they killed. And for my money, Mailer has done exactly the same thing with his obsession with murderers.
>
> That's why, even before the Abbott thing, I'd hated *The Executioner's Song*. I wasn't impressed with the book's style. For me it's very simple: I'm opposed to murder. And I don't see how anyone coming from a Jewish background, with this terrible history of the Holocaust murders, can defend murderers or be that interested in murder. (Manso, 650)

12

God And Murder

*Meanwhile, where is God? This is one of the most disquieting
symptoms. When you are happy . . . you will be—so it feels—
welcomed with open arms. But go to Him when your need is
desperate, when all other help is vain, and what do you find? A
door slammed in your face and a sound of bolting and double
bolting on the inside. After that silence. You may as well turn
away. . . . Why is He so present a commander in our time of
happiness and so very absent a help in time of trouble?*

C. S. Lewis,
A Grief Observed

"Doctor, Doctor, will I die?"
"Yes, my child, and so will I."
Anonymous

Down, down, down into the darkness of the grave
Gently they go, the beautiful, the tender, the kind;
Quietly they go, the intelligent, the witty, the brave.
I know. But I do not approve. And I am not resigned.
Edna St. Vincent Millay,
"Dirge Without Music"

God and Murder—what an odd title for a chapter. I suspect
that nowhere in the books on criminology and victimology
does such a chapter title appear. But where there is Death,
there is God. If there were no Death, there would be no need for
God. When someone we love dies as a result of an accident or
illness, we say it is "God's will." But when someone is mur-

dered, we cannot say that. We know it is the murderer's will.
We are puzzled because we ask, Who gave the murderer his
will to kill? In some way, God, if he exists, must be involved
with crime. For if he is the omnipotent, omniscient, omni-
perfect Being of religious belief, how can he permit the evil of
murder to exist?

In a 1974 Gallup Poll, 94 percent of Americans stated that
they believed in God. In 1982 George Gallup in his *Adventures
in Immortality* revealed that 50 million Americans believe in
God, 100 million believe in life after death, 7 out of 10 foresee a
reward in heaven for a good life, 50 million have had a re-
ligious born-again experience, and 53 percent believe in hell.
In 1981, Research and Forecast, Inc. did some extensive poll-
ing and discovered that 74 percent of those polled were re-
ligious. In the same year that Gallup published his book, Rob-
ert Henry and Ruby Hart Neuhaus claimed in their work that
one-fourth of the American people do not have any religious
belief and half do not believe in life after death. They wrote:

> The belief that external life after death is determined by a per-
> sonal relationship with God established in this life is fading
> with some notable exception, and fantasies or uncertainties
> about life after death seem to hold greater sway than religious
> teachings. (185)

I don't know how these authors gathered their evidence for
this conclusion.

On March 8, 1983, President Reagan told the National
Association of Evangelicals in Orlando, Florida, that it is
preferable for our children to "die now, still believing" in God,
than to have them grow up under communism and one day die
"no longer believing in God." I hope the repellent view re-
vealed in this passage was only an erratic example of the
mindless rhetoric of a politician. Surely Reagan would not
have wished that his own son were dead rather than Red? But
this fatuous remark quoted in the newspapers reveals how it
is always politically wise to be on the side of God.

Bereaved parents who are religious refuse to blame God for
their tragedy. Over and over again we read ghastly stories

about abominable murders and diseases, and God's name is usually invoked with love. Thus after Phil Donahue showed the bodies of the women missionaries murdered in El Salvador, he asked the mother of one of these victims how she felt about God. She said that while at first she could not understand the evil that had befallen her daughter, she came to believe that for some reason God wanted her daughter to die, and she had faith in him, and believed in him. John Gunther, who described the agony of watching his brilliant and charming son die from a brain tumor, records the words of his wife, Frances Gunther:

> I did not for one thing feel that God had personally singled out either him or us for any special act, either of animosity or generosity. In a way I did not feel that God was personally involved at all. I have all my life had a spontaneous, instinctive sense of the reality of God, in faith, beyond ordinary belief. I have always prayed to God and talked things over with Him, in church and out of church. . . . During Johnny's long illness, I prayed continually to God, naturally. God was always there. He sat beside us during the doctors' consultations, as we waited the long vigils outside the operating room, as we rejoiced in the miracle of a brief recovery, as we agonized when hope ebbed away, and the doctors confessed there was no longer anything they could do. They were helpless, and we were helpless, and in this way, God standing by us in our hour of need, God in His infinite wisdom and mercy and loving kindness, God in all His omnipotence, was helpless too. (252)

God in all his omnipotence was helpless too! Amazing, is it not, how the human mind is capable of harboring contradictory thoughts! Frances Gunther absolves her God of all responsibility in the death of her son at the very same time that she describes him as being omnipotent, which means no more or less that he is all-powerful and therefore is responsible for the death of her son. For omnipotence means that God *can do everything.*

Similarly, Max Wylie wrote about God's role in the savage murder of his daughter:

> God had nothing to do with the murder of Janice, anymore than He had anything to do with the creation of the hideous

social deformity that is her killer. (37-38)

Wylie tells us he is a Christian who believes in a higher power, though not the formalized personification to whom the average Christian prays. But he does believe in Jesus Christ. This paradox of not believing in a personal God and believing in Jesus Christ does not seem to bother Wylie. Again note that God had nothing to do with the murder of Janice or the creation of the monster who killed her. God had nothing to do with the tumor in Johnny Gunther's brain; he had nothing to do with the murder of Wylie's daughter.

On their way home to Utica after attending religious services, Pamela Rudin, Erica Hassner, and Ruth Rudelson were killed by a drunk driver. They were religious and were attending a Shabbaton of the National Conference of Synagogue Youth. Pamela Rudin was president of the Binghamton chapter of the Union of Orthodox Jewish Congregations, and Erica was an active member of that group. In their burial service the Kaddish was sung for them, the prayer for the dead, a song of sanctification for the Creator: "Let his great name be blessed forever and for all eternity." There is no mention of death nor any reference to God's mercy. In other words, the religious parents of these dead children were supposed to recite three times a day during the week and twice on the Sabbath those words which bless God. Christians use a form of the Kaddish in the Christian liturgy in the Latin mass of the Roman Church.

When God is blessed in the Kaddish during a funeral, he is obviously being thanked for death as well as life. The young religious people who were killed by a drunk driver in Utica loved God and were on the streets that night because they loved God and refused to disobey his laws by taking a taxi on a holy night. The parents of these dead children have sued the city of Utica for millions of dollars for not shoveling the snow on the sidewalks so that the children were forced to walk in the streets. They could not sue God. He was not responsible.

God was not responsible for the tumor in Gunther's son's brain or for the earthquake that killed millions in the land of the Pope. He is not responsible for the deaths of school children in a bus on their way to summer camp or for the deaths of families as they pray in a church that collapses. When a mother looks at the body of her daughter, cut into little pieces by a maniac, she does not blame God. He is omnipotent but is not responsible for what men choose to do to each other. If seven children in one family die in a bus accident, God is not responsible; man is responsible. But surely there must be some explanation for the existence of a six-foot-nine-inch monster weighing 280 pounds who rapes a child and throws her body off a roof. The act of faith requires a God who has a reason for permitting, if he does not cause, such horrendous events. In Bangladesh the Moslems say God sent the flood to punish the sinners.

For the majority of people in this world it is impossible to live without believing in a benevolent God. How else is it possible to accept what Schneidman correctly calls the "obscenity of death"? How else is it possible to live with the injustice of the slaughter of innocents? That is why even those who are intellectually convinced that God does not exist fall back upon a form of Pascal's Wager. It is wiser to believe in him. If he does not exist, then one has only wasted some time following some silly rituals or believing some wrong ideals. But if God does exist and if he is the kind of God religion describes, he would be ruthless in destroying those who did not believe in him.

I used Pascal's Wager on the second anniversary of my son's death. I tried to think of a special way to commemorate this event. What did I do? I made a donation to Hadassah so that in a synagogue in Israel a prayer would be said for Eric in perpetuity—what is called a Yahrzeit. At the same time I knew that one of Eric's friends had arranged for him to be remembered forever in a Catholic Mass. If a Christian God exists, then Eric's soul can enter a Christian heaven. If a Jewish God exists, then Eric's soul can enter a Jewish heaven. I have not as yet guaranteed his soul a place in a Moslem heaven. But, of course, indulging in Pascal's Wager is merely a form of intellectual cowardice. I cannot bear to accept the consequences of my disbelief; so I make these futile gestures.

As for those who believe, the most freakish, the most horrific tragedy will not shake their belief. Take away their son in a vicious murder, and the family will ask you to donate money to their church. Take away their daughter in a freakish accident, and the family will advise that memorial contributions be made to the Advanced Hebrew Education Fund at Hillel Academy. What will such advanced education teach the Jewish youth about a God who permits such suffering? The Jewish Binghamton newspaper, the *Daily Reporter,* said of the death of the deeply religious Hassner girl: "Why do such things happen? These are questions we cannot answer. We live in a world that is not always fair or just" (Feb. 18, 1981, 2).

If we live in a world that is not always fair or just, who is to blame for that state of affairs? Since God in the Judaic-Christian view is all-powerful, all-good, all-knowing, and perfect, what is his responsibility for the evil we suffer as his created beings?

In the early fourth century the church father Lactantius wrote the following in the thirteenth chapter of his *On the Wrath of God:*

> Either God wants to remove evil from the world and cannot; or he can and does not want to; or he cannot and does not want to, either one; or else, finally, he wants to and can. If he wants to and cannot, that is impotence, which is contrary to the nature of God; if he can and does not want to, that is malice, which is equally contrary to his nature; if he neither wants to nor can, that is malice and impotence at the same time; if he wants to and can (and this is the only one of the alternatives that is consistent with all the attributes of God), then where does all the evil of the world come from? (R. M. Adams, 88)

Where indeed does all the evil come from? For centuries the greatest philosophers have tried to answer this question. Those who are not committed to a Judaic-Christian view of God have no difficulty in identifying the source of evil. They simply accept the existence of two opposite principles, forces, or gods. Typhon was the bad force for the Egyptians; Arimane was the evil force for the Persians. The Yezidi in Syria believe in the goodness of God and the evil of the Devil. They worship the Devil, reasoning that if God defeats the Devil, God will forgive those who did not worship him, whereas the Devil would not be benevolent. The Manicheans and Zoroastrians also believed in this duality of good and bad gods. The Marquis de Sade reasoned that since God is all-powerful and since *evil* does exist, therefore God must be evil. The way to serve God is to be as vicious and malignant as he is. No one would deny that the marquis eliminated the age-old paradox of a good God and an evil world.

Judaic-Christian theology, however, has not been able to eradicate the tension that results from two incompatible beliefs. The Book of Job deals with the question of God's omnipotence and human suffering. But the story of Job is essentially a fairy tale with a "happy" ending that would make sense only to those who have not suffered the tragedy of loss.

Job opens with a bet. The omnipotent God *gambles* with Satan, and Job is the innocent pawn and victim. Satan goads God into testing Job. God says to Satan:

> Have you considered my servant Job, that there is none like him on the earth, a blameless and upright man, who fears God and turns away from evil? (1.8)

Satan answers:

> Does Job fear God for nought? Hast thou not put a hedge about him and his house and all that he has, on every side? Thou hast blessed the work of his hands, and his possessions have increased in the land. But put forth thy hand now, and touch all that he has, and he will curse thee to thy face. (1.9-11)

And God allows Satan to test Job. God says, "Behold, all that he has is in your power; only upon himself do not put forth your hand" (1.12).

In other words, God allows Satan to cause Job's suffering. Since God has prescience, he knows how everything will turn out; yet he makes Job suffer to win a wager. Why would an all-powerful being have to resort to this kind of foul play to prove to Satan that the best of men would love him even in adversity? It is hardly the kind of behavior we would excuse in a human being. While God admits that Job has never sinned, God rebukes him by boasting of his own omnipotence. Finally, he restores Job's fortunes, and he restores his family of seven sons and three daughters. Presumably these are *new* children. There is no indication in the text that God performed the miracle of resurrecting the dead children.

The biblical text says: "He had also seven sons and three daughters." Did God really believe that by giving Job new sons and daughters, he would make up for the loss of the original family? If so, even God didn't know that you can never replace dead children. In any event, the God of Job makes him suffer, and while it is not clear why he does this, it is clear that Job's God is an enigmatic power who has baffled scholars for centuries.

In a sense the message of Job is the message of the eighteenth-century optimists. God insists at the end of Job that whatever he does is right because he is God—an obviously circular argument. But it satisfied Leibniz, Pope, Bolingbroke, and Shaftesbury, who all agreed that "whatever is, is right." God created the best of all possible worlds. What looks to us like evil will be found to be ultimately good. In other words, there really is no evil; private or personal suffering makes for universal good. This simple-minded view has been brilliantly satirized by Voltaire in his *Candide* and his essay "Well, Everything is Well." In this latter work he wrote scathingly of Leibniz's view that even punishment for the original sin of man is a part of God's plan for man's felicity in this best of all possible worlds.

> What! To be driven out of a delightful garden where one could have lived forever if one hadn't eaten an apple! What! To give birth in anguish to miserable and sinful children, who will suffer everything themselves and make everyone else suffer! What! To experience every sickness, feel every grief, die in anguish, and then in recompense to be roasted for eternity! This fate is really the best thing possible? It's not too good for us; and how can it be good for God? (R. M. Adams, 87)

Are we to believe that an omnipotent God who could prevent needless suffering, pain, wars, plagues, droughts, illness, and murder but does not do so is good? John Stuart Mill said:

But when I am told I must believe this, and at the same time call this being by the names which express and affirm the highest human morality, I say in plain terms that I will not. Whatever power such a being may have over me, there is one thing which he shall not do: he shall not compel me to worship him. I will call no being good, who is not what I mean when I apply that epithet to my fellow creatures; and if such a being can sentence me to hell for not so calling him, to hell I will go. (129)

Some Christians in our own age have taken the extreme position that human suffering is a *gift* of God. Thus Joseph Sullivan has written:

It is rather the mark of a good and holy God that he permits so many of his children to undergo that suffering here on earth. Suffering is almost the greatest gift of God's love. (75)

This is the nadir of sophistry that attempts to equate love with suffering. How can we accept the notion of a God who inflicts suffering on innocent children in cancer wards to show his love? The following passage expresses all that has to be said about Sullivan's repulsive doctrine:

I was standing on the veranda of an Indian home darkened by bereavement. My Indian friend had lost his little son, the light of his eyes, in a cholera epidemic. At the far end of the veranda his little daughter, the only remaining child, slept in a cot covered over with a mosquito net. We paced up and down, and I tried in my clumsy way to comfort and console him. But he said, "Well, padre, it is the will of God. That's all there is to it. It is the will of God."

Fortunately I knew him well enough to be able to reply without being misunderstood, and I said something like this: "Supposing someone crept up the steps onto the veranda tonight, while you all slept, and deliberately put a wad of cotton soaked in cholera germ culture over your little girl's mouth as she lay in that cot there on the veranda. What would you think about that?"

"My God," he said, "what would I think about that? Nobody would do such a damnable thing. If he attempted it and I caught him, I would kill him with as little compunction as I would a snake, and throw him over the veranda. What did you mean by suggesting such a thing?"

"But John," I said quietly, "isn't that just what you have accused God of doing when you said it was his will? Call your little boy's death the result of mass ignorance, call it mass folly, call it mass sin, if you like, call it bad drains or communal carelessness, but don't call it the will of God. Surely we cannot identify as the will of God something for which a man would be locked up in jail, or put in a criminal lunatic asylum." (Weatherhead, 10-11)

The conventional view is that man is responsible for evil. Man is a sinner. God never meant that his creations should die, but he was forced to invent death as a punishment for man's sins. One of the most famous exponents of the typical Christian belief that man suffers because he is a sinner is Billy Graham. Graham immediately sought his audience in the aftermath of the great tragedy at Las Vegas. I listened to him perform on television before that audience as he dealt with the question "Why Does God Permit Suffering?" He began by telling the story of Job to demonstrate the mysterious actions of God. But then he went on to insist that man is being punished for not believing in Jesus Christ. Although Graham was careful not to make the explicit correlation, he implied that those who were killed in the fire were sinners. As I sat and listened to his description of a God who punishes his creations for lack of belief, I thought of how he had punished the three children of Mark Chasteen, aged three, four, and five, who were brutally murdered by the depraved Judy. How had those children sinned? Were they murdered because they did not believe in Jesus Christ? Were the millions of Jews and non-Jews murdered in the Holocaust guilty of the sin of disbelief in Jesus Christ? It is horrible to think of a perfect being who has to kill innocent children to make his point. And if the answer is that we are too feeble-minded to understand God's purpose, then we can only ask why God made us feeble-minded. There is nothing in the story of the kind, compassionate Jesus requiring us to believe he would mandate suffering and death for those who do not believe in him. Yet according to Graham, God punishes man for his refusal to believe in Christ—an act that reduces both God and Christ to the status of tyrants.

The theologian Paul Tillich, a Christian existentialist, also examines the question of human suffering in a famous essay, "The Riddle of Inequality." Why, he asks, does the New Testament contain the following words spoken by Jesus?

For to him who has will more be given and from him who has not, even what he has will be taken away. (Mark 4.25)

What does it mean? Tillich recalls that a colleague once described this saying of Jesus as "one of the most immoral and unjust statements ever made!" (36). These words appear four times in the Gospels, and for the writers of the Gospels, who were offended by this text, as we all are, it was a stumbling block, which they tried to interpret in different ways. Probably none of these explanations satisfied them fully, for with this saying of Jesus, we are confronted immediately "with the greatest and perhaps most painful riddle of life, the inequality of all human beings. We certainly can not hope to solve it. Neither the Bible nor any of the great religions and philosophies was able to do so" (36). But Tillich tries to give us a way of living with it after he explores the nature of the riddle. Perhaps Jesus' parable meant that what we *have* is the capacity for growth; if we use what talents we have, then they multiply through growth while unused talents disappear.

All of us have suffered loss—the loss of innocence and youthful enthusiasm, which are a natural part of maturity and which we are not responsible for. But we feel guilty about losses we cause to happen, such as when we lose our love of nature, of knowledge, and of God. "Those who have, receive more if they *really* have what they have, if they use it and cause it to grow. And those who have not, lose what they seem to have, because they really do *not* have" (40).

But Tillich admits that this is not the answer to the riddle of inequality. It does not deal with the question of why some receive more at the outset before the possibility even exists of using or wasting talents. "Why does the one servant receive five talents, and the second, two, and the third, one? Why is one person born to desperate poverty, and another to affluence?" (40-41). The question can be asked not only of individual men but also of classes, races, and nations, and, therefore, the riddle involves political as well as social inequality. Nor does the hope of reform and revolution and a future social utopia resolve the problem of how we live in the present with the riddle of the inequality of the talents of the body and the mind, the inequality produced by our freedom and destiny. Think of the inequality created by the fact that generations who did not have equality were superceded by generations who did.

Nor can the doctrine of racial inferiority be used to justify the inequality of social injustice. Inequality has nothing to do with the phenomenon of the uniqueness of each self. Tillich states:

> He who has witnessed hospitals for the ill and insane, prisons, sweat shops, battlefields, people starving, family tragedies or moral aberrations should be cured of any confusion of the gift of individuality with the riddle of inequality. He should be cured of any sense of easy consolation. (42)

And so we continue to ask questions about the misery inequality produces.

> Why did my child, or any one of millions of children, die before he had the chance to grow out of infancy? Why was my child, or any child, born crippled in mind and body? Why has my friend or relative, or anyone's friend or relative, disintegrated in his mind and thus lost both his freedom and his destiny? Why has my son or daughter, gifted as they were with many talents, wasted them or been deprived of them? And why does this happen to any parent at all? (44)

The main question is not the Jobean question answered by an all-powerful God who really does not answer. We cannot, like Job, accept divine judgment without knowing why or how he judges; we cannot simply accept the view that many are called but few elected. We cannot believe in an afterlife when everything will be set right, because the afterlife is another destiny different from our present life. What solution does Tillich offer after analyzing so brilliantly the *non liquet* nature of the riddle of inequality? What exists, he says, is an ultimate divine unity in which *all* beings participate. Once we become aware of this unity it drives us

> to give, to share, to help. The fact that others fall into sin, crime and misery alters the character of the grace that is given us: it makes us recognize our own hidden guilt; it shows us that those who suffer for their sin and crime, suffer also for us, for we are guilty of their guilt and ought to suffer as they suffer. (45-46)

Translated into plain English, this absurd statement means that I am as guilty of the murder of my son as Deltejo, and that in suffering in prison, he is suffering for me while I also must suffer for my sin!

Tillich concludes with the ultimate insult to his God.

> It is the greatness and the heart of the Christian message that God as manifest in the Christ on the Cross, totally participates in the dying child, in the condemnation of the criminal, in the disintegration of a mind, in starvation and famine, and even in the human rejection of himself. There is no human condition into which the divine presence does not penetrate. This is what the Cross, the most extreme of all human conditions, tells us. (46)

Thus even though finite minds cannot solve the riddle of inequality, the certainty of divine participation gives us the courage to endure the riddle. But what is divine participation? It means that God or Christ participates in the dying child's suffering. Why he participates in it without stopping it, since he is omnipotent and therefore by definition capable of stopping suffering, is not clear. That God chooses not to eradicate suffering is always viewed by the believer as one of those mysteries impossible to fathom. Tillich in the end grasps at the Christian cliché and leaves God in the untenable position of participating in the evil that is supposedly anathema to a "loving" spirit.

Another writer recently tried to explain the relationship between God and suffering. Rabbi Harold S. Kushner wrote a book with the inspired title *When Bad Things Happen to Good People*. His son died at the age of fourteen from progeria. In this work Kushner offered his view of the nature of God and the role that God plays in the drama of human tragedy.

Kushner's explanation was so successful that his book became a best seller, and he appeared on television and gave lectures. I saw him on one of those TV programs and I listened to him and I read his book.

The rabbi is a decent, well-meaning man who has tried to bring solace to those who have suffered tragedies. He admits that he is not a formally trained philosopher. He is simply a religious person who offers his view of the relation of God to human suffering. And what is this view that has enthralled so many readers? Kushner's God does not cause the bad things that happen to us. God does not make us suffer because we are sinners, or because there is a purpose which he has not revealed to us, a pattern into which all of our lives fit, or as a test, as a means of ennobling our personality, or as a preparation for a better life in heaven. Kushner cannot accept the notion of a sadistic God who tests Abraham by requiring him to sacrifice his son Isaac.

The clue to the solution is in Psalm 121: "I lift mine eyes to the hills; from where does my help come? My help comes from the Lord, maker of Heaven and earth." Kushner notes that the psalmist does not say "My pain comes from the Lord" or "My tragedy comes from the Lord." He says "My *help* comes from the Lord" (30-31). Thus, oddly enough, this maker of Heaven and Earth, this creator of this vast world has no responsibility for the bad things that happen. He only has the power to help us when bad things happen.

In his chapter on Job, Kushner contends that God had nothing to do with Job's suffering—the loss of his wealth, and his illness. Kushner ignores the beginning of Job. The author of Job

> believes in God's goodness and in Job's goodness, and is prepared to give up his belief . . . that God is all-powerful. Bad things do happen to good people in this world, but it is not God who wills it. God would like people to get what they deserve in life, but He cannot always arrange it. Forced to choose between a good God who is not totally powerful, or a powerful God who is not totally good, the author of the Book of Job chooses to believe in God's goodness. (42-43)

God, in chapter 40, verses 9-14, is interpreted as saying in the second half of his speech from the Whirlwind: "If you think that it is so easy to keep the world straight and true, to keep unfair things from happening to people, *you* try it" (43).

Undaunted, Kushner accepts contradictory views. Whatever he wants to think, he thinks. At the beginning of his discussion on Job, he describes how Satan challenges God to test Job. God accepts the challenge. Now, if Kushner's God is limited and fallible, why would he accept such a challenge? Why would he inflict such terrible suffering on Job just for the sake of proving a point to Satan? If God is not omniscient and does not know that in the end he can reward Job for his faithfulness, then accepting this challenge makes him seem cruel and egotistical, more interested in proving that he is right than in worrying about the sufferings of his creations. But the crucial point is that God *does* inflict the suffering at the beginning of Job. And he has the power to end Job's suffering. At what point in Kushner's contradictory view does God suddenly not have the power to stop the suffering? Kushner's explanation of God is oxymoronic; he is both omnipotent and impotent. If the misfortunes of Job did not come from God, where *did* they come from? God fights the sea serpent and captures him, but it is not easy for God to do this. If the serpent is a symbol of evil, then the author is telling us that God has a difficult time controlling evil.

> If God is a God of justice and not of power, then He can still be on our side when bad things happen to us. He can know that we are good and honest people who deserve better. Our misfortunes are none of His doing, and so we can turn to Him for help. Our question will not be Job's question "God, why are You doing this to me?" But rather "God, see what is happening to me. Can you help me?" (44)

This limited God seems to have only the power to give us compassion for suffering and anger at injustice. This God does not cause the earthquake, the accident, or the murder. These evils are independent of his will, and he is as sad and angry as we are when they strike us. This peculiar being Kushner has dredged up is curiously impotent at the most crucial times in human history. He has no control over natural laws. He does not cause disease and pain, but he gives us death because immortality would be unbearable for the human race. How a being who mandates death for the whole race suddenly becomes impotent in the face of disease is not explained. God gives man free will—including the freedom to hurt and kill and destroy so that the freedom will be limited. Notice that Kushner makes God all-powerful in relation to the concept of freedom but limited in relation to stopping pain and suffering. This good God obviously has a "black" sense of humor.

Of course, God did not cause Auschwitz.

> I have to believe that the Holocaust was at least as much of an offense to God's moral order as it is to mine, or how can I respect God as a source of moral guidance? (82)

How indeed! Kushner's God was so enraptured with the concept of free will that he did not intervene to save six million Jews.

> I have to believe that the tears and prayers of the victims aroused God's compassion, but having given man freedom to choose, including the freedom to choose to hurt his neighbor, there was nothing God could do to prevent it. (84-85)

Thus this God who has the power to give freedom of choice does not have the power to prevent freedom of choice. Presumably this God was responsible for Hitler's freedom to kill but was not capable of taking away his freedom. Why?

Kushner denies that "God is a person like me, with real eyes and real tear ducts to cry, and real nerve endings to feel pain" (85). But he is the source of our being able to feel sympathy and outrage. Kushner never tells us whether his God is a force, a supernatural being. But one thing is certain: this Being does not create the problem. He gives us the strength to cope with the problem. Then on page 129 Kushner identifies the source of the problem: Fate. That's it. Fate is to blame for everything, but what is Fate? Kushner never bothers to explain what he means by this term and what relation it has to the concept of God. Is Fate more powerful than God? Then Fate is God, or Kushner's God is Fate's servant. Kushner uses these terms blithely indifferent to the thousands of pages written on the subject of Fate, free will, and God by great thinkers through the ages.

If we turn to this God when we are in pain, he will give us the endurance to bear the pain. He gives us strength and patience and hope, renewing our spiritual resources when they run dry. This God who doesn't cause the suffering has the power to make "people become doctors and nurses to try to make you feel better. God helps us to be brave even when we're sick and frightened, and He reassures us that we don't have to face our fears and our pains alone" (129). But Kushner doesn't mention the people I know who are not comforted by the God they believe in, who have no strength and no hope, who live in despair. Some people commit suicide. God does not bring hope to everyone. He obviously can't do everything; he can't make everyone strong and full of hope in the face of tragedy.

Finally, Kushner asks the inevitable question: If God cannot prevent the bad things that happen to good people, "What good is He at all?" This God who can't stop cancer, who can't stop plagues and epidemics, gives us friends and neighbors and family to ease our burden and fill the emptiness. He gives us self-discipline; he gives us altruistic people to help others. He gives us his compassion, and "we must forgive the world for not being perfect"; we must "forgive God for not making a better world . . ." (147). Kushner forgives God for not being perfect, but what Kushner has been describing all along is not God as every trained theologian conceives him. Kushner's God is a figment of his imagination whom he has to create in order to continue to be a rabbi. Having experienced the horror of watching his young son die, he could not accept the notion of an omnipotent, omniscient, all-perfect, omnipresent God. He had to make up a fantasy God of his own, as a small child who is afraid of the dark imagines he has a magic guardian sleeping with him.

Kushner asks on the last page of his book:

> Can you learn to love and forgive Him despite his limitations, as Job does, and as you once learned to forgive and love your parents even though they were not as wise, as strong, or as perfect as you needed them to be? (148)

What an odd analogy! Our parents are imperfect. They are mortal. The very name of God signifies a superior being; if he is imperfect, then he is by definition not a superior being. A heart surgeon seems to be more worthy of worship than the inept, incompetent, limited being Kushner wants us to revere. Unlike Billy Graham, Kushner does not sell sin, but he offers hope at the price of ignorance.

If the free will God gave to man is responsible for human evil, God should at the very least have protected the innocent from the exercise of someone else's free will to commit an evil act. To say that God is not to blame for what man does is to limit his power, and no amount of theological sophistry can obscure the plain fact that the whole notion of free will is invalidated by contradictory and irreconcilable elements. Free will makes sense only if you eliminate the idea of a God who is interested in humanity and accept instead the idea of a clockmaker who made his clock, sold it, and then lost all interest in it. But Western religious people insist on worshipping a God who is good and who cares, despite all the evidence to the contrary. They even invent the doctrine of plenitude to explain the existence of natural evil. Having taken care of human evil with the doctrine of free will—man is free to choose good over evil; that is God's gift to him—they insist that natural evil is simply evidence of God's plenitude. God in his perfection had to create everything—everything means the insects that carry deadly disease, the bad germs as well as the good germs, the tumors that kill, the storms, earthquakes, and fires that destroy. He had to create a universe of beings existing by means of predation. Is there any sane person who watches the animal programs on TV who doesn't recognize that the law of life is hunt, kill, and eat?

Sensitive humans in revolt at the predatory nature of human existence resort to vegetarianism to avoid eating what is slaughtered. Yet the essential functions of life involve hunger, digestion, and excretion. Every animal species survives by feeding on other forms of life. Civilized man has, *in extremis,* resorted to cannibalism. History offers us examples of shipwrecked men who ate each other to stay alive. During the famine in Stalingrad, the Russians ate ground human meat. In the Bashkir Republic the children were fastened to the walls by their fathers to prevent them from devouring each other. Some tribes liked to eat human flesh. In Polynesia and Melanesia feasts were held called "Long Pig," pleasing to the palate. Cyrus Sulzberger reports the answer of a cannibal when a European asked about his degrading habit of eating human flesh. The cannibal said:

> Why degraded? You people eat sheep and cows and fowls, which are all animals of a far lower order, and we eat man, who is great and above all, it is you who are degraded. (154)

The cannibal has a point, for if God created man in his own image, then in some way the cannibals partake of that image along with the civilized being.

God created the swan who lives lovingly and monogamously with his mate, but he also created the bullfrog who eats his own young when he is hungry. Is there not an inherent absurdity in the notion of an all-powerful Being who has to create love and death, digestion and excretion, health and disease, good and evil to fulfill his nature? Did he need Auschwitz, Majdanek, Buchenwald, Belsen, Ravensbruck, Treblinka, and Babi-Yar as well as Paradise? Did he have to produce a universe filled with antinomies? On the one hand, there is the couple married for seventy years with eighty-two grandchildren. On the other hand, there is the Sutherland family with a history of cancer for more than 140 years. (Raymond Sutherland of Miami and his three sons died of cancer.) On the same day that one mother, Mrs. Pagano, won $20 million in a lottery, another mother, Mrs. Carol Stott, lost both of her young sons, aged eleven and sixteen, who were killed suddenly and inexplicably by an unidentifiable illness.

But people believe in God because they want to believe, have to believe, in God. Faith enables them to survive in a terrifying world that ultimately brings annihilation. John Hospers, James W. Cornman, and other philosophers brilliantly refute the arguments used to prove the existence of God: ontological, causal, contingency, utility, teleological. But nothing they say, no matter how irrefutable the logic, would have any impact on those who *must* believe in God.

If it could be shown that belief in God produces peace, brotherly love, and happiness, then religions could justify their existence. Belief in God, even if it originated out of fear, ignorance, or superstition, would be a desirable phenomenon if it helped to civilize mankind. But the history of religion is a record of torture, prejudice, hatred, murder, and war. What men have done to each other in the name of God is despicable. Man invents Gods to escape death and then proceeds to kill those whose faith differs. The Spanish Inquisitors used horrible instruments of torture on heretics before burning them. Protestants in that great age of creativity known as the Renaissance, the age that produced Shakespeare, hanged Catholic priests. While still alive they were placed on the ground, their members cut off, their entrails removed and burned, their heads cut off, their bodies divided into four parts and placed where Queen Elizabeth mandated.

In his essay "Death in the Name of God" in *My Brother Death,* Cyrus Sulzberger describes how Turkish Moslems, Spanish and Irish Catholics, English Protestants, Punjab Sikhs, Buddhist Singhalese, and Cambodian Hindus butchered their religious opponents. In 1922, Hitler announced that it was as a Christian that he was fighting the Jewish poison. We know what he accomplished as a Christian.

Today, in the name of God, Christians, Moslems, and Jews fight each other in Lebanon; in Ireland, in Iraq and Iran, in India and other parts of the world, people continue to destroy each other because of religious differences. As Cyrus Sulzberger notes:

> Regardless of the theology in which he claims to speak any man who aspires to be God's prophet is a false prophet. Any man who assumes the right to dictate another's faith is himself faithless. And yet, disregarding this simple truth, man insists on his cruel joke. He invents religion to escape from death and slaughters those who disagree. History's ears throb with the screams of those who died for godless gods. And we, in our time, with the aid of mechanical devices, have pursued the cataleptic creed of killing because of differences in faith. (101)

Of course, many religious people really believe in a good creator and try to live their lives virtuously. Among the born-again, evangelical, charismatic, neopentecostal Christians, there are spiritually motivated beings who genuinely believe in their religion. But think of what the Guyana tragedy reveals. Mothers were willing to poison their children and die with them to obtain the bliss in heaven that their fanatical leader, Jim Jones, had promised them. Nine hundred people died because of a sick, distorted view of God. Nor should we overlook the Identity Church, a religious organization that teaches that Jews are children of Satan and should be exterminated. Extreme racist religious groups in this country preach hatred of Blacks, Jews, Catholics, Protestants, Atheists, and Communists. Alan S. Katchen records the words of a preacher on a "religious" broadcast over radio station KTTL-FM on January 21, 1983, in Dodge City, Kansas. It was called "Victory with Jesus."

> Yes, we're gonna cleanse our land. We're gonna do it with a sword. And we're gonna do it with violence. "Oh," they say . . . "you're teaching violence." You're damn right I'm teaching violence! God said you're gonna do it that way, and it's about time somebody is telling you to get violent, whitey . . . . You better start making dossiers, names, addresses, phone numbers, car license numbers, on every damn Jew rabbi in this land . . . . And know where he is . . . . You get those road-block locations, set up ambushes, and get it all working now. (3)

But why blame God for fanatics and bigots? The term may, after all, be nothing more than a linguistic ploy to express man's fears of the unknown. Perhaps nothing more than man's arrogance makes him think that his existence has meaning, that his suffering is deplorable, that his life must be in some way directed by a benevolent being who will ultimately reward him in a beautiful and eternal heaven. The humorist Harry Golden explains in *Only in America* why he never scolds a waitress for serving bad food or taking a long time to serve it:

> . . . because I know that there are at least four billion suns in the Milky Way—which is only one galaxy. Many of these suns are thousands of times larger than our own, and vast millions of them have whole planetary systems, including literally billions of satellites, and all of this revolves at the rate of about a million miles an hour, like a huge oval pinwheel. Our own sun and its planets, which includes this earth, are on the edge of

this wheel. This is only our own small corner of the universe, so why do not these billions of revolving and rotating suns and planets collide? The answer is, the space is so unbelievably vast that if we reduced the suns and planets in correct mathematical proportion with relation to the distances between them, each sun would be a speck of dust, two, three and four thousand miles away from its nearest neighbor. And mind you, this is only the Milky Way—our own small corner—our own galaxy. How many galaxies are there? Billions. Billions of galaxies spaced at about one million light-years apart (one light year is about six trillion miles). Within the range of our biggest telescope there are at least one hundred million separate galaxies such as our own Milky Way, and that is not all, by any means. The scientists have found that the further you go out into space with the telescope the thicker the galaxies become, and there are billions, of billions as yet uncovered to the scientist's camera and the astrophysicist's calculations . . . . (21)

In the light of all this, how ridiculous it is to worry about trivia.

Jacques Choron also reminds us of the insignificance of man.

This immensity of the universe makes it rather improbable that man amounts to anything in it. The cosmic insignificance of the whole human adventure is perhaps even more strikingly apparent when we look at it not in terms of space, but in terms of time: when we consider that the age of the earth is estimated to be 2000 to 3000 million years and if, for the sake of our demonstration we equate it to 24 hours, the appearance of life on earth did not take place until 10:51 P.M., the appearance of man a mere 22 seconds before midnight and the whole of "world history"—that is, the establishment of great empires, the founding of great religions, all art, music and science, all the discoveries and inventions—took place in the last 3/10 of a second . . . .

At the same time, the world science presents to us is not only immense and "silent" but a world in which every thing perishes in the end, and where, as William James said, "back of everything is the great specter of universal death." And Russell says that: "All is passing in this mad, monstrous world, all is struggling to snatch, at any cost, a few brief moments of life before Death's inexorable decree." Astronomy tells us of the birth and death of solar systems; biology sees the world of life as "red in tooth and claw" and ruled by the basic law of the necessity of death; paleontology reminds us of the disappearance of plant and animal species; and archaeology brings to us the melancholy message of the ruin of once-great civilizations. Worst of all, physics shows us the universe unwinding toward entropy. (195, 197)

Perhaps science will ultimately discover the fate of the earth. As the theoretical particle physicists bombard the atom and find their mesons, quarks, muons, tauons, pions, kaons, and neutrinos, they also search for evidence of proton decay. Such decay would indicate that all matter as we know it will eventually disappear. Perhaps this will be the solution to the riddle of inequality. We will all go back to the nothing we came from. Heinz R. Pagels may be right when he says: "Theoretical and experimental physicists are now studying nothing at all—the vacuum. But that nothingness contains all of being" (279). It seems futile, then, to worry about God's responsibility for evil. We cannot blame the volcanoes for their eruptions; we cannot blame the earthquakes for their devastations. We cannot blame the atom if it is eventually used to perform a nuclear Götterdämmerung. We cannot arrest God or whatever force created the universe.

When bad things happen to good people, we can only blame specific individuals for their evil acts and arrest them and punish them. In a state of nature, the life of man is, as Thomas Hobbes describes it, "solitary, poore, nasty, brutish and short" *(Leviathan,* chpt. 13). A civilized society uses a form of government to protect the rights of its citizens. And if a government cannot protect its people, then all the horrors of anarchy, war, and murder result. Martin Luther King, Jr. writes in his *Why We Can't Wait* that violence must become as abhorrent to man as eating man's flesh. Hans Vaihinger says we must live *as if* man matters, goodness matters, sanity matters, rationality matters. We must continue to fight against evil and injustice. This is ultimately the true meaning of religion in its purest sense. Otherwise, if we complacently and apathetically accept violence and murder, we doom ourselves to the barbarism that can only lead to early extinction.

Do not, I beg you, forget my son, and the murdered dead like him who fill the graves in every cemetery in this land of the free and the home of the brave. Do not forget the spilling of the blood of one innocent being. Abhor it. Abhor it and work to prevent the murderers in our society from presenting us with the statistics that one person is killed in the United States every twenty-three minutes, and one out of three families is victimized by the scum of society. We spent $5.1 million on the second trial of Juan Corona. When we are willing to spend $5.1 million to prevent murder, we will have at least begun to make the commitment to life instead of death.

Life is a precious gift. Whether we believe that God will offer us immortality or whether we believe that life is nothing more than what the Silesian proverb describes—a chicken perch, short and full of filth—we want to live. The revolting act of murder is a particularly loathsome form of death. Nothing can equal the horror of losing someone you love. Theodore Dreiser has expressed what I felt when I looked at my son's face in the morgue.

> For here, now, is one walking with you. He is tense, alert, strong, charming, alive. Then for a very little while, maybe, he is gone from your presence. And then of a sudden that ever appalling word—dead. He is dead. He or she was alive and now is no more. The look, the feel, the voice, the temperament, the dreams, the plans—all gone. No word, no sound. No trace. The effective and valuable and always amazing body that you knew— dissolved. You stand—astounded—but without answer. (281, 317)

A priest said of Ramses II after his death, "You will live again." In the Egyptian religion to speak of the dead is to make them live again. That is what I have tried to do in this book. Eric, my son, you are dead, but this book will speak of you forever.

Appendix

Transcript of Court Colloquy between Judge Benjamin Altman and William Greenbaum. July 10, 1981. Page 4.

THE COURT: It was made with the understanding it was open before a Huntley, any hearing, and that was your statement on the record.

Now, I am ordering you to hold that offer open, because that was a promise made by the district attorney's office. This is an order of the Court.

MR. GREENBAUM: May I respectfully inquire of your Honor as follows? Your Honor has been made aware on the record of the fact that we are now at a point after the People have been answering ready, steadily, since June 3rd, 1981—

THE COURT: This is only a murder, Mr. Greenbaum, and I have heard it over and over and over again. Only a murder, and we are talking about an 18-year old. Let me tell you this—

MR. GREENBAUM: My inquiry is simple and brief. I would like to know if your Honor would consider this: Tuesday I expect your Honor is going to send us out for a hearing. At that point I think it would be important for the People to know and for the witnesses to know what their schedules will be like for the next few months.

Works Cited

Abbott, Jack Henry. *In the Belly of the Beast.* New York: Random House, 1982.

Adams, Laura, ed. *Will the Real Norman Mailer Please Stand Up?* Port Washington, New York: Kennikut, 1974.

Adams, Robert M., tr. and ed. *Candide; or Optimism* by Voltaire. 1st. ed. New York: Norton, 1966.

Aldridge, John W. "From Vietnam to Obscenity." In Lucid: 180-192.

Alvarez, Alfred. *Savage God: A Study of Suicide.* New York: Random House, 1972.

Amsterdam, Anthony G. "Capital Punishment." In Bedau: 346-358.

Aristotle. "Rhetoric." In *Oxford Aristotle.* Tr. W. R. Roberts. New York: Oxford Univ. Press, 1924. Vol. 9.

Badinter, Robert. *L'Exécution.* Paris: Grasset, 1973.

Barkas, Janet L. *Victims.* New York: Scribner's, 1978.

Beccaria, Cesare. *On Crimes and Punishment.* Tr. Henry Paolucci. New York: Bobbs-Merrill, 1963.

Bedau, Hugo Adam, ed. *The Death Penalty in America: An Anthology.* 3rd. ed. New York: Oxford Univ. Press, 1982.

Berger, Raoul. *Death Penalties: The Supreme Court's Obstacle Course.* Cambridge, Mass.: Harvard Univ. Press, 1982.

Berns, Walter. "The Morality of Anger." In Bedau: 333-341.

Binghamton Evening Press. 16 Sept. 1980: 4A. Alice Mitchell on Eric Kaminsky.

———. 30 Jan., 1985: D1. S. Judy's Threats.

Black, Charles L., Jr. *Capital Punishment: The Inevitability of Caprice and Mistake.* New York: Norton, 1974.

Bowlby, John. *Attachment and Loss.* New York: Basic Books, 1980. Vol. 3.

Braudy, Leo. ed., *Norman Mailer.* Englewood Cliffs, New Jersey: Prentice-Hall, 1976.

Burger, Warren E. Speech to the American Bar Association. Feb.

1981. Houston, Texas.

———. Speech to the American Bar Association. Feb. 1984. Las Vegas, Nevada.

Camus, Albert. *Reflections on the Guillotine.* Tr. Stuart Gilbert. Michigan City, Indiana: Fridtjof-Karla, 1959.

———. *The Stranger.* Tr. Stuart Gilbert. New York: Vintage, 1946.

Capote, Truman. *In Cold Blood.* New York: Random House, 1966.

Cheatham, Wallace. "Declaration of Disclaimer." *Newsletter: New York State Probation Officers Association.* Apr. 1985: 1-14.

Choron, Jacques. *Death and Modern Man.* New York: Collier, 1964.

Cornman, James W., et al. *Philosophical Problems and Arguments: An Introduction.* 3rd. ed. New York: Macmillan, 1982.

Cortland Standard. 8 July 1982: 12. Jeffrey Hart on Bonnie Garland and the Catholic Clergy.

———. 10 July 1982: 4. Elisia Fominas and Murder.

———. 28 Sept. 1984: 9. J. Gould on Manhattan Court.

Cuomo, Mario, M. *Diaries: The Campaign for Governor.* New York: Random House, 1984.

Daily News. 15 Oct. 1981: 16. Bill Reel on rape of a nun.

———. 20 Oct. 1981: C16. Bill Reel on horrors of city crime.

———. 15 June 1981:7. Carol Bellamy on subway crime.

———. 27 Aug. 1981: 62. Bill Reel on Dominicans.

———. 16 Jan. 1982: C17. Koch on great Transit system.

———. 23 Jan. 1982: C9. Mailer on Abbott.

———. 25 Jan. 1982: C17. I. Edelson's letter on Mailer and Abbott.

———. 20 Feb. 1982: C13. Transit cannot be sued.

———. 21 Apr. 1983:1. High murder rate in Wash. Heights.

Daily Reporter [Binghamton]. 18 Feb. 1981: 2. The death of Erica Hassner.

Dershowitz, Alan M. *The Best Defense.* New York: Random House, 1982.

———. "Rev. of W. Gaylin's *The Killing of Bonnie Garland.*" *Psychology Today.* Aug. 1982: 75-76.

Dix, George E. "Expert Prediction Testimony in Capital Sentencing: Evidentiary and Constitutional Consideration." *American Criminal Law Review.* 19 (1981): 1-48.

Dostoevsky, Fyodor. *The Idiot.* Tr. Constance Garnett. New York: Bantam, 1981.

Dreiser, Theodore. "What I Believe." *Forum* 82 (1929): 279-281, 317-320.

Ehrlich, Isaac. "The Deterrent Effect of Capital Punishment: A Question of Life and Death." *American Economic Review.* 65 (1975): 397-417.

Elliott, Chip. "Letter from an Angry Reader." *Esquire* Sept. 1981: 33-37.

Elliot, Gil. *The Twentieth Century Book of the Dead.* London: Allen Lane, 1972.

Eshelman, Byron E., and Frank Riley. *Death Row Chaplain.* Englewood Cliffs, New Jersey: Prentice-Hall, 1962.

Ferrante, James. "Guest Editorial." *Modern Medicine.* 15-30 Mar. 1981: 9.

Freud, Sigmund. "Thoughts for the Times on War and Death." In *Collected Papers.* Ed. Joan Riviere. New York: Basic Books, 1959. Vol. 4: 288-317.

Frost, Robert. *The Poetry of Robert Frost.* Ed. Edward Connery Lathem. New York: Holt, Rinehart and Winston, 1969.

Gallup, George, and William Procter. *Adventures in Immortality.* New York: McGraw-Hill, 1982.

Gaylin, Willard. *The Killing of Bonnie Garland. A Question of Justice.* New York: Simon and Schuster, 1982.

Gibbs, Jack P. "Preventive Effects of Capital Punishment Other than Deterrence." In Bedau: 103-116.

Godwin, John. *Murder USA.* New York: Ballantine, 1978.

Golden, Harry. *Only in America.* New York: World, 1958.

Goodman, Lisl M. *Death and the Creative Life.* New York: Penguin, 1983.

Gray, Barry. "Column on Abbott." *Our Town.* 31 Jan. 1982: 2.

———. "Column on Richard Herrin." *Our Town.* 6 June 1982: 2.

Gunther, John. *Death Be Not Proud.* New York: Harper, 1949.

Harper Study Bible. Revised Standard Edition. New York: Harper and Row, 1962.

Hendin, Herbert. *Suicide in America.* New York: Norton, 1982.

Herzog, Arthur. "My Robe is a Symbol of Mourning." *New York.* 19 Jan. 1981: 24-25.

Hobbes, Thomas. *Leviathan.* Ed. C. B. Macpherson. New York: Penguin, 1982.

Hook, Sidney. *Philosophy and Public Policy.* Carbondale, Illinois: Southern Illinois Univ. Press, 1980.

Hospers, John. *An Introduction to Philosophical Analysis.* 2nd. ed. Englewood Cliffs, New Jersey: Prentice-Hall, 1967.

Hunt, Morton. *The Universe Within.* New York: Simon and Schuster, 1982.

Isenberg, Irwin, ed. *The Death Penalty.* New York: H. W. Wilson, 1977.

Jacoby, Susan. *Wild Justice.* New York: Harper and Row, 1983.

Kanfer, Stefan. "Rev. of Mailer's *Pieces and Pontifications.*" *Time.* 28 June 1982: 73.

King, Martin Luther, Jr. *Why We Can't Wait*. New York: Harper and Row, 1964.

Kipling, Rudyard. *Verse*. Garden City, New York: Doubleday, 1940.

Kübler-Ross, Elisabeth. "Death Does Not Exist." In *The Holistic Health Handbook*. Berkeley, California: And/or, 1978: 348-354.

Kunen, James S. *How Can You Defend Those People?* New York: Random House, 1983.

Kushner, Harold S. *When Bad Things Happen to Good People*. New York: Avon, 1983.

Levine, Richard M. "When Sam and Sergius Meet." In L. Adams, 23-33.

Lewis, C. S. *A Grief Observed*. New York: Seabury Press, 1961.

Lipton, Lawrence. "Mailer: Genius, novelist, critic, playwright, politico, journalist and general all-around shit." *Los Angeles Free Press*. 31 May 1968: 27-28.

Lucid, Robert F., ed. *Norman Mailer: The Man and his Work*. Boston: Little, Brown, 1971.

Mailer, Norman. *An American Dream*. New York: Dial, 1965.

——. *Ancient Evenings*. Boston: Little, Brown, 1983.

——. *The Armies of the Night*. New York: New American Library, 1968.

——. *Barbary Shore*. New York: Universal Library, 1959.

——. *Deaths for the Ladies and other Disasters*. New York: Putnam, 1962.

——. *The Deer Park*. New York: Putnam, 1955.

——. *The Executioner's Song*. New York: Warner, 1979.

——. "Interview." *Mademoiselle* Feb. 1961: 161-162.

——. *The Naked and the Dead*. New York: Rinehart, 1948.

——. *Pieces and Pontifications*. Boston: Little, Brown, 1982.

——. *The Presidential Papers*. New York: Berkley, 1970.

——. *Tough Guys Don't Dance*. New York: Random House, 1984.

——. "The White Negro." In *Advertisements for Myself*. New York: G. P. Putnam, 1959.

——. *Why Are We in Vietnam?* New York: Putnam, 1967.

Manzo, Peter. *Mailer: His Life and Times*. New York: Simon and Schuster, 1985.

Merrill, Robert. *Norman Mailer*. Boston: Twayne, 1978.

Mill, John Stuart. *The Examination of Sir William Hamilton's Philosophy*. London: Longmans, Green, 1889.

Mills, Hilary. *Norman Mailer: A Biography*. New York: Empire Books, 1982.

More, Sir Thomas. *Utopia*. New York: D. Van Nostrand, 1947.

Morris, Herbert. "Persons and Punishment." *Monist*. 52 (1968):

475-501.

Mumford, Lewis. *Sketches from Life.* New York: Dial, 1982.

Neuhaus, Robert Henry, and Ruby Hart. *Successful Aging.* New York: John Wiley, 1982.

New York Post. 6 Sept. 1981: 9. On juvenile escapees.

———. 10 Sept. 1981: 12. Juvenile criminals.

———. 12 Sept. 1981: 2. Juvenile Law and Richard Huttner.

———. 2 Oct. 1981: 5. Judge Burton Roberts and Sentencing Policy.

———. 15 Oct. 1981: 9. No police on subways.

———. 16 Oct. 1981: 3. Koch on rape of nun.

———. 29 Oct. 1981: 10. Rape of nun.

———. 14 Jan. 1982: 7. Wayne Larsen on Adan's murder.

———. 21 Jan. 1982: 30. Ravitch and Dangerous Subways.

———. 23 Jan. 1982: 4. Mailer on Abbott.

———. 12 Apr. 1982: 13. Rape on Subway.

———. 15 May 1982: 17. Richard Herrin the murderer.

———. 21 June 1982: 3. Murder of model St. Antoine.

———. 19 Apr. 1983: 17. Bronx, a modern day hell.

———. 21 Nov. 1983: 14. D'Amato on Subway Crime.

———. 29 Nov. 1983: 14. D'Amato on Subway Crime.

———. 7 Dec. 1984: 49. D. Rabinowitz on C. Isenberg murder.

———. 14 Feb. 1985: 3. Cuomo on bad subway.

New York Review of Books. 6 Dec. 1979: 6. D. Johnson rev. of Mailer's *Executioner's Song.*

———. 19 June 1981: 15. Mailer on Abbott.

New York Times. 16 Sept. 1980: B3. S. Lipkin on Eric Kaminsky.

———. 23 Mar. 1980: A16. A. Dershowitz defends role as criminal lawyer.

———. 18 Jan. 1981: 17. Henahan on subjectivity of music criticism.

———. *TSM.* 8 Feb. 1981: 41. Schonberg on music critics.

———. 7 Apr. 1981: C11. Eli Weisel.

———. 21 Apr. 1981: B1. D. Montenegro on the murder of her daughter.

———. 30 Apr. 1981: C18. Rev. of M. Marlowe's recital.

———. 4 May 1981: A23. Harris Poll on low esteem for lawyers.

———. 14 May 1981: A5. I. B. Singer on Crime.

———. *TSB.* 20 June 1981: 15. T. des Près on Abbott.

———. 17 July 1981: C6. E. Ax on piano competitions.

———. 25 July 1981: 23. R. Baker on crime.

———. 26 July 1981: 26. Kosinski on Abbott.

———. 28 July 1981: B20. Rathblatt on criminal lawyers.

———. 17 Aug. 1981: B4. Mailer on Abbott.

———. 20 Aug. 1981: A31. Schanberg on subway crime.

———. 3 Sept. 1981: A1, A4. Denzer and Crimmins.

————. 16 Sept. 1981: B6. State Commission on Judicial Conduct.

————. *TSB*. 20 Sept. 1981: 36. J. C. Oates on Abbott.

————. *TSM*. 20 Sept. 1981: 38. Kosinski on Abbott.

————. 3 Oct. 1981: 27. McGuire on Juvenile Crime.

————. 6 Oct. 1981: A31. Schanberg on the South Bronx.

————. 10 Oct. 1981: 14. Rev. of Cecil Licad concert.

————. 15 Oct. 1981: C1. On New York City housing.

————. 1 Nov. 1981: A1. Lawyers and court delays.

————. 5 Nov. 1981: B15. Koch on the subway.

————. *TSM*. 31 Jan. 1982: 20. P. Theroux on the subway.

————. 9 Feb. 1982: B4. Koch on subway crime.

————. 19 Feb. 1982: B3. Transit Authority cannot be sued.

————. 18 Apr. 1982: 42. Koch Transit Enemy No. 1.

————. 18 May 1982: C12. Rev. of W. Gaylin's *Killing of Bonnie Garland.*

————. *TSB*. 4 July 1982: 19. Rev. of Dershowitz's *Best Defense.*

————. 7 Sept. 1982: A23. Justice O. W. Holmes on Justice.

————. 17 Oct. 1982: E15. A. Dershowitz on terrorists.

————. 15 Apr. 1983: C31. Rev. of N. Gage's *Eleni.*

————. *TSM*. 17 Apr. 1983: 71. E. B. Williams on Nixon.

————. 26, 28 June 1983: A1, B2. Contempt for the New York City criminal court.

————. *TSB*. 24 July 1983: 27. W. Goodman on Roger Knobelspiess.

————. 21 Apr. 1984: 19. Schanberg on the bad quality of life in New York City.

————. 20 Apr. 1984: A17. FBI Crime Index for the Northeast.

————. 23 Apr. 1984: A1. Justice Murphy on crime.

————. 24 Apr. 1984: 19. Subway lechers.

————. 19 July 1984: B1, B6. On New York City housing.

————. 30 July 1984: A1. Kiley on the decline of the subway.

————. 13 Dec. 1984: A18. J. Greenberg on the Death Penalty.

————. 17 June 1985: B2. Morganthau on Criminal Court.

Oates, Joyce Carol. *Bellefleur.* New York: E. P. Dutton, 1980.

Pagels, Heinz R. *The Cosmic Code.* New York: Simon and Schuster, 1982.

Pascal, Blaise. *Pensées. The Provincial Letters.* New York: Modern Library, 1941.

Pickering, James, ed. *Fiction 100.* 3rd. ed. New York: Macmillan, 1982.

Pileggi, Nicholas. "Open City." *New York.* 19 Jan. 1981: 20-26.

Reiff, Robert. *The Invisible Victim.* New York: Basic Books, 1979.

Ruttencutter, Helen. "Pianist's Progress." *The New Yorker.* 19 Sept. 1977: 42-106.

Saturday Press [Binghamton]. 6 Mar. 1982: 8C. E. Schwartz against the death penalty.

Schell, Jonathan. *The Fate of the Earth.* New York: Alfred Knopf, 1982.

Schiff, Harriet S. *The Bereaved Parent.* New York: Penguin, 1978.

Schneidman, Edwin S. "The Enemy." *Psychology Today.* Aug. 1970: 37-41, 62-66.

——. ed. *On the Nature of Suicide.* San Francisco: Jossey-Bass, 1969.

Schroder, George Alfred. "Norman Mailer and the Despair of Defiance." In Braudy: 82-95.

Schroth, Raymond A. "Mailer and His Gods." In L. Adams: 34-42.

Schulz, Max F. "Norman Mailer's Divine Comedy." In L. Adams: 43-79.

Scott, Nathan A. *Three American Moralists: Mailer, Bellow, Trilling.* Notre Dame: Univ. of Notre Dame Press, 1973.

Shakespeare, William. *The Riverside Shakespeare.* Boston: Houghton Mifflin, 1974.

Shields, Pete. *Guns Don't Die: People Do.* New York: Arbor House, 1981.

Starr, Roger. *The Rise and Fall of New York City.* New York: Basic Books, 1985.

Sullivan, Joseph V. *Catholic Teachings on the Morality of Euthanasia.* Washington, D.C.: Catholic Univ. of America Press, 1949.

Sulzberger, Cyrus. *My Brother Death.* New York: Harper, 1961.

Survivors. Parents of Murdered Children Newsletter. Ed. Robert Hullinger. 1980-1984. 4 Vols. 1739 Bella Vista, Cincinnati, Ohio.

Szasz, Thomas. "The Ethics of Suicide." In *The Theology of Medicine.* Baton Rouge: Louisiana State Univ. Press, 1977: 68-85.

Tanner, Tony. "On the Parapet." In L. Adams: 113-149.

Tatelbaum, Judy. *The Courage to Grieve.* New York: Lippincott and Crowell, 1980.

Tavris, Carol. *Anger: The Misunderstood Emotion.* New York: Simon and Schuster, Touchstone, 1984.

Paul Tillich. "The Riddle of Inequality." In *The Eternal Now.* New York: Scribner's, 1963: 36-46.

Time. 24 Aug. 1981: 3. Niel R. Ayer letter on Mailer and Abbott.

——. 24 Jan. 1983: 28-39. On the Death Penalty.

——. 14 Feb. 1983: 6. Norman Felton letter on forgiveness.

Transcript of Trial. Supreme Court of the State of New York. County of New York. Part 93. The People of the State of New York against Jose Deltejo Defendant. Ind. No. 4606/80. Charge: Murder 2. 100 Centre Street, New York, New York, 8 Dec. 1981. Before Hon. Morris Goldman.

Transcript of Sentence. Supreme Court of the State of New York. New York County. Part 93. People of the State of New York against Jose Deltejo Defendent. Ind. Number 4605/80. 7 Jan. 1982. 100 Centre St. New York, New York. Sentencing before Hon. Morris Goldman.

Trilling, Diana. "The Radical Moralism of Norman Mailer." In Braudy: 42-65.

Twain, Mark. *Autobiography*. Ed. A. B. Paine. New York: Harper, 1924. 2 Vols.

USA Today. 16 Mar. 1983: 2A. On Handguns.

———. 16 Mar. 1983: 2D. Shana Alexander and Jean Harris.

———. 28 Apr. 1983: 3A. Unreported crimes.

———. 12 Sept. 1984: 1D. Mailer and Violence.

Vaihinger, Hans. *The Philosophy of 'As If'*. Tr. C. K. Ogden. New York: Harcourt, Brace, 1924.

Van den Haag, Ernest. "In Defense of the Death Penalty: A Practical and Moral Analysis." In Bedau: 323-333.

———. and John P. Conrad. *The Death Penalty: A Debate*. New York: Plenum, 1983.

Virgil. *The Aeneid*. Tr. K. Guinagh. New York: Rinehart, 1953.

Weatherhead, Leslie D. *The Will of God*. New York: Abingdon Press, 1944.

Willingham, Calder. "The Way It Isn't Done: Notes on the Distress of Norman Mailer." In Lucid: 238-244.

Wilson, James Q. *Thinking about Crime*. 2nd. ed. New York: Basic Books, 1983.

Wolfe, Tom. "Son of Crime and Punishment or: How to Go Eight Fast Rounds with the Heavyweight Champ—and Lose." In Lucid: 151-161.

Worden, J. William. *Grief Counseling and Grief Therapy*. New York Springer, 1982.

Wylie, Max. *The Gift of Janice*. New York: Doubleday, 1964.

Yeats, William Butler. *The Variorum Edition of the Poems of W. B Yeats*. New York: Macmillan, 1966.

Yoder, John Howard. "A Christian Perspective." In Bedau: 370-375.

Index